IVY AND INDUSTRY

# IVY AND INDUSTRY

. . . . . . . . . . . . . . . . . . . . . . . . .

BUSINESS AND THE MAKING OF THE

. . . . . . . . . . . . . . . . . . . . . . . . .

AMERICAN UNIVERSITY, 1880–1980

. . . . . . . . . . . . . . . . . . . . . . . . .

## CHRISTOPHER NEWFIELD

DUKE UNIVERSITY PRESS

. . . . . .

*Durham & London* 2003

© 2003 Duke University Press

All rights reserved

Printed in the United States

of America on acid-free paper ∞

Designed by Amy Ruth Buchanan

Typeset in Carter & Cone Galliard by

Keystone Typesetting, Inc.

Library of Congress Cataloging-in-

Publication Data appear on the last

printed page of this book.

# CONTENTS

. . . . . . . . . . . . . . . . . . . . . . . . . .

PART I   *The Two Missions*

. . . . . . . . . . . . . . . . . . . . . . . . . .

# CHAPTER 1

. . . . . . . . . . . . . . . . . . . . . . . .

*Introduction*

This book considers how the research university and the business corpo-ration grew up together, how they did and didn't get along, and how each has shaped the other's fate. The relationship has been complicated, and its stakes have been large. The research university has played a central role in establishing corporate capitalism and two of its major pillars, commercial technology and organizational management. The research university has also remained a major, if partial, outsider to this business system, having sought to support free inquiry and the pursuit of truth independently of what the market will buy.

The university has had a double role to play, both sustaining and evading the remarkable rise of large organizations in nineteenth- and twentieth-century economic life. *Ivy and Industry* narrates this aspect of the university's intellectual and institutional history from approximately 1880 to 1980. These dates mark two defining moments in the country's economic history, moments that might be described as business revolu-tions. The first revolution forged the multidivisional corporation, the factory labor system, and large-scale bureaucratic management. The sec-ond, at least on the surface, undid many of these innovations, allegedly inaugurating a more decentered "network" society that is arguably more dependent than ever on technological change. The first revolution brought the research university into being as industry's indispensable adjunct. The effects of the second are still in the making. But it is already clear that this second revolution has challenged, if not undone, most of the bases that created the research university as we know it.

This book is shaped by my long-term interest in how institutional and social forces affect individual experience. Here I concentrate on two major domains of experience — work and art, with literature being my major instance of the latter. These domains are far more connected than we realize, particularly in the history that I will tell here, which is the history of the development of the college-educated or professional middle class through the cultivation of its desire for good work. Good work for this population has had many of the characteristics of what the nineteenth century called "free labor" and "craft labor." The core psychological components for university graduates derive from an imagination of work formed in large part by the themes of their college books, themes that included the centrality of freedom to desirable life and work.

The formation of the middle class has been heavily influenced by the university's double role. As I read the record, the university supported economic development, which was largely the province of science and engineering, while simultaneously promoting self-development, which was the traditional province of the humanities. The university was a meeting place for ideas and experiences that normally inhabited different realms, but that multiplied (or diminished) their effects when brought together.

It has been difficult for us to grasp the immensity and complexity of the university's impact on modern society because its various segments — science, humanities, social sciences, administration — are usually treated separately. This book tries to overcome the limits of most existing scholarship by considering these elements in relation to one another. I describe the rise of managerial culture in the university, with some comparison to parallel developments in the commercial firm. I examine the evolution of the humanities through the development of literary criticism over the same period, and I consider management and criticism in their various, although often veiled, relations. I show that for much of the history of academic humanism, aesthetics and labor have been false opposites: the humanities have mattered most when they have provided an aesthetic — and a deeply personal — basis for a craft labor view of professional life. I also describe the relationship of science practice and policy to university administration. The result is a picture of the university as a permanent battleground, and a source of vitality, contestation, "creative destruction," money power, and visions of better worlds. The university is a corporate and a utopian environment at the same time, and has been the central site for considering the possibility that once modernity had irreversibly delivered a world of organizations, the corporate might be made utopian, and the utopian might be post-corporate.

My analysis owes something to my personal experience of these issues. I was lucky enough to graduate from Reed College, an archetypal small liberal arts college which I thoroughly loved, and to get my doctorate with equal pleasure from Cornell University, an archetypal research university, one that played a major role in inventing the concept. I started my first academic job in the fall of 1987 at Rice University, whose interesting liberal arts were drowned out by its science and engineering, a neighboring archipelago of medical complexes, and Houston's corporate center. My next job took me to the Santa Barbara campus of the University of California, the original "multiversity" with ties to industry as complex and elaborate as any in the United States. This trajectory has brought me a varied institutional experience, and has convinced me that though the humanities were central only at Reed, they have a pervasive effect even in the "triple helix" where the university intertwines with industry and government.

This trajectory has also taken me through a crucial transitional period for my field, the university, and American society. The late 1980s brought a false spring to the market for PhDs in literature, one followed by a long hot summer of "culture wars" which damaged what I felt were two of literary academia's crucial contributions to the outside world. The first consisted of theories of interpretive knowledge, which enable nonreductive, qualitative analyses that science could not perform. The second consisted of theories of identity, which explain so much about social and cultural change, not to mention everyday life. The culture wars put both sets of theories on the defensive, ultimately threatening the quality and the quantity of scholarly output. I think that these theories — and the larger field of literary studies — have yet to recover, and I have written this book in part to help that recovery along.

The year 1989 also marked the end of the cold war, since which the United States has more perfectly concentrated on commerce and more completely adapted to business leadership. During the decade that followed, the nation witnessed the rise of the "new economy" and a financial boom. The recession of the early 1990s intensified awareness of the university's dependence on external funds, and the boom of the later 1990s encouraged the university to look to business for its best growth opportunities. The boom also enhanced the status of business prescriptions for university ills, offered a stock-market cure for endowment anxieties, and encouraged pundits to look to high-tech entrepreneurs for the keys to the American knowledge economy.

This seemed like great news for higher education — who was closer to knowledge than the university? Industry was quick to explain how the university could benefit. Scientific and technological fields never had better prospects for sponsored research and lucrative licensing agreements. The bachelor's degree rose in value as labor markets tilted toward high-tech. The university was struggling, many industry leaders claimed, because of uncontrolled costs, poor coordination, and non-entrepreneurial management, but these were things that industry could fix. Perhaps private businesses with more efficient structures could carve off the university's more commercializable functions if the university couldn't keep up with changes in industry. As the university became relentlessly more complex — "a college campus now resembles a medium-to-large municipality, with an array of public works, social services, and market-sensitive functions"[1] — industry offered itself as the master of this complex organization. It had invented the multidivisional corporation in the nineteenth century and then reinvented it for the twenty-first, and knew how to make complexity pay. Firms had the recipe, they said, for transforming complicated, long-term research and teaching into major revenues. The commercialization of teaching and research would revitalize these services just as deregulated capitalism had revitalized the overall economy. Business also mixed carrots in with its sticks: new management ideas, private funding, research partnerships, royalty agreements, manufacturing and marketing, and varieties of profit sharing. By the late 1990s, business was extending the Internet gold rush into the university through "distance learning" — whole courses, degrees, and schools could be put on line and go anywhere, anytime, over the web and into your home computer. As an example of the reformist tone, Michael Milken, junk bond king of the 1980s, turned himself into Michael Milken, creator of "social value" in the 1990s through the educational holding company he called Knowledge Universe.

Business came to the university bearing three gifts: the management of complexity, financial control, and entrepreneurial opportunity. It threw in a relatively new visionary turn. For example, a business professor at Duke University who had recently taken leave from his faculty position to spin off an executive education company described some nearly ideal post-university working conditions: brilliant colleagues, improved pay, stronger staff support, broader, more challenging audiences, equity stakes, genuine ownership of one's ideas, built-in leisure for thought and research, and a group dynamic far better than that of academic departments.[2] Business was promising the university true efficiency, opportunity, *and* intellectual freedom — a kind of "free labor" — along with, eventually, its obsolescence.

While analyzing these developments, I was also thinking about the status of the humanities. In the first years of my career, English studies became a journalistic whipping boy while suffering acute fiscal crisis. When financial recovery began around 1995, at least in the University of California, growth and opportunity were increasingly defined in fiscal terms. I was struck by the apparent absence of strong noncommercial visions of higher education among educational leaders. I was struck also by the apparent muteness of the humanities. Weren't humanists the ones who had done so much to orient life on earth around individuals and society rather than God, and then, after 1800, to orient it around people rather than industrial production? Didn't literature always show a hardcore interest in freedom, autonomy, self-development, and happiness? Perhaps literature's answers were sometimes economically naïve or rooted in the past. But even when professors told us to follow Chaucer, Shakespeare, and Milton, they were in effect telling us to follow pioneering geniuses where genius meant the power and courage to think without limits and to make new rules. Literature was where you could watch fearless people ask, in the words of the South African writer Mark Mathabane, "how do you become your own liberator?" Literature allowed you to explore their answers too.

With this in mind, I had some serious questions about what literary studies were going to do in the more explicitly commercial university. I wondered whether literary studies could affect the ways and the extent to which the university was becoming commercial. Along with others, I started to explore how commercialization was affecting the university's intellectual independence.

I approached these questions through several axioms. At the start, I knew enough about the history of higher education to know that capitalism's esteem for performance, production, profit, measurement, and management was not an alien intruder on campus. I was thus not searching for literary and cultural study that existed outside of capitalist economics. I also thought that commerce as such was not only inevitable but also good, since it was at bottom a central form of human exchange and of mutual aid. I was morally opposed to core elements of capitalist commerce: its enormous inequalities, its exploitation of so much labor, its consistent conflicts with democracy, all of which seemed to be getting worse. At the same time, capitalism's large organizations and orchestrated workforces wrought daily miracles of invention, production, and distribution. The forces of innovation and transformation that I loved in the humanities appeared in different and often captive and yet impressive forms in the modern corporation. Both locations — the corporation and the university — sponsored the true wonder of sociable, even socialized, creativity.

In short, I did not seek a humanistic consciousness that would be free of — undetermined by — the economy and its organizations. To the contrary, I was looking for ways in which the humanities had and would confront and modify economic and organizational life. I thought that this confrontation would be led, within higher education, by its ancient stress on what I'll call *human development*. I felt that human development was more important than ever in an unjust world where information technology and diverse cultures were both of increasing importance.

I sought this strength in the humanities because it was a historical sponsor of these ideas. In spite of its many failings, it also retained insights that had been abandoned by the commercial vision of education. I felt that public economic thought in America in the 1990s was misguided in trying to address (or suppress) the cultural and psychological components of national issues through economic growth. In that sense, the 1990s were much like the 1950s, when the leadership of an affluent society naïvely governed itself through "the paramount position of production."

I also felt that corporate styles of management were very hard on their own people, and that they were equally hard on academics. Most forms of management I'd examined were profoundly anti-humanist. To me humanism meant most fundamentally that economies should be evaluated by the human conditions they produce — for employees, consumers, citizens, the ones left out, everyone affected. The discipline of economics couldn't measure human conditions, but that was all right, as long as its practitioners realized that they needed to get the data elsewhere, meaning from the public, from the humanities, from "qualitative" approaches to social life. Not only did economists usually seem uninterested in this, but I wasn't sure the humanities were set up to do the job. I had been surprised by academic humanists' weak response to attacks on so-called political correctness. I had been alarmed by our ambivalence toward our own colleagues' research on race, sexuality, colonialism, and multiculturalism. These fields combined the analysis of social relations with a focus on personal identity. If humanists didn't care about personal identity, who should? If we didn't care about the sociocultural conditions that helped or harmed identity, who would? Well luckily, lots of people cared, but we were their main representatives in the university, and we could have been doing much better.

Personal identity was, I was sure, a core issue of the information age. The corporate restructuring of the 1980s and 1990s had been accompanied by identity-based social movements, and this was more than coincidence. Many of the latter used the decentralized, flexible organizational structures that were of increasing interest to business. But many humanities academics acted as though these movements were irrelevant if not actually dangerous to academic standards and behavior. Multiculturalism drew fire through the mid- to late 1980s and early 1990s, as did antinuclear peace groups, environmentalists, and AIDS activists. Opponents of multiculturalism and "PC" denounced the replacement of "rigorous standards" with "self-esteem," and it became clear to me that this phony tradeoff encouraged these opponents to cast strong personal and cultural identities as a threat to the management of society. It was true that difference and complexity spelled trouble for economic and political structures based on uniform principles and homogeneous subjects — on "treating everyone alike." But this claim begged the question of the value of this uniformity. Should the internal complexity of individuals and cultures be factored into the governing of society? The attacks on affirmative action in the mid-1990s continued to raise the question of whether personal experience, position, and identity should adapt to "due process" and similar notions of administrative uniformity, or whether administration should adapt to changing social identities. As the decade wore on, identity had a harder time holding its own.

In the midst of this, diversity was going mainstream. Social activists, academics, corporate managers, and others from various walks of life began to define diversity as an asset. Business was interested in the value of multicultural and multinational workforces for global enterprise. Activists were interested in old and new forms of identity-based prejudice and exclusion. Artists, writers, and musicians wanted society to honor creative work from all the country's various and sometimes marginalized communities. Public spectacles like the hearings on the confirmation of Clarence Thomas reminded everyone of the continuing relevance of identity politics to most realms of social life.

Social theorists were drawing out one crucial implication: the increasingly knowledge-based, borderless, "network society" made the self more rather than less important. Alain Touraine wrote that "in a post-industrial society, in which cultural services have replaced material goods at the core of production, it is the defense of the subject, in its personality and in its culture, against the logic of apparatuses and markets, that replaces the idea of class struggle" — or intensifies it. In his widely cited analysis of "the rise of the network society," Manuel Castells made a similar point. "New information technologies are integrating the world in global networks of instrumentality. Computer-mediated communication begets a vast array of virtual communities. Yet the distinctive social and political trend of the 1990s is the construction of social action and politics around primary identities, either ascribed, rooted in history and geography, or newly built in an anxious search for meaning and spirituality."[3]

This book, then, is motivated by three further beliefs. First, even decentralized forms of management will not adequately reflect or govern existing identities because they will fail to contain the larger social transformations on which these identities rest (the information revolution, post-industrial production, the mixing of cultures, increasing social inequality, and so on). Second, to imagine a just version of the post-managerial society, we will need to face a central problem for its inhabitants in and out of science, and particularly for this society's professional and managerial class, or PMC: a deep and pervasive crisis of personal agency. Third, the autonomous university is a crucial site for imagining desirable forms of free agency for the present and the future. The humanities, in particular, should be a leader in this work within the university.

I have divided the book into three parts. Part I, "The Two Missions," tells the story of the research university's double emphasis on economic and human development. In contrast to accounts that invoke a disinterested university later pulled into a worldly orbit, I describe the university's constitutive financial dependence on outside sources and its strategies for dealing with this original state. I recount the development of liberal humanism and the uses to which the university put its narratives of human freedom. I show the connections between humanist aestheticism in the American university and persisting ideals of craft labor. Craft labor ideals were not, I claim, an add-on gesture toward the labor movement, which was largely ignored (or despised) in the university. These ideals were instead part of humanism's imagination of a realm of unalienated individual and collective activity. At its best, humanism summoned the arts as a domain where unalienated experience — freedom as such — could be experienced in the present time, and not wait for the future changes that would give them social existence.

The humanities, however, were insufficiently aware of how actual social conditions would forestall their ideals indefinitely. Part II describes the rise of the most decisive of these conditions, which I call the managerial condition. Management became the privileged, sophisticated mediator between the university's main projects of economic and human development as described in part I. My focus is on the movement from "administration" to "management" in large universities and the distinctive forms that management took on campus. I continue by analyzing the quiet permeation of literary studies by management concepts, and consider the damage done by the concepts of the New Humanism and of meritocracy, both of which hamstrung individual agency and a fuller notion of merit. I am more positive about management in chapter 6, suggesting through an analysis of the rhetoric of agency in big science that university bureaucracy supported high levels of both individual and collaborative innovation. I end this section by considering a strong form of humanist non-managerialism and a counter-reaction within literary academia, led by its New Critics, against those remarkable possibilities.

Part III considers the changing relation between science and industry after World War II, noting both strong humanist values and their confinement by the financial and political logics of postwar science policy. The final chapter looks at the corporate version of the humanities' freedom narrative, and asks how literary academia might get its freedom narratives back. The research university's most important result by far is its graduates, most destined for some segment of the professional middle classes. *Ivy and Industry* asks whether this middle group can really be the agents of history rather than the servants of it — the servants of the top executives and owners and moguls and political players who make the major decisions. Where the university's middle class acts autonomously, can it side, to put it bluntly, with those injured by the university's funders? Part III suggests that middle-class agency was a hotter topic in industry than in the university, to the disadvantage of the independent — and socially radical — forms of agency envisioned by the linkage of aesthetics and craft.

This book reflects my interest in avoiding the waste of existing literary and cultural resources by redirecting rather than abandoning them as weak or corrupt. My procedure is conservative in this sense even as my aims are not, and it has involved me in a difficult and occasionally discouraging process, particularly where I broach the central concept of humanism itself. I argue, starting in chapter 3, that humanism has often revolved around a radically emancipatory vision for human potential, one recovered in metropolitan modernity by the American and French Revolutions, by British Romanticism, by the abolitionist and civil rights movements, by decolonization struggles, all in different ways and in the company of others. At the same time, humanism has helped to justify colonization abroad and draconian social control at home by depicting foreign lands, domestic immigrants, people of color, and workers as defective or un-civilized or unteachably barbaric. If humanism cannot be equated with racism and imperialism, it is continuously associated with them, and with a cofactor to which the United States, especially these days, is prone— cultural exceptionalism, or more accurately cultural supremacism. Hu-manism's impact has therefore varied widely, and in this book my starting point for handling its contradictions is to treat it, restrictively, as a *theory of American middle-class possibilities under industrial capitalism*.

The middle class is an endlessly debated category, which gives me reason to say a few simple things about my use of the term. "Middle class" most generally refers to people of middle to upper income who have at least some college, and who have historically been majority white and white-identified, culturally speaking, though exceptions have been as im-portant as the rule. My "middle class" is largely made up of the "university middle-class," or more familiarly the "professional middle-class," which by and large does knowledge work for a living. This class centers on professionals in the narrower sense: doctors, lawyers, and engineers who retain a version of guild structure in order to evaluate and restrict mem-bership, to define their body of knowledge, and to regulate standards of practice. Yet I do not limit my discussion to them. The middle class includes business people, from support staff to chief executives, and I will favor the term PMC where that is more descriptive. I also mean "middle class" to invoke a crucial feature of professional life—a plausible expecta-tion of real autonomy in the performance of work. Much professional organization has devoted itself to self-governance *within* large organiza-tions, and this wish for autonomy has coincided, in theory, with the sense that autonomy depends on some kind of peer-group democracy, though of a highly managed kind.

It is also true that the professional middle class is internally divided, and is, in particular, divided over the role of the market. Will it be market forces or the members of professions that set fees, define work projects and conditions, and so on? To the extent that the middle class has increasingly allowed market objectives to define its goals, it has tended to define autonomy less in terms of self-governance than in terms of income levels and managerial position: "market" professions are actually not reducing management so much as they are joining it. Throughout these changes, parts of the middle class continue an older tradition of defining professional skills through their *social* value. In the case of the humanities, the value lies even further from the market, involving aesthetic, spiritual, intellectual, or other personal values — the mysterious, indispensable contents of self-development as such. While many sociologists think the market has conquered the middle class, I believe that the middle class is at war with itself over its response to the market. The university, the sciences, the humanities are one place where this quiet but pervasive war is now taking place. The outcome will decide whether the middle class will help the rest of society continue the evolution of autonomy and democracy as forms of life, or rather help our increasingly narrow political system to reduce these to market functions.[4]

My analysis has the unwanted effect of focusing attention on an Anglo-American academic mainstream at a period in history when its monopoly on literary attention has finally started to erode. Here I do not discuss the liberal arts colleges where many of higher education's most radical possibilities were conceived and put in place. I ignore important developments at remarkable colleges all across the country, from Evergreen and Reed in the Northwest to Spelman, Howard, and Fisk in the South. I thus bypass the major centers of African American education during this period. Given the racial segregation that defined the student bodies and faculties at research universities, my story here is largely about the white middle class. My discussion of racial transformations at the research university will appear in a companion volume on the later twentieth century.

Here I attend to the pillar of the middle class, the overstudied, oversimplified professional middle class, because most recent work has blinded its members to their own antagonisms toward the economic system they support, and especially to their history of implicitly radical expectations for individual life. In the United States, these radical expectations do not appear in the form of radical politics. Excavating the minor and silent notes of this radicalism will try the patience of some of my readers, including some who are closest to my own sense of the terrible incompleteness of human emancipation in our own time. My hope is that this book contributes to a better synthesis of recessive yet visionary humanistic perspectives with their recent, irresistible antihumanist critiques.

My experience of literature has been of perennial and intense enjoyment. I have learned from it that enjoyment forms the core of creativity and innovation. It is obvious to me that much of our current economic turbulence comes from widespread efforts to manage the unmanageable — to manage the subtlest forms of human freedom on which all new knowledge and, we are told, economic prosperity depend. In my opinion, the future will be good only if we can figure out how to achieve free agency for an entire society within the complex organizations through which we do our work. Our society is managed, if not controlled, by a middle class bound, one that frequently tolerates the bondage of others. Yet literature has always been about the struggle for agency in intricate social states, and its authors and critics and protectors have as much to contribute to building a better future as do the country's leaders, who direct an army of technologists.

# CHAPTER 2

. . . . . . . . . . . . . . . . . . . . . . . . . . .

## *A Permanent Dependence*

Most university graduates are happy to have the skills they acquired in school. But many also talk about their college years as a time of awakening to a larger world, to the histories of art and science and peoples, to unknown capacities in themselves, to new forms of ambition and of hope. Such alumni are interested in how various economic or social changes affect their alma mater's ability to continue the teaching mission that they think helped create their own adult selves.

When they think this, students and alumni are aligned with an inaugural purpose of the research university—the teaching of reason to selves and citizens. In most descriptions of its rise, the modern research university was an institution apart from the world. The university allowed the rational self to evaluate everything freely because the university protected its faculty from political and commercial power. More accurately, free inquiry was the domain of the faculties that lacked worldly power, faculties now associated with the humanities. The faculty of reason could be developed and instilled in those fields where politics and commerce were held at bay. When politics and commerce intruded on these faculties, that would damage the development of reason.[1]

When one alumnus of Harvard took an interest in how his university was adapting to a commercial age, he didn't like what he saw. "The men who stand for education and scholarship have the ideals of business men. They are, in truth, business men. The men who control Harvard to-day are very little else than business men, running a large department store which dispenses education to the million. Their endeavor is to make it the *largest* establishment of the kind in America."[2] This kind of outcry became increasingly familiar in the 1990s as the "corporate university" crystallized in many minds as a threat to the greater goals of higher education. This particular quotation stands out because of its date. It was published in 1909, and its author, John Jay Chapman, had attended Harvard during the long presidency of Charles W. Eliot that began in 1869.

The university has always symbolized independent thought, but it has never been an independent institution. Government support increased in scale and visibility after World War II, but it began long before. The same is true of business patronage. When we talk about the research university, the term "corporate university" is largely redundant. The research university has never been anything like a monastery or an ivory tower. It developed after the Civil War in partnership with business and government. The laments of Chapman and his contemporaries demonstrate that the research university was not invaded by business agendas recently, but was constituted by business agendas from its inception.

In the late nineteenth century, American capitalism underwent what we could call its first corporate revolution. This revolution created the modern form of business enterprise, in which relatively small firms were replaced with large, intensively managed corporations. The business historian Alfred Chandler has argued that the corporation "took the place of market mechanisms in coordinating the activities of the economy and allocating its resources." The economy became increasingly dominated by the practices of bureaucratic control. Chandler identified two core features of the corporation: "it contains many distinct operating units and it is managed by a hierarchy of salaried executives." The hierarchy consisted of an "entirely new class of businessmen" — "middle and top managers." "As late as 1840 there were no middle managers in the United States — that is, there were no managers who supervised the work of other managers and in turn reported to senior executives who themselves were salaried managers."[3] The corporate revolution created a new economic infrastructure and a new class of people to operate it.

The research university was a central component of this rising industrial system. It was a vital subcontractor, providing technical and organizational knowledge for the new business organizations. It promised renewal to a rising industrial economy that in the last third of the nineteenth century was racked by two extended depressions. It also supplied the people who would fill these new management roles. It created managers, people who had the independence to manage others and the malleability to be managed themselves.

But the university did not simply fuse with this system as a supplier. It sheltered much non-utilitarian knowledge and research driven by pure curiosity. It harbored free thinkers and a few dissidents, and some non-capitalist and anti-capitalist forms of understanding. The university taught the new middle classes of professional and organizational workers to see themselves as justified exceptions within an industrial labor system where the scientific management associated with Frederick Taylor was regimenting ordinary worker self-direction almost out of existence. The university gave its graduates the means to see themselves as humanizers. It gave them an expectation of humanized working lives for themselves in an era of routinized administration and managerial concentration.

Throughout this book I will be discussing the university's double-edged industrial role. This role extends back to the first corporate revolution after the Civil War, and to the nineteenth-century university's material dependence on it.

· · · *Four States of Dependence* · · ·

Most descriptions of university-business relations since 1980 note the increase in corporate influence on campus. A good initial case can be made for this claim. In the crucial case of funding for research and development (R&D), federal data show that "industrial support of R&D in colleges and universities grew from 2.6 percent of total academic R&D in 1970 to 6.9 percent in 1995," and by the early years of the twenty-first century was approaching 10 percent of the total.[4] In the University of California, industry support hovers just below 10 percent of the total. It has continued to rise during the past five years, although, as we will see, its forms have changed. Such figures refer to overall R&D funding; the proportion of non-defense research on campus from corporate sources is higher. Even those numbers underplay the concentration of business investment in advanced forms of technology with the highest visibility on and off campus. Business has also become increasingly vocal in calling for changes in university funding and governance. Some industry leaders have decried "political correctness" on campus (although industry has not been so supportive of rollbacks of affirmative action). Universities have been increasingly eager to show their adherence to "business" standards of accounting, labor efficiency, and getting "results." At the same time, in the 1990s public funding for universities began to stagnate or decline. In one report's representative words, "All sources of revenues for the research university seem to have reached a plateau or even to have begun to decline. The biggest declines are in two important sources of support for research: state appropriations and profits from medical services. Federal grant support has [also] begun to shrink."[5] Taking such trends as a whole, many observers have questioned what seems to be the university's increasing subservience to business priorities.

One of the best studies in this vein is *Academic Capitalism*, whose authors summarize the mechanics of the situation:[6]

> As the economy globalized, the business or corporate sector in industrialized countries pushed the state to devote more resources to the enhancement and management of innovation so that corporations and the nations in which they were headquartered could compete more successfully in world markets. Business leaders wanted government to sponsor commercial research and development in research universities and in government laboratories. . . . [At the same time], the flow of public money to higher education was receding . . . As the share of federal funds for higher education decreased, the states picked up some of the burden, but not all, because the states, too, were spending the bulk of their moneys on entitlement or mandated programs such as health care and prisons. After 1983, states periodically experienced fiscal crisis (state income failed to match state expenditures) that precipitated restructuring in higher education. In 1993–94 several states, for the first time, experienced an absolute decline in the amount of money expended on higher education . . . Restructuring often put increased resources at the disposal of units and departments close to the market, that is, those relatively able to generate external grants and contracts or other sources of revenue. [These conditions] encouraged faculty and institutions to direct their efforts towards programs and research that intersected with the market.[7]

We could call this scenario the "dependency thesis": changes in the economic environment intensify the university's state of financial dependence, which boils down to a dependence on market revenues. Universities that license their inventions to business firms are dependent on market dynamics and on the firms that dominate markets. Administrators logically come to value business thinking, to think more like business people, and to invite business people to join and shape their work.

As we start off, it's worth distinguishing four dimensions of the university's dependence on business.

1. *The commercialization of university campuses.* Those old, sometimes amateurish but locally operated student cafeterias, bookstores, and memorabilia counters are increasingly assimilated by national chains. On many campuses, Burger King or Panda Express serves the food, the Gap makes the school T-shirts. The bookstores, when not run by Barnes and Noble, crowd books with brand-name sportswear and computer supplies. Coke or Pepsi signs an exclusive distribution deal that covers all campus food outlets and dormitories, the sports teams display the logo of Nike or whatever corporate sponsor bought the equipment, and student mailboxes are filled with pre-approved applications from Visa and Master Card.

David Noble has likened this commercialization of educational precincts to putting Calvin Klein shorts on the statue of Jesus.[8] Like Noble, I regret the extent to which students are addressed as retail customers, and the large proportion of work time they spend maintaining the middle-class levels of consumption they had enjoyed through their parents. At the same time, I've found that most students can distinguish between education and advertising, learning and consuming, and I reject generalizations about their diminished commitment to knowledge, their reduced attention spans, and their reduced intellectualism. In any case, I will have little to say about this most visible (but superficial) layer of business's campus presence.

2. *Research partnerships between university scientists and individual companies.* These partnerships include sponsored research, in which the company supports research initiated and conducted by a faculty member, and collaborations in which the company pays for new campus facilities where university personnel conduct research largely chosen in concert with the company. Researchers may come to be influenced as much by market factors as by research problems; they may be steered by potential profits rather than by mystery and curiosity. Faculty may become accountable to their corporate partners and investors in addition to, and sometimes ahead of, their professional and university communities.[9] Nearly all kinds of research partnerships have their roots in the nineteenth century, and offer opportunities and risks that have long shaped knowledge, society, technology, and the economy. Most research and development has always taken place in industry, which today "performs 70 percent of the nation's

total R&D" while "academic institutions perform about 13 percent."[10] The university can come to depend on industry for research funding and infrastructure and, to some extent, for its research problems as well. In addition, the university depends on industry to produce and market its inventions.

3. *Managerial influence on university administration.* Universities have periodically borrowed from the business world efficiency measures modeled on factory management, or cost accounting techniques that apply profit-and-loss measures to academic units. The 1990s in particular saw various attempts to employ "bottom-line" thinking in the delivery of educational services to the student customer, and to apply various management trends like "total quality management" and "reengineering" to university bureaucracies. The university, in this dimension, depends on the corporation for its organizational self-knowledge and for organizational reform. It may apply the standards of for-profit enterprise to its nonprofit activities.

4. *The culture of entrepreneurship.* Academic entrepreneurs may come to regard financial self-interest as a legitimate motive for academic activity, on the theory that self-interest in no way damages the impartiality and freedom of research long associated with the university. Academic research becomes increasingly intertwined with profit possibilities, meaning that commercial standards help to define research agendas and social utility. When this happens, business's instrumental goals, shortened time frames, visible results, measurable outcomes, financial rewards, and top-down decision-making seem both valid and valuable in the university community. Successful faculty become "businessed," praise enterprise, steer their research toward commercial problems, look for private funding, partner with potential investors, and concoct vehicles for equity stakes. As these activities come to seem more important or at least more urgent than basic research, they may distort or block basic research even as they offer new opportunities, revenues, and public goods. In this dimension, the university may become culturally and psychologically dependent on industry for its notions of success, influence, and development. It may become dependent on industry for its sense of its core product — useful (and lucrative) technology — and its social value.

In this volume I will be analyzing these last three forms of business influence: technological development; managerial administration, including financial control; and entrepreneurial visions of the public good. I analyze *managerialism*, by which I mean a cluster of principles of organizational life that combines these three elements. Each of these has cultural and ideological strength in its own right, and their joint strength has been magnified by their association with business's financial power.

The university's financial dependence raises doubts about its intellectual independence. What happens to basic research when industry offers greater rewards for commercial research? What are the structural effects on science and non-science professions when their priorities are increasingly set, and their work increasingly reviewed, by markets instead of peers? How does commercial dependence change the activity of the researchers themselves? How do psychological states of dependence change the questions asked and the knowledge produced? How can an industry-oriented university sustain nonprofit visions of modern life, including the traditional university staples of curiosity-driven research and human development? We can best answer these questions by understanding the history of business's presence on the nation's campuses.

## · · · *From College to Corporation* · · ·

Historians have been unable to find a period in which colleges and universities were fully in the hands of educators who ignored business input. Although the "old college" was often under the sway of its founding church and saw itself as serving public functions, college leaders generally favored governance by boards of trustees largely composed of prominent professionals and businessmen.[11] They espoused the college's public mission while protecting the college's governing body from the often powerful claims of what we'd now call the "stakeholders" — the community, the taxpaying public, the students, the staff, and the teaching faculty. Regardless of the insularity of campus life, the college did not live apart from business so much as it furnished sites for the application of business methods to public ideals.

The legal foundation for private control of higher education was formalized in 1819. The source was the U.S. Supreme Court's decision in *Trustees of Dartmouth College v. Woodward*. John Wheelock, the college's beleaguered president and son of Dartmouth's founder, had asked the legislature to investigate the behavior of the board, which retaliated by firing him. In 1816 the legislature "passed and the governor approved a law that changed the name of the institution from Dartmouth College to Dartmouth University and brought the institution . . . under more effective state control." There was significant popular hostility to the trustees, and in 1817 the New Hampshire Superior Court "decided that Dartmouth was indeed a public corporation, that its trustees were public officers responsible to the people and therefore subject to legislative control. The court rejected the notion that a corporation charter was a contract; it could find no precedent and, moreover, such a notion put a public institution beyond public control."[12] The trustees fought against this public control of Dartmouth by appealing the decision to the Supreme Court, where John Marshall wrote a decision that restored Dartmouth College's status as private property.

Dartmouth, Marshall wrote, was an "eleemosynary corporation," and such corporations are for "the management of private property, according to the will of the donors. They are private corporations. A college is as much a private corporation as a hospital; especially a college founded as this was, by private bounty. A college is a charity. . . . The government, in these cases, lends its aid to perpetuate the beneficent intention of the donor, by granting a charter, under which his private charity shall continue to be dispensed, after his death."[13] The crucial, lasting legal cornerstone was the court's finding that a public charter was like a private contract. Though a corporation be chartered by an act of the legislature, the legislature could not interfere in its legal operation without its members' consent. Justice Story used the analogy of marriage: the legislature can make "general laws regulating divorces upon breaches of that contract." But the legislature cannot "dissolve such a contract, without any breach on either side, against the wishes of the parties, and without any judicial inquiry to ascertain a breach."[14]

The *Dartmouth* case had an enormous impact on the related histories of the college and the corporation. It established that chartered educational and business institutions resembled each other in one crucial way: both could be governed as if they were the private property of their internally appointed officials. The case "established that corporations had private rights, including protection from changing the content of a charter. If the Court had decided on the basis of the equally plausible principle that the state had a continuing interest in holding the corporation accountable to the public, corporate history would have been very different indeed. There might have never arisen an entity with the rights, entitlements, and responsibilities that we recognize as the modern private corporation, much less one that would have come to dominate the economy and society."[15] The decision gave the American college the legal status of a private business at the same time that it affirmed business's autonomy from the public will. The old college's autonomy and success became increasingly associated with its similarity to private business.

· · · *Public Like Private* · · ·

The *Dartmouth* decision ratified an existing tradition according to which boards of trustees assumed their independence from their constituencies inside as well as outside the college. This was understandable: no organization wants to be constantly second-guessed by outsiders, even if they formally represent the public, and a board's financial ingenuity was a great asset to struggling institutions. But most colleges made systematic attempts to insulate their boards from direct public scrutiny and accountability; they insulated their boards from faculty, staff, and students as well. In seeking this kind of freedom from both customers and employees, college boards resembled business proprietorships.

When members of California's "college movement" wrote up the compact for the College of California in 1860, they were explicit about the trustees' constituency: "Rule I. Such trustees shall be elected from time to time as shall fairly and equally represent the patrons and contributors to the funds of the Institution, provided, (1) A majority of them shall always be members of evangelical Christian churches, and (2) Not more than one-fourth of the actual members be of one and the same Christian denomination."[16] Balance required the presence of a range of Christian faiths but not a range of college constituents. The later description of the University of California Regents would read differently, but there would be similar attempts to shield the Regents from popular intervention.

For example, in his inaugural address as UC's second president in 1872, Daniel Coit Gilman put the legislature in a subordinate place. "He asked the Regents to be 'the power behind the throne,'" and suggested that they might choose instructors and develop "new departments and schools" in the same way that they would construct buildings and invest the money. The members of the legislature, by contrast, were to pay up while staying out of the way. They were to provide "steady, munificent, and confiding support." But "'quick to help and slow to interfere' should be their watchword."[17] In spite of many legislators' doubts about nontechnical education, they generally obliged Gilman and his successors by leaving the governance of the university to private parties.

The California legislature made one serious nineteenth-century attempt to get back in the game, and it occurred early in the university's

history. In 1874 it formed a body to investigate the university's management, starting with the possibly self-dealing behavior of a wealthy Regent
who was supervising the construction of the College of Letters. One
historian of UC attributes the inquiry to the spread of Henry George's
populism in tandem with the agitation of "two dissatisfied professors,
Carr of the agricultural department, and Swinton of the literary." Carr felt
that Gilman was violating the Morrill Land Grant Act by allocating only
about 10 percent of his budget to agriculture. (Carr and Swinton were
soon fired from the faculty, which, this historian reports, "practically
ended the internal disharmony.") The report vindicated the university
and, in the process, described the possibility that the president be elected
by the faculty as "productive of great evil."[18] The report affirmed that the
university's legitimate subjects went well beyond its agricultural and mechanical base. It tied the university's comprehensive scope to the multitude of the university's funding sources, sources that included federal
grants, state appropriations, and "private gifts."

When a new state constitution was enacted in 1879, the university was
granted operational independence from the legislature. For UC to be
great, its advocates held, its leadership would need to be buffered from
both the faculty and the public. This buffer has often protected the university's academic freedom, though it has by no means secured it. Business
leaders, however, were not excluded by these prohibitions. Their presence
helped the university defend itself as a key component in the development
of California business. By the middle decades of the nineteenth century, "a
passion for economic expansion and development motivated both business and education."[19] A public university's dependence on public moneys
did not end its dependence on business support.[20] To the contrary, the
two dependencies increased together.

### · · · *Endless Insecurity* · · ·

The United States has always had more than its share of colleges, and
these have had more than their share of money trouble. Private colleges,
even the wealthiest, were never wealthy enough to buy their freedom.

Up through the late nineteenth century, most colleges were supported
by private organizations, religious and otherwise, and these were often
too small to keep the college in one piece for long. Colleges lacked the
popular support of the parish church and the steady income of the local
candle factory. Virtually none could afford to pick and choose their stu-

dents, and most addressed themselves to local and denominational constituencies. A large number of small colleges competed with each other for a limited number of interested students, and also competed with mechanic institutes, lecturing societies, and other educational groups offering a more practical kind of teaching. Before the high school system took root in the Northeast and Midwest in the last two decades of the century, colleges lacked a public pipeline for appropriately trained young people. Colleges regularly vanished from the world, leaving their grounds and buildings to fall into disrepair or be converted into something useful like an orphanage. In the 1850s, a decade when it might now seem impossible that the entire United States could have supported seven hundred colleges, seven hundred colleges disappeared.[21]

Until massive federal support was established during World War II, the university's fiscal crises of the 1930s and 1990s were the norm rather than the exception. Modest stability required the support of external benefactors and patrons. Sometimes these external benefactors were religious denominations. Sometimes they were men of wealth. When Eliphalet Nott, the president of Union College, gave the school $600,000 of his own money in 1854, he made Union the wealthiest college in the United States before the Civil War.[22] Many colleges depended on bailouts from benefactors for their survival, and the search for these was perpetual.

Where churches and individuals left off, government picked up. Even the wealthiest private colleges have needed regular government injections: "On over one hundred occasions before 1789 the General Court of Massachusetts appropriated funds for Harvard College, which clearly was not capable of taking care of itself. Indeed, Harvard, Yale, and Columbia could not have survived the colonial period without support of the state. . . . In the case of Bowdoin and Williams, each of which received $30,000 as the result of the same legislative act, state aid underwrote whatever solvency the two institutions attained during the period."[23] Public subsidy similarly floated Rutgers, the University of Pennsylvania, Hamilton, and the City College of New York. "In 1785 Vermont gave a half township . . . to Dartmouth, a college in neighboring New Hampshire." Princeton got permission to operate lotteries in three states. Even wealthy Union College, after receiving Nott's $600,000, accumulated another $385,000 from state-authorized lotteries while Nott was president. A new college meant a new demand for state support, and this rule was so unbroken that when Massachusetts chartered Amherst College in 1825, it expressly stated that the charter could never be construed as a "pledge" of "pecuniary aid."[24]

Later in the century, the University of California overspent its original endowments and income within its first three years.[25]

Business and government have played parallel roles in supporting higher education throughout its history. Their support was the only thing standing between colleges and universities and their fiscal demise. Without external patronage in both private and public forms, the end was merely a question of when.

### · · · *Numerical Identity* · · ·

After the Civil War, higher education began to undergo its long revolution. The result was the unique kind of modern research university that still reigns in higher education. The last four decades of the nineteenth century saw two waves of major foundings. The Morrill Act of 1862 offered federal resources to start public universities devoted to "the agricultural and mechanic arts." The act gave a new and lasting momentum to the idea of college education for a growing middle class. It offered higher education unprecedented security. It also allowed the founding of universities on a whole new scale and scope. The Morrill Act was the impetus behind the founding of the University of Illinois (1867), the University of California (1868), and Cornell University (1865).[26] It was complemented by a booming interest in the university systems that had produced major scientific advances in Europe, especially Germany. The vision of pure research was embodied in the founding of the Johns Hopkins University in 1876, an event most historians regard as a turning point for higher education. The 1880s and 1890s witnessed a second wave of major foundings, one that included Clark University in 1887, Stanford in 1891, and the University of Chicago in 1890.

These foundings were propelled by great purposes, and by various descriptions of what these purposes were. The new universities set themselves apart from the older colleges in two ways. The first was the lack of a core identity. The university offered not identity but totality, and its leaders deliberately avoided a single or unified description of the university mission. Ezra Cornell's founding vision was of "an institution where any person can find instruction in any study." The first president of Cornell, Andrew D. White, claimed that "four years of good study in one direction are held equal to four years of good study in another."[27] Daniel Coit Gilman defined the University of California as "a group of agencies organized to advance the arts and sciences of every sort, and train young men as scholars for all the intellectual callings of life."[28] Within the vision of a comprehensive wholeness of learning, leaders combined moral and practical goals in the company of new ambitions for the creation of scientific knowledge.

The legislative impetus behind the public university, the first Morrill Act, encouraged states to establish "land grant colleges." The act had established the basic pattern for the combination when it dedicated its grants to institutions "where the leading object shall be, without excluding other scientific and classical studies, . . . to teach such branches of learning as are related to agriculture and the mechanic arts."[29] The bill's chief sponsor, a congressman from Vermont, had said that his purpose was "to offer an opportunity in every State for a liberal and larger education to large numbers, not merely to those destined to sedentary professions, but to those much needing higher instruction for the world's business, for the industrial pursuits and professions of life."[30] Every president has emphasized some elements over others, but the excitement, the promise, and the compelling need for expensive, gigantic, general campuses came from the offering of all the callings, all the research, all the schools of useful *and* liberal culture — all the intellectual goods of past and future under one big roof.

The research university, through its basic structure and goals, was born as a miscellany that would be funded for its inclusiveness. This in turn insured the absence of an intellectual, religious, functional, or socioeconomic core.[31]

It wasn't easy to find general qualitative measures of progress for a "group of agencies." Academic fields advanced according to their internal assumptions, methods, goals, and standards, and much of the time these were at odds with the standards and goals of other fields. Many fields were in turn internally divided about these measures, making outside judgments even trickier. Any given administrator was incapable of making professionally substantive judgments about nearly all the disciplines in the university. Quantitative measures, on the other hand, could be applied to any area. Better yet, they were already central to American understandings of social progress — territory controlled, size of population, level of national income, and so on. In the undergraduate curriculum, a unified set of standard requirements of study was gradually replaced by the "elective system," and by 1900 this had become a general (though contested) hallmark of the research university. In the administration of departments, qualitative judgments were replaced with numbers — size of undergraduate enrollments, number of courses or students taught per faculty member, rate of growth in enrollments, and, later, scores on teaching evaluations, numbers of publications, size of research grants, and so on.

The research university eventually learned how to instill an "alma mater" identity in its alumni and alumnae, to use sports, regional links, and other social connections to create loyalty to something that had an everyday life for students and employees, tied to their familiar sections of the campus. But institutional experiences and personas did not enable operational unity or coherent development. Universities were increasingly governed through bureaucratic administration, quantitative measures, and client demand.

····· *The Growth Imperative* ·····

The second distinctive feature of the research university was its devotion to economic growth. Quantitative measurement was part of a larger post–Civil War American culture that prized expansion and growth above nearly all else. Growth was an especially pressing issue during the age of incorporation that followed the Civil War. Both waves of university founding coincided with major economic depressions, in the 1870s and the 1890s. Trapped in the pursuit of resources in times of stagnating and shrinking economies, universities cast themselves as vehicles of much-needed economic recovery.

Research universities increasingly defined their own success in these same quantitative terms. More students meant more tuition revenues, but also required more facilities, which laid claim to the increased revenues. Expanding academic disciplines needed more faculty and more laboratories. Professional schools offered new forms of knowledge, useful training, and new revenues, but also required additional buildings and ever-improving equipment. Growth was also part of a competitive system in which universities ranked themselves against their peers, poached faculty, imitated successful programs, and dreamed of glory. Between 1900 and 1920 revenues at the fifteen leading research universities increased by a factor of five.[32]

Growth was not simply a form of measurable change. It was a spirit, a desire, a vision, and a way of life. In 1897 President Eliot of Harvard wrote, "I find that I am not content unless Harvard grows each year, in spite of the size which it has attained." "Quality being secured," he added, "the larger the quantity the better." Historians of higher education have noted the similarities between the development of the university and the rise of big business. Laurence Veysey observes that "Eliot's keen eye for numbers was almost universally shared by academic administrators."[33] Roger L. Geiger concludes that higher education "was no less a growth industry during these years than steel or oil."[34]

Constant growth required consistent management, which meant the constant growth of management. Academic growth was matched if not exceeded by administrative growth.[35] Administrations grew in two waves that more or less matched the waves of founding mentioned earlier; each increased the attachment to the existing corporate model. "The first occurred in the late [eighteen] sixties and early seventies," Veysey writes, "when Andrew D. White [of Cornell], Charles W. Eliot, and James B. Angell [of Michigan] came to power. Eliot and Angell, especially, represented a new style of worldly sophistication . . . Their aggressiveness, their concern for budgets and public relations, their interest, for example, in the statistics of their establishments, set what was then an entirely new standard."[36] Strong management of the research university has always gone hand in hand with a systematic focus on fundraising and funds.

The second stage enhanced business specialization. Administration became differentiated into budgeting, accounting, fundraising, alumni activities, personnel relations, facilities management, and other functions. At Columbia, around 1900, the "president's chambers" became the "president's office." New offices opened in most universities to conduct the new practices of organized fundraising and the solicitation of alumni gifts. As the structure became more articulated, more structure was required to communicate and mediate among different parts. The administrative system developed its own internal metabolism. It established clearer boundaries between itself and the university's academic functions. I'll have more to say about this separation of knowledge and management in later chapters, but it is so familiar to us in part because it was well under way in the 1890s. By 1900 university administration had achieved something very close to its current form.[37]

Finance was always the centerpiece of university administration. William Rainey Harper, the founding president of the University of Chicago, was particularly clear about this. "The university of the twentieth century," he wrote, "is compelled to spend a hundred thousand dollars where the institution of the nineteenth century spent ten thousand." The result, he concluded, was that "the great university cannot be conducted except upon a business basis and with large funds for expenditure." The business basis required an apparatus that would allow the university to function like a business. "The business of a university, with eight or ten millions of dollars which continually require to be reinvested, is therefore equivalent to the work of two or three large banks, and the strictly banking part of the business transactions thus involved is not inconsiderable."[38] The university's banking sector had to track its real estate investments, trade in stocks and bonds, collect rents and maintain rental property, and manage a dozen other financial sectors that Harper expertly detailed.

None of this is meant to suggest an intrinsic contradiction between financial and educational values. Growth and education are compatible, and finance is part of any institution's operation. Harper is an interesting example of the combination: he was an organizational diva who also crusaded for the liberal arts. In the morning he would devise managerial solutions to business problems during a dozen appointments. In the afternoon he would teach classical languages to undergraduates. The University of Chicago was simultaneously the creation of Rockefeller's monopoly oil money and of liberal arts advocacy. Nonetheless, we can say that university research and university finance grew up in continued, muted struggle. They grew by different standards and yet grew side by side, mutually suspicious and interdependent.

The research university increasingly defined institutional success through quantitative measures resembling those of growth industries in competitive markets. Of course the advancement of knowledge remained the university mission, and it was invoked by financial officers in trustee meetings no less than by literature professors in their classrooms. Each academic field maintained its own non-financial definitions of intellectual progress. Administrations rarely operated by confronting or ignoring these intellectual definitions. But the advancement of knowledge is hard to define and measure, differs drastically from one area of knowledge to the next, and is usually contested within each field. Administrations set up parallel measures, ones that were simpler and more legible to taxpayers and legislators, and that became institutionally more powerful than any discipline's self-descriptions. Research universities assumed that research would exist within the parameters of its business system, helping the processes of administration to become increasingly unlike internal intellectual practices and increasingly like business practices outside them.

Quantitative measures meant no harm, but they tacitly reduced the intellectual singularity of academic fields. Academic success became something best communicated with the methods of cost accounting. Whatever the cultures of specific fields, their common culture was dominated by quantitative measures of recognition and growth. The members of a field, and their consciousness of themselves, became dependent on the university's financial status and on the quantitative system that managed it.

### · · · *Growth without Profits* · · ·

Universities shared their formative years with those of corporate America, and they acquired many of the procedures of the corporation. But they were not actually business corporations. Profits were not "job one," and universities, operationally, were nonprofit institutions. Education did not function like a commodity in a capitalist economy. It was labor intensive, and thus the difference between labor costs and revenues for the product was fairly small. Education's labor force, though often mistreated, had enough social status to protect it from the more extreme forms of exploitation in the manufacturing economy. One discipline after another was professionalized in the 1880s, and one core motivation was to protect the relative autonomy of intellectual work. As we will see, faculty preserved many of the practices of self-managed labor that were common among craft workers in earlier periods.

The colossal profits of the concentrated industrial economy remained unavailable to the university. They could never take advantage of the fount of capitalist value — surplus value extracted from each unit of production multiplied by huge, standardized product runs. On virtually every count, the university was closer to an older artisanal economy than to the newer factory model.

Because they played by different economic rules, universities and corporations aspired to very different scales of resources. The table on the next page is crude, but it illustrates the difference in size between the most prominent universities of the turn of the century and some examples of prototypical business corporations (mostly railroads).[39] Many of the companies on the list were ordinary enough to disappear in the next wave of consolidation, and yet they overshadowed even the wealthiest research university. In terms of their overall function, universities and corporations played entirely different games, and were separated by orders of magnitude in their resources and returns.

Universities had a number of available funding sources, but the only one that was under their direct control was tuition revenue, and even that

University Endowments and Capitalization of Industrial Firms, in Millions, 1890s and 1917–1919

---

*1890s*

| Harvard (1899) | $12.615 | New York, New Haven & Hartford Railroad | $110 |
|---|---|---|---|
| Chicago | 5.726 | Reading Rail Road | 670 |
| Cornell | 6.756 | Atchison, Topeka & Santa Fe Railroad | 647 |
| California | 2.878 | Norfolk & Western Railway | 120 |
| Yale | 4.942 | American Tobacco (plug only) | 97.691 |

*1917–1919*

| Harvard | $44.569 | New York, New Haven & Hartford | $694 |
|---|---|---|---|
| Chicago | 28.364 | Reading Rail Road | 500 |
| Cornell | 16 | Atchison, Topeka & Santa Fe Railroad | 847 |
| California | 7.254 | Norfolk & Western Railway | 343 |
| Yale | 24.05 | American Tobacco (all) | 164 |
| Stanford | 33.26 | American Ice | 35 |
| Michigan | 1.329 | Standard Oil of New Jersey | 574 |

---

was dependent on custom, student income, and the price of peer institutions. Too much rode on tuition to give steady comfort. For many years after 1900, Penn and MIT continued to use tuition to cover 90 percent of their budgets. Even at Harvard, which has been the wealthiest university in the United States since 1870, the figure was close to half.[40] Tuition could be set internally in response to the university's own desires and needs, but it never generated surplus cash flows of the sort that corporations used to fund their own growth. No matter the prestige or health of the institution, tuition would never turn into capital. It covered a portion of educational costs in the same way that sales covered costs in a retail store. Nor could universities raise funds in other ways common in business, such as by selling equity shares to the public on a stock market.

In short, universities did not directly participate in the commodity system that is the major long-term source of the growth of capital. They took on a vast new set of activities and expenses without access to the financial machinery that supported these activities in corporations. The small size of the university's asset base, noted above, was the central symptom of its dependent position within a capitalist economy.

Other sources of funds — state governments, loyal alumni, private benefactors—were even less subject to the university's control. In 1899 state appropriations were nearly 90 percent of Wisconsin's budget and 95 percent of the University of California's.[41] By the 1870s many state legislatures realized that they would have to contribute regular funds to university budgets, but it was not until after 1900 that these contributions evolved into "substantial recurrent investments for the expansion and improvement of [university] facilities." Private donations were erratic, highly localized, and often given for restricted purposes. Johns Hopkins and Stanford tried self-reliance in the 1890s, meaning that they tried to live on their endowments, and as a reward suffered perpetual money trouble.[42]

· · · *Soft Taylorism* · · ·

Since they couldn't turn money into capital, universities focused on controlling costs. Decades of federal grant growth and steady tuition increases make it harder for us to see this, but universities never moved far from a small-business adherence to the virtues of austerity. A university is labor intensive; an increase in "customers" or research production generally requires a proportionate increase in personnel. The bulk of any university budget is payroll, and payroll has been a prime target for every kind of financial discipline.

The American university tradition of low faculty salaries goes back 370 years. An equally old tradition has allowed colleges and universities to save money by letting faculty go and herding leftover students into remaining courses. Colleges often cut faculty benefits, and this could mean anything from reducing pensions to eliminating a professor's right to graze one milk cow on university grounds.[43] When salaries rose after World War II and again in the 1960s, largely because of federal infusions of funds into technological fields, payroll costs were contained by expanding the use of non-faculty instructors, especially teaching assistants enrolled in doctoral programs. Since 1980 universities have controlled payroll costs by increasing the use of nontenured and part-time instructors at not quite double the rate of full-time faculty.[44]

The research university broke with the college by organizing itself to produce knowledge, and it has always been attracted to forms of labor discipline modeled on commodity production. By 1900 most business leaders equated discipline with some version of what came to be known as Frederick Taylor's scientific management. Taylorism meant at least three things: the "time-motion" studies that broke the production process down into its component steps; a preoccupation with improving labor "efficiency" by refining each of these steps; and minute external control of each worker through the supervision of every step of production. Taylor, propelled by humanitarian impulses, offered business an apparently scientific basis for the separation of labor from management and for management's autocratic power over labor.[45]

Taylorism has always been attacked by critics outside and inside business, but it has never been vanquished. It did not need to be adopted in a literal or complete way in order to act as a regulative ideal. This was true in professions and universities as well as in factories. The standard of excellence became "efficiency": Veysey concludes that "for about twenty years after 1900, 'efficiency' (often in the phrase 'social efficiency') held sway as the most frequently used noun in the rhetoric of university presidents." Taylor, widely considered the author of scientific management in the factory, shaped the development of university administration as well.

The historian Clyde W. Barrow has unearthed an interesting part of this story. In 1905 President Henry S. Pritchett of the Massachusetts Institute of Technology published an article called "Shall the University Become a Business Corporation?" Although he admitted that faculty-led European universities were actually more efficient than their more "business-minded" American counterparts, Pritchett argued that faculty management of large universities would be a setback for higher education. Businessmen, he claimed, were far superior to faculty as administrators, for "no type of man has been developed who is a wiser councilor than the businessman of large sympathy and of real interest in intellectual problems." In the following year, prompted largely by Pritchett, Andrew Carnegie endowed the Carnegie Foundation for the Advancement of Teaching, kicking off a new era of externally funded university research.[46] The foundation's first president was Pritchett.

Pritchett wrote to Frederick Taylor in 1909 seeking advice on sponsoring "an economic study of education." Taylor suggested that the study be directed by a mechanical engineer named Morris L. Cooke. In his report, *Academic and Industrial Efficiency* (1910), Cooke held that "the problem of academic efficiency was in principle no different from that of industrial efficiency because 'all large and continuing causes rest upon formal organization and upon some assured machinery of administration.' Organization was primarily an engineering problem. Administering this organization was the function of management. . . . Organizational efficiency demanded that a worker not 'produce any longer by his own initiative,' but 'execute punctiliously' the orders given by management, 'down to their minutest details.' . . . Professors 'must be governed and measured by the same general standards that generally obtain in other occupations.'" Cooke made a number of recommendations, including one to abolish tenure on the grounds that it screened inefficient workers from management intervention.[47]

It turned out, of course, that management could give orders regulating the physical labor of manufacturing more easily than it could dictate the motions of office work. Many administrations gave it a try, but the more complex or conceptual the work became, the more difficult it was to devise the single most efficient procedure or the know-how to enforce it. Some labor is more easily broken into minute component parts than others, and the general category of white-collar work required more subtle methods of orchestration.

Though direct and detailed supervision of teaching and research did not generally take root in universities, efficiency-oriented business management did. The result of the first stage in the development of the modern research university was to establish the baseline assumption that business thinking as a form of practical reason is better for university decision making than the thinking of faculty and staff. Scientific management did not become a set of regulative techniques in higher education so much as it served as the standard of objective efficiency by which existing faculty and staff practices might be regularly judged.

Over the decades, university faculty have generally consented to this definition of efficiency. Departments and their faculty may not have much contact with the procedures of cost accounting, but its standard was always in place. The result was not that education was run "like a business" but that business remained the standard of efficiency in administration. University subjects, and particularly the arts and humanities, did not develop alternative systems for valuing their activities as they managed to find shelter from the financial standard. In downturns, administrators would always have recourse to an efficiency model that treats educational workers as fungible, in the same way that business treats labor in general.

The university's dependent status is well known to its funders both private and public, and they expect payroll economies to come early and often. In the 1990s accusations of waste were directed at universities from large sectors of the business community. Such criticism might seem odd coming from industries that pay top executives many millions of dollars a year, twenty-five-year-old assistant budget directors more than senior professors, and average salaries in the boardroom five hundred times greater than the average wage on the factory floor. (By contrast, the ratio of highest to lowest salaries in the university is generally ten to one, and about four to one from the top to the bottom of faculty ranks.) But such charges fit with a long tradition in which patrons expect universities to follow low-wage, short-rein labor strategies to match their low-profit activities.

· · · *The Professions and Their Customers* · · ·

Quantitative measures were the first method of managing the early research university. A second was the elaborate process of fundraising. In contrast to their European counterparts, American research universities could not even aspire to surviving on public support. From the start they pursued two major groups of clients: the students, who formed the largest single income source by paying tuition, and wealthy donors of the kind who had helped found major universities like Cornell, Johns Hopkins, Chicago, and Stanford.

In the 1990s many observers suggested that universities had to get "close to the customer," as though this were a new idea. But good customer relations was a business concept that had been part of the research university since its beginnings. The place of the customer was large enough to have been included in the formation of professional standards. Critics of the client-oriented university in the 1990s generally invoked professional standards against commercial ones, and yet most professions have always been attentive to commercial concerns.

The professions developed in opposition to the political sphere's influence on the use of knowledge. Educators and professionals tended to dislike the precedence that politics gave to monetary interest or speculation over knowledge and principle. Cornell's early president Andrew Dickson White complained that "no one can stand in any legislative position and not be struck with the frequent want in men otherwise strong and keen, of the simplest knowledge of principles essential to public welfare." Universities sustained and expanded the professions as guilds. That offered, in Gilman's terms, "objective standards for achievement by banishing partisanship in mental labor and eliminating monopolies of thought."[48] At the same time, the professional's distrust of politics did not entail a rejection of market forces. Burton J. Bledstein's research on the history of the professions led him to conclude that "its client orientation emerged as the outstanding characteristic of the American university, and the clientele included the broad range of people with middle-class aspirations."[49] The professional orientation of the research university actually encouraged responsiveness to its customer base.

Bledstein carries this argument a step further. Not only were university leaders receptive to market forces, but they at times led those forces themselves. "Some of the evidence suggests that university presidents such as Eliot, White, and William Rainey Harper at the University of Chicago introduced businessmen to techniques of corporate promotion and exploitation unfamiliar even in the commercial world."[50] This is not to say that educators and professionals pursued market profits in the same way as commercial business: the development of professional protocols, peer review, and other mechanisms enforced major differences. Nonetheless, the university's financial dependence helped to insure that its client would also be its customer. The university and the professions would control the treatment while practicing under the laws of supply and demand.

The most influential mingling of faculty and client took place in the fields of industrial research. Industry had started to fund university research as early as 1900, and its financial presence increased consistently thereafter. One leading historian of the phenomenon discovered that "cooperation between universities and industry became the urgent message of the science-based industries, the engineering profession, and technical-school educators from roughly 1906 on."[51] Another has noted, "An examination of corporate donations to individual research universities during the interwar years . . . reveals that they were commonplace by the early 1920's and became more frequent as the decade progressed."[52] Industry was most interested in sponsoring research in particular specialties with tangible benefits: "while American business in general could not be convinced of its vested interest in pure science, individual firms made thousands of investments in specific aspects of university science."[53]

University-industry ties took a variety of forms. Among the earliest were research institutes, which were affiliated with universities but were funded largely with industry support. The first and most important of these was the Mellon Institute at the University of Pittsburgh, established in 1913.[54] Another kind of tie was the "Industrial Fellowship" system, instituted at the University of Kansas in 1907. Under this plan, "a member of the chemistry staff [of the university] was appointed for a two-year period to work exclusively on a problem defined by the sponsoring company, which would underwrite the cost. Any discoveries made during the fellowship period became the property of the company, and all patents were assigned to it."[55] As the years passed, an infrastructure was developed to support a range of university-industry collaborations. In the first decades of the century, academic scientists, led by "Vannevar Bush and his MIT colleagues, created models for academic consultation (the one-fifth rule), patenting, and firm formation."[56]

Ties between industry and universities formed early in engineering. MIT, for example, established its department of electrical engineering in 1884. In 1887 Thomas Edison "donated materials, machines, and dynamos for departmental instruction, and additional equipment was secured from Westinghouse."[57] University-industry interactions became increasingly common as MIT and similar institutions saw their graduates staff university and industrial laboratories, making it more likely that each side would recognize mutual interests. In 1907 MIT's electrical engineering department established the Visiting and Advisory Committee, which included representatives of GE, AT&T, Westinghouse, Chicago Edison, Boston Edison, and similar firms. A departmental brochure in 1910 described the department as ready to undertake both basic research and "some of the more distinctively commercial investigations under the patronage or support of the great manufacturing or other commercial companies."[58] In 1920 the department instituted its Technology Plan, "whereby industry could take advantage of the resources of the Institute in exchange for a standard fee." Under the plan, MIT "was obliged to function as a clearinghouse of information for industry, providing ready access to both technical knowledge and the possessors of that knowledge."[59]

Such partnerships spread to other universities both before and after World War II. Their impact on the university system ranged from minor at older, élite liberal arts universities and highly diversified public universities to transformative at others, such as the wealthy but underachieving institution founded in honor of Leland Stanford Jr.[60] Whether visible to the rest of the university or not, industry partnerships were a persistent part of life in the areas of technical research most interesting to industry, centering on electrical and chemical research in the earlier part of the century, and on biotechnology and computer engineering at its end.

· · · *The Business Baseline* · · ·

Research universities never stopped trying to control their financial destinies. They arose through business contributions and partnerships and governmental funding, and continued to look for other and larger sources. They began to cultivate alumni in earnest after World War I. They helped develop the system of private philanthropy that supported major research in science and engineering until the federal government finally weighed in during World War II.[61] They pitched their "products" to every state legislature in the country, and generally showed enormous creativity in keeping higher education going in the face of the ups and downs of public support.

It can still be said, without distorting this remarkable history, that none of these efforts changed the basic structure of dependence on external funds. Whether public or private, rich or poor, every university devoted enormous effort to sustaining the flow of funds from unpredictable external sources. The funding chase remained a central fact of university life. Success or failure in one chase led to the same result next year: another chase.

The university's historical situation is complex and even contradictory. Above all, it has always been dependent on an external financial environment: "American universities," Carol Gruber concludes, "have been particularly responsive to outside influence because of their pattern of lay government and their dependence for funds on donors . . . and on legislative bodies."[62] As part of this tie, the university must be like a business but not be a business. It must be intellectually independent while remaining financially dependent. It must offer products and services that business cannot provide yet be receptive to business practices. These paradoxes have not interfered with the university's social function, but they have shaped that function's content. Above all, we can say that the research university has spent the past hundred years bringing an increasing proportion of the American workforce into the business system while also giving its members a partial haven from the system.

The dependence on external funds has gone hand in hand with a specific business model. We can now itemize its core features:

1. The business corporation provided the basic standards of financial and administrative efficiency.
2. The corporation also furnished the chief standard of success, which was growth. There were intellectual measures, of course, but the growth standard was persistent and public. Growth largely determined distinction: there are virtually no examples of universities that stagnated or declined in wealth or size while rising intellectually.

3. Since the university could not achieve financial independence in the manner of a business corporation, its growth depended on successful customer service.

4. The starting point of university budget strategy was controlling the cost of academic labor. Its primary response to fiscal crisis would be austerity rather than reinvention or debt-based investment.

5. Market forces were seen as compatible with the highest professional standards. There would be no deep contradiction between the market and truth, the outcome of unfettered research. Those who felt that commerce usually distorted the pursuit of knowledge could expect no influence in the university and, in many cases, no employment. Genuine knowledge would always, at least potentially, be a saleable product. The university-trained professional middle class would, in general, assume continuity between higher learning and the market system.

In short, the research university had to live by the rules of administration, growth, customer service, labor austerity, and market demand. It would produce graduates rather than capital—intellectual capital some would call it now. These graduates formed a new middle class that could creatively manage an evolving society of organizations. But to produce these graduates the university could not engage in the activities of corporate production, and its frontline workforce, its faculty, remained in the awkward, even contradictory position of being corporate employees and self-employed at the same time. The research university bridged the corporate and non-corporate worlds, preparing people for market success through the non-market activities of research and teaching. The university had to be simultaneously useful and original, cooperative and independent. It had to transform its financial dependence on outside clients both public and private into a basis for intellectual freedom. But how, exactly, could it do this?

Much of the answer lay with the humanities, including literary academia. As we will see, the humanities disciplines were not simply a marginal or backward sector at the utilitarian university, but central to its special identity.

. . . . . . . . . . . . . . . . . . . . . . . . . . .

## CHAPTER 3

*The Humanist Outcry*

Business has often held that higher education would be better were it more like business. Businessmen have always felt perfectly free to give money to universities while also denouncing them. Andrew Carnegie endowed education quite generously, and yet publicly deplored the college focus on "the barbarous and petty squabbles of a far-distant past, or trying to master languages which are dead." He contrasted this worthless study with the noncollegiate efforts of the "future captain of industry . . . hotly engaged in the school of experience."[1] Wealthy donors often taxed the funds they gave to higher education with ridicule for some of its defining practices.

During the debates about higher education in California in the 1860s, many participants made it clear that they couldn't see the point of any kind of college work. "What is the good of going to college? Whatever the good may be, does it pay? Will it pay in such a country as this, in California, and in this last half of the nineteenth century? Mining, farming, the mechanic arts, railroads, steam navigation, electro-magnetic telegraphs, politics, commerce — are not all these practical matters to be learned by use, and operated by men of practical experience?"[2] Liberal arts seemed a wasteful and roundabout way of teaching the production skills that wrested wealth and civilization from a reluctant nature.

· · · *A Dual Mission* · · ·

Such criticisms were common enough to exasperate even the top administrators who were most familiar with business opinions. In his presidential inaugural address at the University of Nashville in 1825, Philip Lindsley felt compelled to argue that only "liberal education" would save students from the "level of a mere labourer at task-work." On the verge of becoming president of the University of Michigan, Henry Tappan was less tactful. "The commercial spirit of our country, and the many avenues of wealth which are opened before enterprise, create a distaste for study deeply inimical to education. The manufacturer, the merchant, the gold-digger," he lamented, "will not pause in their career to gain intellectual accomplishments. While gaining knowledge, they are losing the opportunities to gain money." Writing in 1885, after fleeing the second presidency of UC for the first presidency of Johns Hopkins, Daniel Coit Gilman felt the need to insist that material progress depended on fundamental research, which came from labs that "were the creation not of industrial fabrics, not of mercantile corporations, not even of private enterprise, but of universities and that the motive which inspired their founders and directors was not the acquisition of wealth, but the ascertainment of fundamental law."[3]

Over the decades, university leaders never stopped trying to define the university's unique contribution to business and society at large. The need for distinction was accompanied by a need for independence. How would the university define its special and important place in society, and then defend it? How would it be supported and yet left sufficiently alone to do its work?

Historians have noted that this project was complicated by the variety of competing views of the university mission inside the university itself. Higher education never offered a united front, and neither did any particular university. Generally speaking, historians have made do with describing overall long-term trends. They see the university as having moved gradually from moral and cultural goals to economic and scientific ones. For example, Veysey writes, "Of the several definitions of the academic community, the one centering in mental discipline had now died, but not without bequeathing fragments of itself to the other three. By 1910, utility and research, uneasily joined together, held sway at most major institutions away from the eastern seaboard, but in so bland and official a fashion as to discourage the more ardent professorial advocates of social change, on the one hand, and of pure investigation, on the other. Finally, culture felt the illusory exhilaration of a few recent victories, but it lagged far behind in terms of actual influence, and it was soon to prove handicapped by its tie with the genteel tradition."[4] Historians largely agree with Veysey's description of a widespread institutional movement toward science and utility, one which continues today. But though the description is accurate about the university's public face and financial practice, it is only part of the story. The research university owed its rise to its contribution to economic development. But it promised a second benefit to its constituency, one whose influence has been less noticed. That promise was self-development.

· · · *The Trouble with Humanism* · · ·

Self-development has never seemed a major university mission because it has seemed subjective and irrelevant to economic development. At times it has seemed worse than irrelevant — more like an active impediment. The self appears on the side of pleasure rather than productivity; its interests are what must be repressed in order to build civilizations. Freud's influential elaboration of this dichotomy in *Civilization and Its Discontents* (1930) can be read as a conventional brief for the university's standard role. The humanities would seem best limited to addressing desire, the better to sublimate it into productivity.

This sense of the humanities' limits was cemented by the anti-humanist critiques of the 1970s and 1980s, but historians had long regarded the humanities as preparatory and anti-modern even when they sympathized with their goals. Their placement of the humanities rested on a stark contrast between liberal and specialized knowledge. Specialized knowledge was associated with the inexorable rise of the professions and the power of business. Liberal knowledge was associated with the past, remnants of tradition, or the basic cultural literacy and adolescent self-formation that stood as prerequisites to modern, scientific, productive learning.[5]

Historians have thus tended to treat the humanities' vision of liberal culture as a version of moral education, a kind of education central to the old college but marginal to the knowledge-creating, science-based university.[6] As the United States became an industrialized and global power, it was not clear how the humanities disciplines would play a role. National prominence rested increasingly on scientific rather than narrative knowledge, and specifically on the technosciences. Moral education was thought replaceable by professional social science. The humanities remained important to national identity, but as a kind of primary school preceding scientific maturity. Teaching Emerson and Dickens offered instruction in great national traditions and furnished a unifying cultural identity in the face of the alleged threats of immigration and pluralism, but it did not exactly produce knowledge. Society could hold the humanities responsible for national unity precisely by granting them a tradition-based domain. Actual social policy would be hammered out through social science research and analysis, as later exemplified by the Chicago school of sociology. The humanities were not thought to shape the future, as science did, but to provide a starting point in the past.

If the "humanities" were static or in decline, it seems cruel to put any weight on the accompanying intellectual framework known as humanism. Historians have linked humanism to the side in literary studies that since about 1880 has argued against the centrality of professional methodology.[7] They have described humanism as conservative moral education and as a version of religious thought.[8] Modern critics continue to maintain the fundamentally professionalist contrast between "professional discourse," which has merciless analytical and experimental procedures, and liberal or "literary culture," based on the "value of tradition that is presumably universal, normative, and above controversy."[9] As a result of irreversible modernization, we have been told, humanism became a backwater, attracting nostalgic, timid thinkers who ruled themselves with a mournful resentment over the replacement of high art by democracy and religion by science.[10] Humanism, in these readings, was relegated to university departments that had "no obvious extrinsic value," or to the undergraduate curriculum, or to the classroom, or to the liberal arts college that ignored research.[11]

We can call this the remainder theory of humanism. Humanism became a function of left-over things: custodial, traditionalist, normalizing, anti-professional, anti-intellectual, anti-modern, and above all, obsolete, something suited to the basic training of half-formed young men and women. Nineteenth-century classicism is seen as liberal in the sense of assuming a tradeoff between "public action" and "internal self-perfection" while preferring the latter.[12] Much evidence does suggest that the research university developed by defining humanism as an institutional backwater. By 1900 most educational leaders had proclaimed a historic shift from a liberal to a scientific core and from moral to professional training. Benjamin Ide Wheeler, president of the University of California from 1899 to 1919, wrote that by the 1880s, "the college was tending fast toward absorption in the specialized subjects, and the old ideals of the liberal culture shrank back into the freshman and sophomore years, disputing the ground as they retreated, but slowly and surely yielding in a failing cause."[13]

Humanism's institutional faltering was assisted by the absence of a stable outlook. One historian of the term, Tony Davies, nicely summarizes the problem: "The several humanisms—the civic humanism of the quattrocentro Italian city-states, the Protestant humanism of sixteenth-century northern Europe, the rationalistic humanism that attended at the revolution of enlightened modernity, and the romantic and positivistic humanisms through which the European bourgeoisie established their hegemony over it, the revolutionary humanism that shook the world and the liberal humanism of the Nazis and the humanism of their victims and opponents, the antihumanist humanism of Heidegger and the humanist antihumanism of Foucault and Althusser—are not reducible to one, or even to a single line or pattern."[14] Humanism appears on nearly every side of many centuries of debate, the patron of beneficial and lethal forms of self-development. Some of the time it embodies the outdated concepts of a preferably superseded past—foundationalist, anti-feminist, ethnocentric, logocentric, heteronormative, transcendentalist, and anti-political.[15] Similarly, it seems to reject always pluralist and hybridized modern societies in the name of purified élites, its ideals requiring the backdrop of degraded others. Humanism seems to set its enlightenment against an image of the brutish masses, and to define non-Western societies as culturally incapable of self-rule. There has been as a result carceral humanism, racist humanism, fascist humanism, imperial humanism—"All humanisms, until now, have been imperial," Davies concludes.[16] All humanisms have been, in some way, *disciplinary* humanism, constructing manageable subjects. All humanisms have been, in some way, *supremacist* humanisms, entangled in the user's attempts to justify the superiority of a national status, an opposition to strangers, a way of life. As a result, nearly all varieties of progressive and left-wing criticism now share a broad suspicion of humanism, a suspicion hardened by the rise in the 1980s of yet another backward-looking humanism, this one remarkably similar to the political and economic views of the Reagan administration.

### · · · *Contradictions and Dialectics* · · ·

It is far easier to dismiss humanism as contradictory and conservative if we treat it as a static structure, removed from historical forces and from the thoughts and feelings of humanists. In reality, like all systems of meaning, humanism has never been static. Its internal incoherence reflects the constitutive pressures of history and individuals. Stuck in the world as it is, humanism reflects standing conditions and even naturalizes them. At the same time, it looks to things that do not exist in society and yet do exist in criticism and in imagination. The idea contains the vision, as do the experiences that humanism claims to explain, whether experience occurs in a union shop or a university laboratory or corporate office, and whether it is fragmentary or sustained. The experience contains both an ideal and an emotion, the affective correlative of freedom and the other concepts I will shortly ascribe to liberal humanism. In the affect, however dimly, the ideal acquires actual form.

Humanism's contradictions form a dynamic of conflict and change, and we can see this when we look at humanism historically, so that its limits coexist with an unterminated process of self-overcoming. I will be referring here not to Italian Renaissance humanism or Heidegger's (anti)humanism or the humanism of the French Revolution but to humanism during succeeding waves of corporate transformation in the United States. Humanism is both a system of concepts and an identity; it expresses central aspects of American middle-class identity, one proper to what later came to be called the professional-managerial class (PMC).[17] As such, humanism came to express this middle class's sense of its difference from — and superiority to — other classes: these university types were not labor, and they were not masters either, not those great capitalists and other sovereigns who followed their financial self-interest rather than science and truth.

Humanism is historically specific, reflects a class position, and as a dialectical movement represents an active relation between history and subject. Like other such concepts, humanism reflects not only historical conditions but the agency of a subject encountering history through its own concepts. When we treat humanism as a set of static, fixed contradictions, as a symptom of supremacism or nostalgia, we treat middle-class university graduates as static and as passive recipients of ideas, stripped of their energy. We are omitting the subject's agency, though it is a key part of a process of transformation in which the very regressions and stupidities contained by the concept "humanism" form part of the basis of critique, of negation, of overcoming. Humanism is both nostalgia and negation, an experience of the present and the future, the existent and the imagined, bound together in the erratic reversals that form middle-class consciousness.

University humanism is best seen as the self-consciousness of the Euro-American PMC after the Civil War, with its reactionary elements and its upheavals in continuous collision. The old does not simply rule the new in a remaindered system of thinking, but continuously cedes ground to the new that the form of the old foretells, dwelling in the present as an elaborate metaphor for what is to come. In the process, the individual experiences the conjunction of her historical location with her own experience and interests. She equally experiences her own non-identity with herself, a sense of pieces that don't fit with what is known to exist, a knowledge of her historical unconscious that does not reveal its content. The imagination arrives with surprise at the unfamiliarity of the actual — the unfamiliarity of historical processes and of ourselves. The imagination arises from its own alienation, negating it and then negating this negation in a conception of an unalienated state — a conception that arises in part from its actual experience.

The dialectical imagination clarifies the function of an ideal version of a concept.[18] The ideal is an index of the inevitable difference between an idea's aim and its effects. The ideal exists in permanent tension with its embodiments, sometimes improved by these, sometimes tormented by what they have sacrificed. Ideals are saturated with desire that the ideal be true, and that this truth be realized. The ideal incarnates the truth of the desire, reflected in the gap between desired and actual states. The ideal's capacity to surpass the actual reflects the process of idealization itself, in which the psyche acts *as if* the usual restrictions on its own interests were unnecessary. Ideals are tied to the positive affect of *interest,* to a particularly strong version of this affect — an actually experienced state in which the conflict between one's interest (or desire) and "civilization" seems not to exist. In this state, the self *feels* the non-necessity of these restrictions, and intimates a condition in which civilization does not present itself as a restriction to the self.

By reading the history of humanism in this light, I hope to avoid the understandable tendency of recent decades to simplify humanism to a conservative core, stripped of its liberal, romantic, even revolutionary elements.[19] This will make it easier to see that liberal humanism persisted, and still persists, to unsettle professional and managerial life, often acting as a critical or antagonistic position, jostling its institutional superior, the technosciences, while drawing on radical and noncapitalist traditions.

· · · *Humanism and Radical Freedom* · · ·

Nineteenth-century humanists knew the founding meaning of liberal: "Originally, ['liberal' was] the distinctive epithet of those 'arts' or 'sciences' that were considered 'worthy of a freeman'; opposed to servile or mechanical."[20] A liberal art is the cause and the expression of human freedom. Advocates returned repeatedly to this conjunction between liberalism and freedom.

Humanism and classicism were often focused on conservation, and their teaching could be rote beyond belief.[21] In addition, uses of liberal often tied the concept of the free person to "upper class status."[22] In their classical origins, the liberal arts were a belief system for owners of slaves. The main feature of the free citizen's liberty was leisure (*otium*), which stood in opposition to commerce (*negotium*, or non-leisure).[23] Freedom was freedom from commerce, but the value of this conception was destroyed by its dependence on the forced labor of others. When "liberal" appeared in the term "liberal arts," it described the goal of "general intellectual enlargement and refinement" linked to a mechanism of repression, including repression of the non-European.[24]

And yet, at the same time, the liberal arts represented a memory and a dream of freedom — an art of freedom, freedom as expressed most perfectly in art. The first modern research university was founded in Berlin between 1807 and 1810 by the romantic humanist Wilhelm von Humboldt. Humboldt was interested in consolidating German national culture. Although his project can be read as subordinating knowledge to national agendas,[25] Humboldt was interested as much in sustaining self-development while making it a feature of public life. The university was to be a special institution for deploying thought, defined as unconditioned freedom, as a principle of the nation. The free self would also be the free citizen.[26]

Building on the ideas of classical humanism and German philosophers, including Kant, Fichte, and Schiller, Humboldt defined freedom in part through his theory of the imagination.[27] The imagination was most broadly the human ability to see though existing determinants, starting with time and space. In its ordinary activity, the imagination "consists in making present what is absent, preserving in thought what is past, rendering real what is immaterial." These everyday functions do not "traverse the boundaries set by real, limited existence itself." But "even if imagination leaves nature as it is, nevertheless it must free it from all conditions limiting and restricting its existence."

What does it mean, we might wonder, that the imagination honors "real, limited existence" while freeing it from all limiting conditions? The answer is that the imagination depicts actual existence under the aspect of freedom. Its operation reveals the freedom present within actual conditions. The revelation of freedom takes the form of the observer's own emotional transport. The imagination, Humboldt wrote, "must eliminate the constrictions that hinder the free soaring of our spirits."[28]

The crucial point is that the humanist imagination, as articulated by Humboldt and kindred writers, sought emancipation rather than transcendence. The imagination does not claim to reveal a realm beyond earthly laws and contingencies, or deny determination in ordinary life.[29] It instead offers the reader the experience of herself as free. Freedom appears as affects that overwhelm the self, overwhelm, that is, the usual restrictions and repressions that the self places on its own movement. The aesthetic imagination, in Humboldt's reading, allows the self to experience itself as autonomous, as spontaneously unconfined. The spontaneity reveals autonomy as a deeper feature of the self's being than its confinement.[30]

The permanent, if often repressed, theme of nineteenth-century humanism was the way that art allows selves to posit their own freedom. Art expresses the individual's capacity to modify conditions rather than simply be modified by them. Samuel Taylor Coleridge, for example, defined the imagination as the power to create and re-create. Sometimes the imagination stems from the "conscious will" and sometimes it is tied to the "eternal act of creation in the infinite I AM." In either case, the imagination is "essentially *vital*" in the sense of having its own power of determination.[31] Ralph Waldo Emerson, though given to tying imagination to the perception of divine essences, wrote that "the poets are . . . liberating gods." "Therefore we love the poet, the inventor, who in any form . . . has yielded us a new thought. He unlocks our chains, and admits us to a new scene."[32] As the literary theorist Frank Lentricchia concluded, "Haunting the humanist tradition from Schiller to [Northrop] Frye is the specter of a deterministic vision which, by deriving human being wholly from the historical or the natural order, appears to deny us the power to build our 'home' freely in culture." "Aesthetic humanism" refuses this state by holding that the "'consummation of his humanity,' as Schiller puts it, depends upon man's ability to free himself from all determinations." This emancipation appears in "the aesthetic creative impulse," again using Schiller's terms, which "is building unawares a third joyous realm of play and of appearance."[33] In the nineteenth century, this stress on freedom was central to the arts' effort to define their differences from industrial progress.[34]

A clear modern description of this humanism appears in Hannah Arendt. The Roman *humanitas,* she writes, carried such a strong sense of "the integrity of the person as person" that "human worth" was more basic than truth itself. The idea is encapsulated in a saying of Cicero: "I prefer before heaven to go astray with Plato rather than hold true views with his opponents." Arendt explains: "What Cicero in fact says is that for the true humanist neither the verities of the scientist nor the truth of the philosopher nor the beauty of the artist can be absolutes; the humanist, because he is not a specialist, exerts a faculty of judgment and taste which is beyond the coercion which each specialty imposes upon us. This Roman *humanitas* applied to men who were free in every respect, for whom the question of freedom, of not being coerced, was the decisive one— even in philosophy, even in science, even in the arts. Cicero says: In what concerns my association with men and things, I refuse to be coerced even by truth, even by beauty."[35] By recalling this classical core, the humanities disciplines represented radical freedom within the client-centered university. This freedom meant freedom *from* science and from commerce on behalf of persons in all their relations.[36]

This notion of freedom appears even in the university's administrative precincts. Charles W. Eliot, Harvard's longstanding president, was a pioneer of the controversial elective system of undergraduate education in which students had some choice in selecting their course of study from a wide range of disciplines (now reconstructed around research specialization). Eliot defended his system by arguing, "If election by the individual . . . works well in practice, it is of course to be preferred to any method of selection for the individual by an authority outside himself, since freemen are best trained by the practice in freedom with responsibility." The elective system, he wrote, "provides on a large scale an invaluable addition to human freedom, and provides this precious freedom for the most highly trained, and therefore the most productive and influential, persons."[37]

Similarly, William Rainey Harper, founding president of the University of Chicago, used humanism to redirect social Darwinism. The leading Darwinist Herbert Spencer had written that "all evil results from the nonadaptation of constitution to conditions," and much of the university's mission was to adapt students to the industrial systems they would face upon graduation.[38] Demanding "individualism" in higher education, Harper insisted that the system must adapt to each individual student. Universities must engage in "the scientific study of the student himself" so that the course of study could be tailored to the student's unique characteristics.[39] The result would be that even in practical fields like business, university graduates would have a "career" in which, like university investigators, they would "develop their own methods of work."[40] This kind of humanism tried to harness even adaptationist biology to its notion of freedom.

Administrators tended to mix aesthetic humanism with professional development, and freedom with the American tradition of "free labor." I will soon turn to this linking of aesthetics and labor, but will first take up the other core features of liberal humanism.

### · · · *Experience and Self-Development* · · ·

Liberal humanism had a second feature: it placed a premium on experiential knowledge. C. S. Schiller, writing in 1903, claimed that the humanist was "sure to be keenly interested in the rich variety of human thought and sentiment, and unwilling to ignore the actual facts for the sake of bolstering up the narrow abstractions of some a priori theory of what 'all men must' think and feel. . . . The humanist, accordingly, will tend to grow humane, and tolerant of the divergences of attitude which must inevitably spring from the divergent idiosyncrasies of men."[41] The more familiar meaning of liberal as tolerant of diversity derives from liberal as close to experience.

"Experience" remained one of the pillars of modern humanism, running through phenomenology and existentialism in Europe, and through psychologists and literary critics in the United States like William James, John Dewey, and Lionel Trilling. Trilling drew on the tradition when he claimed, in his preface to *The Liberal Imagination,* that the imagination sees sentiments and ideas as virtually the same thing. Humanism encouraged Trilling's definition of liberalism as "concerned with the emotions above all else," and as therefore trying "to establish emotions, or certain of them, in some sort of freedom."[42]

For James, the core "humanistic principle" is that "you can't weed out the human contribution."[43] But James meant something specific by this. He insisted on the priority of individual experience to anything "archetypal and transexperiential," including preestablished rules. "The essential service of humanism," he wrote, is to have seen that "experience as a whole is self-containing and leans on nothing."[44] Concepts such as the "central unity," which conservative humanists like Irving Babbitt used to identify literary masterworks, struck James as the residue of a habitual idea to which "most of us grow more and more enslaved." Consciousness certainly depends on familiar patterns, but must not be captured by them.

While Babbitt attributed greatness in art to a perfect balance of opposites, James traced it to balance's disruption: "Genius, in truth, means little more than the faculty of perceiving in an unhabitual way."[45]

If the self's experience was central to the creation of "truth" and "reality," then that experience had to be opened up. James and other humanists did not see experience as determined by regulatory forces such as the discourse of experience; it was possible to reduce if not eliminate regulatory habits. The most important of these, ironically, was the desire for a truth that existed independently of context. James located the "spirit of humanism" in a "temper of renunciation" of fixed truth external to the self. "For humanism, conceiving the more 'true' as the more 'satisfactory' (Dewey's term), has to renounce sincerely rectilinear arguments and ancient ideals of rigor and finality."[46] "Truth" is brought on by a feeling of satisfaction, or what Silvan Tomkins and later psychologists would call enjoyment.[47] Tomkins argued that the more important regulatory force is the affect of shame, which forces the subject to curtail his or her interest. James and Tomkins agreed that the point was not so much to find experience that transcended context as to find a context that would not predetermine experience. "If there be a God," James wrote, "he is no absolute all-experiencer, but simply the experiencer of widest actual conscious span."[48] Freedom of interest is the natural divine.

Dewey venerated experience to the point of making it the judge of efficiency. "Ultimately," he wrote, "social efficiency means neither more nor less than the capacity to share in a give and take of experience. It covers all that makes one's own experience more worth while to others, and all that enables one to participate more richly in the worthwhile experiences of others."[49] Efficiency was to be defined in terms of experience, and not the other way around. Humanism meant something radical here. Experience was prior to economic measures of productivity. Properly understood, experience could serve as a basis for rejecting the notion of efficiency as a quantifiable reduction of input. The humanities were prior to economic rationality.

The concepts of experience and freedom came together in liberal humanism's third feature — its goal of individual self-development. This goal was limited by its application to one segment of the population, generally Anglo-Saxon males. It was, however, within its restricted context, quite intense. At Amherst, President William Augustus Stearns wrote, "The end, or aim of education . . . is not primarily to produce greatness in partial directions, great mathematicians, great philologists, great philosophers, but in the best sense of the term, great *men — men* symmetrically and powerfully developed. . . . The whole man comes into our consideration. The design is, by discipline and culture, to make men."[50] George Peterson has argued that "men symmetrically and powerfully developed" into the "Whole Man" had long been the objective of the liberal arts college. The Whole Man "represents the belief that man can find genuine joy in music, read Goethe, Newton or Tacitus with perception, and still lead a useful life, and that man will be *better* because he can do these things. Only such a man can live with himself without boredom. He is not frustrated by the triviality of his thoughts nor disgusted at his need to convert knowledge into social advancement. By acquainting himself directly with the best of man's creations, he has liberated himself from servitude to others' judgments. He has achieved the freedom of mind which enables him to front life as a personal matter between himself and his experience, not something rendered harmlessly bland by its conformity with other lives."[51] Self-development rested on mental freedom, which it in turn increased. Academic freedom, defined as "freedom of inquiry," was dependent on a prior freedom of mind. The principle of free participation was secondary to the personal capacity for freedom itself, which self-development allowed.

University leaders often separated knowledge creation from self-development, for which they nevertheless retained a privileged place. At Chicago, Harper insisted that "the university is the place for men who have come to know themselves, and who have learned what they can do and what they cannot do," and defined the college as the "place for the student to study and test himself."[52] Harper was so concerned with the process of self-making that his university sometimes sounded like a college. "The university, as priest, is a mediator between man and man; between man and man's own self; between mankind and that ideal inner self of mankind which merits and received man's adoration. The university, like the priest, leads those who place themselves under its influence, whether they live within or without the university wall, to enter into close communion with their own souls — a communion possible only where opportunity is offered for meditative leisure. The university guild, of all the guilds of working men, has been the most successful in securing that leisure for contemplation, consideration of society and of nature, without which mankind can never become acquainted with itself."[53] Like the college, Harper claimed, the research university is founded on knowledge of self and hence on the liberal arts. For this reason, he added, "the university is in deep sympathy with every legitimate effort, made by other guilds of workingmen, to secure shorter hours of labor and longer hours for self-improvement."[54]

Self-development expressed itself in liberal humanism's fourth major category, individual agency. *Agency,* most generally, is one's capacity to respond to stimuli, where the response is not determined solely by the stimulus itself. Freedom does not mean the sheer absence of determination, although one of its major symptoms is the ability to initiate one's own stimuli rather than simply react to those of others. Free or independent agency refers to agency in a system with a high degree of complexity, meaning that the system allows a high proportion of "independently variable states." "The freedom of a feedback system" Tomkins wrote, "should be measured by the product of the complexity of its 'aims' and the frequency of their attainment."[55] "Free" agency, again, is not agency that escapes determinate forces, but agency that has a wide range of options within that system of forces. The enabling factor is not the quantity or force of one's will but the state of one's interaction with the system. Agency can be defined as the capacity for equitable interaction.

Without using this more recent terminology, nineteenth-century university leaders described independent agency as the hallmark of the college graduate. One of the more conservative of the early university presidents, Andrew S. Draper of the University of Illinois, insisted that university education was no longer "culturing" but "trains one for *work.*" Draper valued liberal education because it provided "native resourcefulness and versatility, sound training and serious study, discrimination in means and methods, and rational applications to real things in life, in ways that bring results of some distinct worth to the world. It makes little difference *what* one does, but he must do something."[56] Universities must produce graduates who are capable of enormous labor and discipline. But their graduates must also be capable of directing this labor on their own. Both the "strenuous" and democratic visions of adult life stressed the need for the autonomous will.

University leaders made this point repeatedly. At the University of California commencement of 1875, president le Conte said, "Education needs a man who is a master not merely an imitator and an operative, in his work. . . . It elevates his trade into a profession, raises it to the dignity of a liberal art."[57] At Harvard, Charles Eliot wrote, "The prime object of university methods of teaching to-day is to make the individual student think, and do something himself, and not merely to take in and remember other people's thoughts; to induce the student to do some thinking and acting on his own account, and not merely to hear or read about other people's doings."[58] Some administrators stressed the higher learning and others stressed manifest destiny. Very different overt goals shared a common humanist purpose — independent agency, defined by the continuous struggle to evade determinism in thought and feeling.[59] The university taught individuals to encounter nature, psyche, and society with powers of interest that only they could sustain.

Liberal humanism's fifth term is enjoyment, which it associates with exercising free agency. We might assume that enjoyment occurs when one achieves sovereignty or command, when one seems utterly liberated from external compulsion or able to exert compulsion over others. But enjoyment is a more comprehensive experience than this. A range of psychologists that includes Freud as well as many behaviorists have associated enjoyment with the reduction of a stimulus. I take this to mean that enjoyment consists of reducing a potentially unmanageable stimulus, that is, a stimulus that insures the self's inadequacy. The self's implicit goal is not sovereignty so much as self-sufficiency, not domination so much as not-being-dominated. Enjoyment consists of the experience in which one's agency does not feel controlled, impaired, or coerced by external factors. Agency is the capacity for equitable interaction, and enjoyment occurs when the self experiences it.

This notion of enjoyment is implicit in many humanist touchstones. In the mid-nineteenth century, the archhumanist John Henry Cardinal Newman identified the place of enjoyment by invoking Aristotle: "'Of possession,' [Aristotle] says, 'those rather are useful, which bear fruit; those *liberal, which tend to enjoyment.* By fruitful, I mean, which yield revenue; by enjoyable, where *nothing accrues of consequence beyond the using.*"[60] Newman is usually read as calling for knowledge "for its own sake," or knowledge without use. In fact, he is calling for knowledge for enjoyment. Enjoyment does not preclude use. To the contrary, enjoyment consists of self-sufficient use. Enjoyment marks the use that does not need to be more than what it already is. Enjoyment means an experience of something that is *not inadequate* in relation to what it "should" be. Enjoyment thus expresses use not determined by external or superior forces.

Newman was famously not a political radical, but in defining enjoyment he came surprisingly close to Karl Marx's concept of "use-value." In a capitalist world, Newman imagined enjoyment as the experience of the absence, the non-necessity, of the accumulation of additional value. Enjoyment reflected the absence of surplus-value in the object, the absence of capital accumulation, the absence of the need to accrue a greater quantitative value. Knowledge "for its own sake" thus meant knowledge not haunted by a use deemed more valuable by the external world. The knower felt enjoyment when the experience of the object was enough, was adequate to the object, and did not require the supplement of science, quantification, or commodity status. Enjoyment meant dwelling in a system in which the relations one already experienced were enough for knowing the object.

The meaning of enjoyment can be stated in another way. Enjoyment expresses non-alienated use. Newman left the podium often enough to see that the world of industrial production was full not simply of utility but of external compulsion. Enjoyment signals the absence of bondage to another's designation of the value of what one has experienced.

In sum, liberal humanism rested on five interwoven concepts: the free self, experiential knowledge, self-development, autonomous agency, and enjoyment. It's true that liberal humanism imagined conditions of freedom that did not require the demolition or transcendence of the increasingly corporate nineteenth-century industrial order. Humanist notions of liberal culture played a conservative role on most social questions. It discredited its own ideals because of the ease with which most academic adherents applied them only to whites, to men, to the middle and upper classes, to Christians. Humanism's betrayals, however, existed in contradiction with its radical standards for developing human potential. The contradiction preserved these ideals in the same moment in which they were denied.

### · · · The Professors Agree · · ·

Discord has always been part of literary study, where one paradigm never simply replaces another and where improvement is not measurable like a computer's processor speed. While Richard G. Moulton of Cambridge and Chicago called science the salvation of literary study, Woodrow Wilson of Princeton called science its destruction. What is more interesting was the ongoing humanism of the science-loving, professionalist camp of literary scholars. They rejected "belletristic" perspectives while keeping humanist goals.

Moulton is a case in point. In *Shakespeare as a Dramatic Artist* (1888), he argued that "literary criticism should follow other branches of thought in becoming inductive." By this, Moulton meant starting "with the observation of facts" and demoting to "sidelights" the "*à priori*" ideas, instinctive notions of the fitness of things," and other features of impressionistic or appreciative criticism. At first glance, it looks as if he wanted to depersonalize literary study and impose standard procedures copied from laboratory science. But Moulton's intention was quite different. The standardizers, he wrote, are actually the belletrists, who practice what Moulton calls "judicial" criticism. This criticism "compares a new production with those already existing in order to determine whether it is inferior to them or surpasses them." Moulton's brand, the "criticism of investigation," "makes the same comparison for the purpose of identifying the new product with some type in the past, or differentiating it and registering a new type."[61] Judicial criticism seeks to "watch against variations from received canons" while investigative criticism "watches for new forms to increase its stock in species." Moulton's science model was closer to botany than to physics, but it explicitly valued variation and diversity.

For Moulton, judicial criticism misunderstands how literature works. It thinks literature expresses moral laws in the sense of "external obligations," restraints of the will. But law, as understood in science, is actually a principle immanent in the object being studied. "The key to the distinction," Moulton wrote, "is the notion of external authority. There cannot be laws in the moral and political sense without a ruler or legislative authority; in scientific laws the law-giver and the law-obeyer are one and the same."[62] This was a remarkable injection of liberal — even radical — humanism into a scientistic outlook. Judicial criticism subjects the author to external standards. Scientific criticism sees the author as making his or her own laws. The artist follows nothing except his or her own artistic agency. On this point, the artist and the scientist are agreed. "Art is legitimate," Moulton claimed, "only when it does not obey laws."[63]

Since he gave a central place to diversity and autonomy, it's not surprising that Moulton should have flatly rejected the "judicial attitude of mind." Belletrists think of themselves as great appreciators, he wrote, but actually their mentality is "highly unreceptive, for it necessarily implies a restraint of sympathy."[64] Because they judge rather than observe, they fall behind the constant flux and difference that marks literary innovation. More accurately, they lack the power essential to comprehending the creativity that literature supremely expresses. "Dr. Johnson lecturing Shakespeare and Milton as to how they ought to have written — these are to us only odd anachronisms. It is like a contest with atomic force, this attempt at using ideas from the past to mould and limit productive power in the present and future."[65] History shows this by heaping ridicule on the incessant errors of judicial criticism, which never learns "*that literature is a thing of development.*"[66] Scientific criticism, to apply our term to Moulton, is more fully humanistic than belletristic criticism, for it foregrounds the combination of freedom, experience, and self-unfolding that animates literary work.

Moulton is more on a mission than most, but these same progressive aspects of humanism can be found scattered throughout research-friendly literary criticism. James Morgan Hart defined the German university as a "system of freedom"—freedom of learning and freedom of teaching.[67] Martin Wright Sampson, in a dull discussion of curricular reforms in the English department at Indiana, described the question of systematic study as "how shall I learn to apprehend literature, that thereby it may influence me?"[68] Charles Mills Gayley, in an equally dull discussion of the same issue at Berkeley, called for including "the methods of the laboratory" to "weigh aesthetic values or to trace the development of literary organisms."[69] Bliss Perry at Harvard, raving happily about "our vast industrial democracy," envisioned a union of "the generous spirit of the amateur with the method of the professional. In the new world of disciplined national endeavor upon which we are entering, why may not the old American characteristics of versatility, spontaneity, adventurousness, still persist?"[70] The Teddy Roosevelt tone, once again, reflected among more dubious things a belief that literature enabled both individual agency and the taking of pleasure in it.

English professors certainly differed in their views about literature, tradition, labor, politics, and industry. But there was much agreement that literary study needed to evade economic laws. In his MLA presidential address for 1912, the Dante scholar Charles Hall Grandgent defined the function of critical education as much more than helping "men and women to perform efficiently their daily economic task . . . If the only object of life is to stay alive, of what use is it to live at all? The ideal of economic efficiency is best realized by a machine. But the individuals we have to deal with are not machines: they are human beings of almost infinite capacities, destined to be citizens and parents. They must be capable of living the life of the spirit, of appreciating the good things in nature, in conduct, and in art . . . The higher we rise in the scale of development, the less conspicuous the purely economic aspect of the individual becomes."[71] This critique of commerce wasn't simply nostalgic and conservative. It held out for a notion of individual capacity that could not be embodied by normal wage labor in a capitalist industrial system.

### · · · Professional Craft Labor · · ·

Liberal humanism, in short, advanced a notion of individual freedom that it undermined and sustained. It thus could not be reduced to a straightforward élitist conservatism. Many of its adherents addressed modern society and wanted to bring it closer to humanist ideals through modern, even scientific methods. The setting for this activity would be the scientific-humanist university, which would reform and even surpass the industrial system by combining economic with human development. Few university humanists opposed capitalism in a systematic way, and yet they espoused freedoms that lay beyond the boundaries of its modes of production and management.

But how would humanists influence society outside the classrooms that they dedicated to the study of art, literature, and history? The usual means was the promotion of the arts and their history: the university, many said, was an ideal forum for cultivating arts appreciation and a lifelong love of beauty, truth, and feeling. And yet it is misleading to read humanism through a gap between aesthetics and experience that developed later in the history of literary criticism. Without damaging the aesthetic's integrity, we are now in a position to grant that the aesthetic functioned for many devotees as a principle of freedom, of free judgment, of free agency, of autonomy for the entire self in all its activities.

Some humanists sought to shelter art from industry and labor. Others, including many university leaders, sought their conjunction. The real debate was not about whether art should inhabit a separate sphere, but about how its principle of freedom could inhabit all others. Many felt that humanism included the humanization of labor, broadly speaking. And when brought into conjunction with labor, liberal humanism's concern with freedom overlapped with American traditions of "free labor" or craft labor. In the university, craft labor appeared not in its artisanal form but in the form of professionalism itself.

The humanities professor was in most ways a nineteenth-century "small producer." Most of his work was conducted under his own supervision, and he set most of his own output goals. His work was evaluated by kindred practitioners at discontinuous points in the work process, and infrequently so. The old college resembled the workshop rather than the factory, where senior colleagues would ideally train and cultivate younger colleagues in both individual and collaborative work processes that were largely under the younger workers' own control. Mechanical aids were introduced at the professor's discretion, as were nearly all curricular changes and other features that outsiders might deem "improvements." College "management" left its "workers" largely alone. Faculty were certainly not immune from political and other types of interference, but no less immune than craft workers in other artisanal systems, which were always conservative in the sense that any individual was susceptible to the judgments of his or her peers, especially those of senior members who claimed to speak for the group.

The labor historian David Montgomery has detailed the status of iron rollers in the 1870s in a way that also clarifies the craft-worker features of faculty labor: "Within the context of mechanized industry and hired wage labor, some skilled craftsmen exercised an impressive degree of collective control over the specific productive tasks in which they were engaged and the human relations involved in the performance of those tasks . . . They exercised this control because they fought for it, and their position in that struggle drew strength from the workers' functional autonomy on the job, from the group ethical code that they developed around their work relations, and from the organizations they created for themselves in order to protect their interests and values."[72] Faculty had to fight as well, but their struggle was quieter in part because they possessed status advantages that other artisans lacked. Artisans and faculty shared the goal of functional autonomy, which included autonomy in creating the job's working conditions and aims.

Nineteenth-century Americans were acutely aware of the connection between the free self and free labor. Much of this awareness arose from the struggle over chattel slavery, which itself overlapped with "free labor" ideals held by working people of various backgrounds. The New England Transcendentalist Orestes Brownson observed in 1841 that "the mission of this country [is] to raise up the laboring classes, and make every man really free and independent."[73] Free labor theory claimed that freedom required freedom from dependence on capital or centralized political power. It also claimed that the quality of production turned less on technology or scientific management than on the expertise of the worker freely deployed. Production efficiency often depended on craft work not yet made "efficient" by Taylorization. The labor historian Herbert Gutman, noting the high proportion of immigrant workers in American factories, suggested, "It may be that America's extraordinary technological supremacy — its talent before the Second World War for developing labor-saving machinery and simplifying complex mechanical processes — depended less on 'Yankee know-how' than on the continued infusion of prefactory peoples into an increasingly industrialized society."[74] The academic humanities offered a parallel set of "premodern" resources, ones in fact crucial not only to critiques of modernity but to making modernity "work."

Craft-labor ideals found their middle-class form in professionalization. Professionals did quite a bit of unacknowledged borrowing from various labor theories of the nineteenth century United States, many of them anti-managerial. Virtually all academic disciplines were professionalized in the last three decades of the nineteenth century, more or less at the same time that industrial workers were developing, defending, and losing craft-labor practices for large-scale production. Literary studies were in the thick of this movement — the Modern Language Association was founded in 1883. Contrary to a polarizing tendency in some readings of university history, professionalism did not arise in opposition to liberal humanist attitudes. Professionalism was indeed self-consciously modern and scientific in a way that liberal humanism was not. But professionalizers were themselves absorbing or adapting the humanist self rather than replacing or rejecting it.

The most remarkable overview of this tendency came from the historian Burton J. Bledstein. The professional claim to authority, Bledstein reported, "derived from a special power over worldly experience" associated with science. "Professionals controlled the magic circle of scientific knowledge which only the few, specialized by training and indoctrination, were privileged to enter, but which all in the name of nature's universality were obligated to appreciate."[75] Nonetheless, while science grounded the professions' effectiveness and authority, humanism grounded its personal and cultural value. "Professionalism was also a culture which embodied a more radical idea of democracy than even the Jacksonian had dared to dream. The culture of professionalism emancipated the active ego of a sovereign person as he performed organized activities within comprehensive spaces. The culture of professionalism incarnated the radical idea of the independent democrat, a liberated person seeking to free the power of nature within every worldly sphere, a self-governing individual exercising his trained judgment in an open society. The Mid-Victorian as professional person strove to achieve a level of autonomous individualism, a position of unchallenged authority heretofore unknown in American life."[76] As a student in college, the future professional was not exactly imbibing Jacksonian democracy. He was, however, absorbing liberal humanism. Professional freedoms were developed in tandem with liberal freedoms. Professional knowledge was scientific and humanist at the same time.

Professionalism has always been a labor system. As such, it defined freedom through its version of craft labor. Although the professional differed in some ways from the tradesman and the craftsman, they were all to define their own work and not the other way around. "The professional person absolutely protected his precious autonomy against all assailants, not in the name of an irrational egotism but in the name of a special grasp of the universe and a special place in it. In the service of mankind—the highest ideal—the professional resisted all corporate encroachments and regulations upon his independence, whether from government bureaucrats, university trustees, business administrators, public laymen, or even his own professional associations. The culture of professionalism released the creative energies of the free person who was usually accountable only to himself and his personal interpretation of the ethical standards of his profession."[77] The professions were modernized craft labor, and as such would form the exception in an economy where work was more intensively extracted and managed every day. Even as many professions helped to eliminate craft labor in industry, they sought to incarnate its principles.

· · · *The Promise of Mass Education* · · ·

Professionals were astute about a central feature of late-nineteenth-century modernity: a mass society was coming to be governed by its large organizations. Democracy in any direct sense was being superseded by expert systems which would apply science and engineering to social problems, ideally harmonizing interests through professional techniques.[78] This progressive vision was important in the university, where many thought that specialized knowledge could replace conflict-ridden political interests as the preferred source of social order.

Even granting that organizations could or should replace political free-for-alls, the question remained as to how inclusive these organizations would be. Would they recognize expertise that did not emerge in the controlled environment of the university but in the field, the workshop, or the factory floor? Would university professionals argue that craft work standards should be applied to professionals and production workers alike? In practice, would higher education entail a move toward mass education?

Free labor theory had its limits, especially racial limits. But at its strongest it insisted that craft labor standards could survive only if applied across the entire society. Christopher Lasch has offered a crucial interpretation of this point. The ideal of "free labor"

> was nothing less than a classless society, understood to mean not only the absence of hereditary privilege and legally recognized distinctions of rank but a refusal to tolerate the separation of learning and labor. The concept of a laboring class was objectionable to Americans because it implied not only the institutionalization of wage labor but the abandonment of what many of them took to be the central promise of American life: the democratization of intelligence. . . . The reintroduction of a kind of clerical hegemony over the mind would [block that promise], reviving the old contempt for the masses and the contempt for everyday life that was the hallmark of priestly societies.[79]

The faculty of the old college had long been a kind of priesthood, and there is no evidence that it harbored widespread free labor tendencies. The same priestly function structured the research university, demarcated leading from laboring Americans. And yet within this élitist vision of a new professional middle class, there remained the idea that higher education would spread craft-labor practices to new elements of society. Though these elements assumed white, male, and middle- and upper-class subjects, they regarded craft labor as essential to modern life.

Craft labor was no panacea. Among other things, it reinforced the "family wage" model that damaged women's social status as both workers and mothers.[80] Freedom of thought and conscience, freedom of love and worship, were of little value unless tied to political and social freedom. Individuals lived simultaneously in their intellectual, personal, and interpersonal spheres. Freedom would not look and feel the same in private and in public — liberal political theory was right about this. But self-development required freedom in both spheres of existence and passage across the boundaries that only partially distinguished them.

In *The Souls of Black Folk* (1903), W. E. B. Du Bois insisted on the connection between self-development and public justice:

The function of the Negro college, then, is clear: it must maintain the standards of popular education, it must seek the social regeneration of the Negro, and it must help in the solution of problems of race contact and cooperation. And finally, beyond all this, it must develop men. Above our modern socialism, and out of the worship of the mass, must persist and evolve that higher individualism which the centres of culture protect; there must come a loftier respect for the sovereign human soul that seeks to know itself and the world about it; that seeks a freedom for expansion and self-development; that will love and hate and labor in its own way, untrammeled alike by old and new. Such souls aforetime have inspired and guided worlds, and if we be not wholly bewitched by our Rhinegold, they shall again. Herein the longing of black men must have respect: the rich and bitter depth of their experience, the unknown treasures of their inner life, the strange rendings of nature they have seen, may give the world new points of view and make their loving, living, and doing precious to all human hearts. And to themselves in these the days that try their souls, the chance to soar in the dim blue air above the smoke is to their finer spirits boon and guerdon for what they lose on earth by being black.[81]

"Social regeneration" depended on "developing men." Political freedom required freedom of self-development. Genuine emancipation required economic and political self-determination, which in turn required levels of self-development that had previously been reserved for the few.

Humanism fluttered through the modern university on two wings. One was élitist and insular, dreaming of a band of classical brothers united in a spiritualized Greco-Christian Anglo-Saxonism. The other wing was radical, insisting on carrying the freedoms of art into work as the center of everyday life, and of doing this for the entire population. Academic humanists might try to free their radical from their conservative wing. If they did, they would have to do it in the increasingly businesslike universities in which they worked.

PART II  *The Managerial Condition*

. . . . . . . . . . . . . . . . . . . . . . . . . . .

# CHAPTER 4

. . . . . . . . . . . . . . . . . . . . . . .

## *The Rise of University Management*


### *The Bureaucratic Revolution*

The end of the Civil War inaugurated a "new economy" the likes of which the country had never seen. This economy emerged from a mixture of new technologies and new forms of administration. The economy developed as it did because firms were able to bureaucratize the administration of their new technologies.

Bureaucracy was something of a magic bullet that solved a variety of problems at once. It increased firms' control over their markets. It coordinated dispersed systems of production and distribution and made these more efficient. It allowed firms to reap great economies of scale. And it increased the firm's power over politics, society, and its own employees.[1]

Business and government intended that the research university should provide both technology and the power to manage it, including above all the management of collectivized work. Capitalism's longstanding tendency was to take relatively autonomous workers and harness them to a common process. Unlike earlier forms of cooperative labor, which tended to reflect the social structures in which they arose, the capitalist form famously organized cooperation around the needs of production for profit. During the infancy of the research university in the United States, Karl Marx was arguing that "co-operation itself, contrasted with the process of production carried on by isolated independent workers, or even by small masters, appears to be a specific form of the capitalist process of production. It is the first change experienced by the actual labor process when subjected to capital."[2] Although cooperative labor had always existed — think of Roman roads, Mayan cities, and plantation cotton — capitalism required a new scale and sophistication in labor management.

The coordination of collective labor became business's central challenge. Although populists, socialists, and many others tried to keep a community or democratic basis for labor cooperation, the main power of coordination was inexorably absorbed by the corporation.[3] This function helped determine the corporation's basic structure as that which "contains many distinct operating units and . . . is managed by a hierarchy of salaried executives."[4] By 1900 the business corporation had established the elaborate bureaucratic systems that allowed this cooperative labor, and the enormous value it created, to be harnessed, extracted, and controlled. There was nothing historically necessary or maximally functional about this trajectory, but it did reflect the general balance of social power and came to dominate the socioeconomic environment.[5] The university contributed both ideas and trained personnel to this bureaucratic system, which needed people that could thrive in spite of, or perhaps because of, its restrictions.

Robert H. Wiebe's description of this new bureaucratic world identified one crucial requirement: continuous adaptation. Bureaucratic ideas, he wrote, were "peculiarly suited to the fluidity and impersonality of an urban-industrial world. They pictured a society of ceaselessly interacting members and concentrated upon adjustments within it. Although they included rules and principles of human behavior, these necessarily had an indeterminate quality because perpetual interaction was itself indeterminate. . . . Thus the rules, resembling orientations much more than laws, stressed techniques of constant watchfulness and mechanisms of continuous management. . . . Now change was interaction and adjustment, forming elaborate and shifting multilinear patterns."[6] Wiebe overstates the indeterminacy of actual practice, but illuminates the crucial context through which the autonomous, flexible self moved—interaction with a multitude of people, factors, and structures. The graduate would be useless unless he felt at home in the economy, and he would not feel at home unless he were comfortable with managing and being managed in turn. He could not manage and be managed unless he were less an individualist or artisan than an organization man.

The bureaucratic revolution mounted a direct challenge to traditional notions of craft labor. With the development of the factory system and Frederick Taylor's mechanical efficiency studies, individualism came to seem an impediment to valuable labor rather than its precondition. The worker couldn't depend on his or her judgement, desire, or skill to achieve the best possible output, but needed external supervision. Bureaucratic control required not only a supervisory system but supervisors, not only management but managers. Managers would be autonomous enough to run this system without actually standing outside it. Managers were people who possessed knowledge—especially operational knowledge—that would be used to supervise workers who lacked this knowledge. Managers were knowledge workers. But their knowledge functioned within organizational terms.

Where would these managers come from? The institution most involved in developing the kind of person, autonomous and manageable, who could develop and apply knowledge in a bureaucratic environment was of course the research university.

### · · · The Discipline of the Knowledge Worker · · ·

Managerial efficiency and technological research rose together to the top of university priorities. This was a predictable effect of the university's economic environment.

By the final third of the nineteenth century, Marx had come to see all modern industry as knowledge industry. "Modern industry," he argued, "makes science a productive force distinct from labor and presses it into the service of capital."[7] The evidence for technology's central role was everywhere to see. As the century came to an end, corporations had begun to systematize their research efforts. This involved orchestrating collective scientific labor, of course, and allowed corporations to shift some of their research effort from applied to fundamental inquiries. "Before 1900 there was very little organized research in American industry, but by 1930 industrial research had become a major economic activity."[8]

A "knowledge economy" is an economy in which sustained profit depends on research-based improvement in the production process. In this sense the United States was a knowledge economy in the nineteenth century. If we narrow the definition so that it specifically denotes an economy in which business firms organize and manage research in the same way they manage production, the United States was a knowledge economy by 1930. Universities were crucial providers of knowledge and knowledge workers alike.

One of David F. Noble's essential insights in his classic book *America by Design* (1977) was that knowledge and the knowledge worker were brought together under one engineering vision of comprehensive corporate management. Parts of this story are familiar, as management practice took shape through Frederick Taylor's scientific management, and through efforts associated with the "human relations" of the 1920s, to reduce invasive supervision and increase job satisfaction. Industry sought not only to engineer its own research but to engineer usable research undertaken by others. Industrial firms looked not only to "trade associations, semiprivate institutes, independent contractors, government bureaus, and private foundations," but to universities. They were especially dependent on universities for expensive basic research.[9] University administrators who desired industry support might feel some need to graft industry's management views onto their own institutions.

If they did, industry was not shy about providing material. Frank Jewett, the head of Bell Labs, defined systematic research as "cooperative effort under control."[10] Dugald Jackson, a GE scientist and chair of the electrical engineering department at MIT, recalled in 1935: "Standardized manufacture demanded 'that the operations of groups of employees and machines . . . be associatively joined, and that individual whims . . . be restrained. . . . The disciplinary relations within the manufacturing organization must be definite and strict.' Dexter S. Kimball, manager of GE's Pittsfield plant, Dean of Engineering at Cornell University, and a leader in industrial management, had this insight when he noted with some urgency that 'the extension of the principles of standardization to the human element in production is a most important and growing field of activity.' "[11] Even workers that handled advanced technology needed strict control from managers.

The same discipline applied to college-trained engineers. "If science was to be effectively controlled, scientists had to be effectively controlled; the means to such control was the fostering of a spirit of cooperation among researchers second only to a spirit of loyalty to the corporation. . . . The content of the education had to provide the training necessary for technical work, especially for the early years of employment; it had to instill in the student a sense of corporate responsibility, teamwork, service, and loyalty."[12]

Many industrial managers felt that the university was falling short in preparing individuals for corporate forms of fitting in. Companies like General Electric and Westinghouse had, by 1900, developed supplemental training courses that transformed engineers from soloists to team performers. These courses retrained graduates who, fresh out of university, "did not know how to adapt themselves to new conditions, . . . to adjust

their personalities to the wishes and desires of their superiors." In corporate school, they learned "to work first for the success of the corporation,
and only secondarily to consider themselves, and . . . to subordinate their
own ideas and beliefs to the wishes and desires of their superiors," — that
only then could they "really be efficient." In short, engineers learned that
"Self-forgetfulness is what is required."[13]

Without assuming that these views also dominated engineering education, we can still detect a strong tendency to see the free agency of the
early knowledge worker as damaging the efficient use of that knowledge.
University engineering programs knew that corporate employers would
see self-direction as a dysfunctional leftover from college days.

It shouldn't be surprising then that some top university administrators
wanted to run the university as a business. In 1900 the *Atlantic Monthly*
published this kind of call from a frustrated but safely anonymous administrator: "When the directors of a great commercial corporation or of
some transportation company find it necessary to call a new man to the
presidency or to the position of general manager, he is at once given
almost absolute authority to all executive details. . . . The educational
executive or manager, however, has no such freedom of choice as to his
associates, has no such right of way." The educational administrator, the
author complains, is blocked by the tradition that places the professor
"quite beyond the reach of complaint," which presumably includes ready
dismissal. The disappointed author correctly noted that nearly every other
organization put its members under the exclusive control of one man, and
wondered why universities should be different.

The author struck a perennial note in business-oriented criticisms of
higher education: modernization means business, and business means
centralized authority. The university will fall behind, he concluded, "unless the business of education is regarded in a business light, is cared for by
business methods, and is made subject to that simple but all-efficient law
of a proper division of labor and of intelligent and efficient organization,
— a division of labor which brings men who are students of the classics, of
the sciences, of the literatures, of philosophy, of history, under the wise
direction and immediate control of the man who is necessarily and most
desirably a student of humanity; [and who is given] an authority entirely
commensurate with his responsibility."[14] For this writer, the research university's diversity of goals and subjects made top-down command more
necessary than ever.

*· · · Not Just a Business · · ·*

Yet most university leaders believed that the university could be businesslike and work with business while refusing to become a business. Individual units such as engineering might form partnerships, but the university as a whole would stand apart. The university had to serve the needs of the larger business community while offering training, services, and environments that business could never provide.

University leaders knew that they were preparing most of their students to enter the era's business system and often advertised this service. At Chicago, President William Rainey Harper wrote, "No man who is acquainted with the facts will deny that today special opportunities of the highest rank, in business, are opening to men of college training." While business could use people of every educational level, the "college man" was equipped go beyond "business life" to possess a "business career." University training "is intended to develop in the man systematic habits; to give him control of his intellectual powers; to fit him in such a manner that he may be able to direct those powers successfully in any special direction."[15]

These leaders also understood the premium that business placed on technical training, specialized expertise, and the capacity for change. In this respect, 1900 was hardly different from 2000. Capitalism is fundamentally dynamic, and big future earnings always lie in some "new" economy rather than in the old. University leaders generally accepted technology and change as the basic parameters of specialized knowledge. At the same time, they insisted that the university had a unique niche in the economy and played a unique role.

Presidents with otherwise different theories of education broadly agreed that the university was special. The liberal Eliot insisted that a university's "trustees are not themselves expert in any branch of the university" and should "always maintain a considerate and even deferential attitude towards the experts whom they employ." Eliot rejected the idea that a university could be treated like a market in which services are always for sale at the right price. The personal qualities of "a first-rate university teacher"—"quick sympathy, genuine good-will, patience, and comprehensive learning"—cannot be bought.[16] At the University of Illinois, President Andrew S. Draper did call for a tight financial rein on faculty. "When teachers are not supported by student fees, but are paid from the university treasury without reference to the number of students they teach

. . . there is no automatic way of getting rid of teachers who do not teach." But despite his conservatism Draper admitted that "the university cannot become a business corporation, with a business corporation's ordinary implications. Such a corporation is without what is being called *spiritual aim,* is without moral methods . . . The distinguishing ear-marks of an American university are its moral purpose, its scientific aim, its unselfish public service, its inspirations to all men in all noble things, and its incorruptibility by commercialism."[17] Most presidents agreed that for the university to be useful to society or even to business, it would need to be something other than a business itself. It would have to combine technical training with the training in personal qualities like "quick sympathy, genuine good-will, patience, and comprehensive learning" that underwrote the transmission and creation of knowledge.

As the decades passed, university leaders became if anything more concerned with protecting the university's independence. The full-service university was engrossed in a web of constantly multiplying external entanglements. The stabilization of public funding after 1900 increased legislative involvement in campus politics. World War I brought new political pressures, including demands for political loyalty that cost many faculty their jobs. The interwar years systematized the funding of science by foundations, and World War II introduced the federal government as the new gorilla among external patrons. University administrations needed to combine solicitude and vigilance on a number of fronts at once.

In the early 1960s, President Clark Kerr at California offered a famous warning about the increasingly prosperous university's decreasing autonomy: "Federal support of scientific research during World War II," he wrote, has had a greater impact on higher education than any event since the land-grant movement was enshrined in the Morrill Act of 1862.[18] Kerr detailed the ways in which an indirect form of "federal influence" operated through a nearly irresistible structure of financial opportunities to reduce "the authority of the department chairman, the dean, the president, [and] . . . faculty government."[19] The research university had become a "federal grant university" in which direct state control was avoided in favor of a much more effective system of financial rewards and penalties: "The university, as Allen Wallis, president of the University of Rochester, has remarked, becomes to an extent a 'hotel.' The [federal granting] agency becomes the new alma mater. The research entrepreneur becomes a euphoric schizophrenic. . . . There are . . . especially acute problems when the agency insists on the tie-in sale (if we do this for you, then you must do this for us) or when it requires frequent and detailed progress reports. Then the university really is less than a free agent. It all becomes a kind of 'putting-out' system with the agency taking the place of the merchant-capitalist of old. Sweat shops have developed out of such a system in earlier times and in other industries."[20] This is a harsh assessment of a federal partnership that was, after all, a cornerstone of UC's research prominence. But Kerr had come to feel that federal support had evolved into a shadow government. The early 1960s were arguably the summit of the research university's wealth and power, but it was at this moment that Kerr feared a systemic loss of independence.

Public criticism wasn't the only threat to university sovereignty: positive funding sources threatened it too. The purpose and identity of the research university were shaped through decades of self-defense against even the supportive attentions of business and government.

### · · · From Autocracy to Administration · · ·

University leaders generally believed in the university's special function and personnel, but they did not find models of conduct in pure craft work or the artistic personality. How would they be able to serve their social and corporate clientele while maintaining their distinctive functions and methods? Leaders were quite certain that the creation of new knowledge and the transmission of advanced skill required a kind of employee freedom not widely admired in business. The development of the technology that allowed Taylorization could not itself be Taylorized. Humanism could draw on both craft labor and artistic traditions for its own vision of the autonomous life that linked creation, thought, and labor. A similar concern for autonomy, however differently expressed, was driven by the university's interest in securing its own unique processes.

The compromise between autonomy and management appeared in the university's rejection of hard Taylorism. In the business world, Taylorism produced opposition in early "human relations" thought. By the 1920s, for example, Mary Parker Follett was arguing that management should replace command with "integration," in which the "desires [of both sides] have found a place," so that "neither side has had to sacrifice anything."[21] Figures such as Elton Mayo and Kurt Lewin would continue the internal resistance to Taylorism into later decades. But years before the anti-Taylorist movement in management theory, many university leaders were denouncing autocratic management as an outdated practice. By the early years of the twentieth century Charles W. Eliot of Harvard had become emphatic on this point: "The president of a university should never exercise an autocratic or one-man power. He should be often an inventing and animating force, and often a leader; but not a ruler or autocrat. His success will be due more to powers of exposition and persuasion combined with persistent industry, than to any force of will or habit of command. Indeed, one-man power is always objectionable in a university, whether lodged in a president, secretary of the trustees, dean, or head of department. In order to make progress of a durable sort, the president will have to possess his soul in patience; and on that account a long tenure will be an advantage to him and to the university he serves."[22] For Eliot, the president-as-ruler didn't fit with the structure of the modern university. About twenty years before liberal management theorists began to criticize autocratic Taylorism, Eliot was defining the leader as a coordinator, facilitator, and supporter.

The university was defining a modernization based on a structural diversity that autocracy couldn't manage. Laurence Veysey notes that universities were experiencing organizational modernity first hand: "Both intellectually and in terms of its structure, the American university was becoming too diverse easily to define — or to control. The adherence of academic leaders to varying educational philosophies, the emergence of crystallized departments of learning, and the presence of larger number[s] of students all contributed to this result."[23] Eliot was ahead of many of his peers in accepting diversity as systemic rather than deviant.

Autocracy was somewhat more workable in industry, where units could congeal around common functions and measurable outputs. But industry's concern with efficiency also inspired systemic approaches that supplanted and partially replaced the autocrat at the top. In the late nineteenth century, business had discovered that mechanization required more rather than less management; "scientific management" arose to deal with complex coordination problems in operations, ones that the most powerful individual could not solve.[24] Even in industry, autocracy had its limits.

The university was a more complex case, for it was a collection of often unrelated disciplines, projects, and research techniques that lacked the common culture of either the small college or the industrial firm. Unlike the college, the university could presume neither a common purpose nor a set of unifying psychological identifications. Unlike industry, the university could not aspire to tight functional integration. The university was also unable to use the accounting and operational techniques that increased integration in industry.[25] The result made administration vitally important to the university's function. As Veysey put it, "Bureaucratic administration was the structural device which made possible the new epoch of institutional empire-building without recourse to specific shared values . . . Techniques of control shifted from the sermon and the direct threat of punishment toward the more appropriate devices of conference, memorandum, and filing system . . . the multiplicity of cleavages demanded a general submission to regulation, from top to bottom, if all vestiges of order were not to disappear. Bureaucratic codes of conduct serves as a low but tolerable common denominator, linking individuals and factions who did not think in the same terms but who, unlike the students of the 1860's, were usually too polite to require threats."[26] By 1910 bureaucracy had become the research university's standard infrastructure. It was a disjointed bureaucracy, a collection of fragments linked indirectly. In this disarticulation, university administration would find its liberalism. To succeed within it, administrators would need managerial skill rather than collegial familiarity or autocratic strength.[27]

### · · · The Meaning of Management · · ·

The term "management" has never been widely accepted as applying to universities, but in reality it described key practices of university administration.

Management is a common but complicated word. The English term comes through several steps from the Latin word for "to handle," as in handling horses (which in turn derived from *manus,* "hand"). By extension it generally implied the training and supervising of something of lower capacity. Only after World War II did "management" come to mean the handling of people in *organizations,* and the handling of systems and processes along with them. "Administration" was used far earlier, and remains dominant in universities.

The first fact about management, then, is that it refers to the "right disposition of things" in a *differentiated system* or "economy." In this way, it is another word for what the historian and philosopher Michel Foucault called the "art of government." Government, he wrote, initially referred to the governance of a family and all its various members. Government seeks "an end which is 'convenient' for each of the things that are to be governed." Government gradually transferred practices that managed the household to the management of the state. Its goals exist in a "complex composed of people and things," and these goals, and the relations through which they are produced, are invariably plural. Government is bound up in reciprocal ties and multilateral influence, no matter how unequal. The "things with which in this sense government is to be concerned are in fact men, but men in their relations, their links, their imbrication with those other things which are wealth, resources, means of subsistence, the territory with its specific qualities, climate, irrigation, fertility, etc.; men in their relation to that other kind of things, customs, habits, ways of acting and thinking . . . accidents and misfortunes."[28] Management exists to regulate and coordinate a system that consists of disparate elements, dynamic relations, and multiple ends.

Foucault described a second crucial feature of management. The art of government departs from an older notion of authority as sovereignty, embodied in the prince. "The prince stood in a relation of singularity and externality, and thus of transcendence, to his principality." The goal of exercising power is for the prince to maintain a relation of control to what he owns. Under the sovereign, subjects and objects must obey the law that descends from the sovereign power. "The end of sovereignty," Foucault wrote, "is in sum nothing other than submission to sovereignty." "On the contrary," he continues, "with government it is a question not of imposing law on men, but of disposing things: that is to say, of employing tactics rather than laws . . . — to arrange things in such a way that, through a certain number of means, such and such ends may be achieved."[29] The art of government evolved into political science as it confronted the question of "populations," of masses and the inevitable failure of singular, top-down decrees. Government aims at *prosperity* in the broadest sense — at maximizing desirable outputs while maintaining order.

Taking these two features together, we can see that management expresses two major structural aspects of the rising research university. It is decentralized, having diverse elements that must be coordinated yet not assimilated. And it favors (ostensibly neutral) coordination over the commands of a sovereign. Management is theoretically a *post-sovereignty* form of authority. It is also the range of techniques that would allow the fully systematic coordination sought by industrial engineers.

The key word is *theoretically:* sovereignty is rarely abandoned in managerial practice. As Foucault observed, "sovereignty is far from being eliminated by the emergence of a new art of government, even by one which has passed the threshold of political science; on the contrary, the problem of sovereignty is made more acute than ever."[30] Management in practice refers to a hybrid situation in which sovereignty has been complicated rather than eliminated. Power has been decentralized and dispersed in managerial systems, and changes as it moves from level to level and point to point. But much power remains "transcendental" or external to its sites of application. In my usage, the term "management" refers to this *mixed* situation of decentralized structures combined with authority that does circulate horizontally and indirectly but predominantly from the top down.

### · · · *Faculty as Labor* · · ·

Speaking abstractly, universities developed a liberal version of available management options. University administration revolved around strong personalities while taking on the major, consistent features of business management. It was hierarchical. It yoked personal relations to explicit, impersonal procedures, procedures which treated individual exceptions as anomalous. Official authority arose from the office rather than from the person. This person, in theory, functioned through his or her specialized expertise. He or she held personal power to the degree to which expertise fit with the larger structure. Finally, the system decentralized power without eliminating the nonconsensual control of superiors over inferiors, that is, without eliminating sovereignty.

The university has had an orthodox chain of command. It had trustees and a president at the top, provosts and deans next, then heads or chairs of departments, rank-and-file faculty, staff, graduate students, and undergraduates. This academic staff was accompanied by a parallel business staff, marked, as Veysey notes, by "its own internal gradations. . . . Generally speaking, power flowed downward throughout this entire organization." Certain faculty wielded what Weber called "charismatic" influence that could override bureaucratic structure and procedure, but only temporarily.[31] Top-down power governed policy making and major decisions. Well before World War I, the term "administration" came to refer to "the president, deans, business staff, and often to a number of senior professors who regularly supported the president's wishes." This group also shared a distinct "state of mind" that had them charging themselves with institutional custody and planning.[32]

Administration was open to selected, individual members of the faculty. The existence within every faculty of a semi-flexible subset of leaders has sometimes been used to suggest that managerial forms do not apply to faculty governance. But disproportionate personal power was fully compatible with managerial procedure. For every junior person who obtained power or resources, there was a senior faculty member or administrator that had exercised an authority to give those things. The senior giver retained sufficient sovereignty to be the source of the gift, which was what distinctive resources generally remained.

As a group, faculty were subordinate to the administrative system. Faculty leadership generally lay with a few trusted "senior" professors rather than with the faculty as a whole or with their legislatures, whose power was generally limited. Even the most influential faculty members, lacking an administrative post, spoke for "the faculty" rather than for the institution as a whole, which was spoken for by the administration. The university's business operations were separated from academic operations, such that the faculty as a whole had negligible input into financial planning and management.

The individual faculty member who lacked important political alliances was powerless and even vulnerable. It wasn't until after World War II that faculty tenure was regularized: for example, the University of California had no formal tenure until 1958.[33] Faculty served in decision-making positions more or less at the pleasure of the administration. The professional standing of faculty did not so much increase their authority as ratify their status as skilled employees.[34] The subordinate position of faculty "was revealed by the fact that whenever an insurgent movement to 'democratize' the structure of an institution took place, it was described as a revolt.'"[35] "The professor had his own quite real dignity," Veysey assures us, "but it was apt to become most apparent when he sat in his book-lined study, not when he met for formal discussions of policy."[36]

Faculty belonged to the professional middle class, and yet they occupied the *position* of labor. Faculty were distinct from and subordinate to management, which retained limited but real authority over their individual affairs. Faculty were sequestered from the business end of the university. When faculty sought authority over the institution as a whole, the move was viewed as it would have been in industry — as insurrection. This system of management was liberal, in the sense that daily faculty labor was not closely supervised, and individuals had the kind of control over the content of their work associated with artisans and professionals. But this individual autonomy did not change the facts of institutional power.

Faculty often contrasted themselves with nonacademic staff, and this contrast allowed them to see themselves as something other than labor in the sense of the clerical, administrative, technical, and facilities workers who kept the university running. Faculty proclaimed their operating principles of collegiality and consent, their research pursued in a "community of scholars," and their teaching as a "high calling." They asserted control over the curriculum and similar matters, and retained many guild privileges by comparison to nonacademic staff. Faculty also retained enormous *supervisory* responsibility. Faculty acted as supervisors to the lowest-status academic workers known as students. Faculty in effect worked on the shop floor, face to face with the students who played the role of "frontline" personnel.

We might therefore think of university faculty as a special kind of "labor aristocracy." Faculty had real control over their individual work and local supervisory authority. But this did not allow faculty *as a group* to wield decision-making power. Faculty occupied a contradictory class location, owning and not owning their academic capital, managing and being managed by turns.

· · · *Divided Governance* · · ·

The underlying reality of the faculty's position as labor was both embodied and concealed by the university's dual management system. The business side generally adapted the corporate look of its particular era, drawing on the practices and the personnel of the business world. The academic side depended on craft skills that remained in the possession of individual faculty. Some academic functions, like lower-division humanities teaching, could be done with untenured labor and be directly controlled by administrators. Other academic functions, like complex and costly scientific research, were utterly beyond the capability of administrators and remained in faculty hands. In spite of constant interaction and negotiation between administrators and faculty, their spheres remained distinct. This meant a reciprocal hands-off ethic, and it also meant, to repeat, the faculty's general exclusion from direct managerial power.

In the absence of this kind of power, how did the faculty protect their positions? The general solution has been a dual system of governance that has sometimes been called "shared governance." Much emphasis was placed on faculty control of academic matters and their right of consultation on policy issues.[37] When it was working normally, a more descriptive term would be *divided governance*. Much of the faculty's sense of freedom and protection depended on the maintenance of this structural division.

Divided governance originally emerged from profound concerns about academic freedom. At the University of California, increasing anger among the faculty at the interventions of President Benjamin Wheeler culminated in the faculty "revolt" of 1919–20, which created UC's Academic Senate.[38] Not far down the road, Mrs. Leland Stanford aroused national attention in 1915 when she got the economist Edward Ross fired for his views on the gold standard.[39] As the century wore on, academic legislatures at various universities, along with the American Association of University Professors, sought to reinforce academic freedom by splitting academics from administration.[40]

As the century advanced, divided governance became the bedrock of academic freedom. In a study based on faculty interviews, Burton R. Clark found that most assumed a clear distinction between business and academic affairs. "The flowering of white-collar bureaucracy [is] largely on the side of 'business' affairs — finance, purchasing, accounting, property management, transportation — and such operations as 'student personnel services.'" On the academic side, "professors look at alternative technologies and decide what is best for their needs. Collectively, they decide on production and distribution, and whether to innovate or continue with the old."[41] Though they had little control over business, faculty members said, they had direct control over academics, which they could prevent from being driven by procedural and financial concerns. But this perception was largely the result of divided governance itself. It was the division that allowed academics to fulfill the wish of most faculty members for the autonomy of their professional sphere. In reality, the larger determinants of academic life were political and financial and, as in other organizations, beyond their reach.

After World War I, some version of divided governance gradually formalized a boundary between educational and business affairs. Business considerations exerted steady pressure on educational policy, but the boundary did correspond to what was in and out of the faculty member's power. She was left with two kinds of freedom: the freedom to manage her individual academic and professional concerns, and the freedom to avoid management contexts where she would be powerless. Faculty were labor within the overall administrative context. They were managers and self-employed professionals in their academic domain. Academic management avoided the Taylorization of its academic functions, but it did this less by democratizing than by dividing authority. Faculty had local and specific craft freedoms in the quasi-private spaces that they sheltered from general management.

··· *Bureaucracy or Democracy* ···

Many faculty have thrived under divided governance. They've had plenty of freedom to do their own work, and they know that they have more personal freedom than they would in nearly any other job. The system has worked particularly well in the sciences, where the university has long served as a kind of communal infrastructure underwriting faculty entre-preneurs. But there are some built-in costs to this kind of freedom, costs that are often overlooked. I'll discuss three of them: a preference for bureaucracy over democracy, a permanent vulnerability to business influ-ence, and a weakening of individual agency.

Most faculty members were inclined toward spending their time in the classroom and lab, where they had freedom and influence, rather than in the larger institution, where they had little of either. They became cynical about mechanisms of participation, like academic senates that spend enormous time ratifying or slightly modifying decisions already made by administrators. Studies have shown that white-collar workers as a whole, when suddenly given authority in contexts where it had long been denied, have difficulty believing in their own authority.[42] Sometimes they have good reason. Their freedom depends on customary protections and guild privileges that are strengthened by a cumbersome bureaucracy. Most fac-ulty members experience university administration less as a system of governance or coordination than as a kind of bomb shelter: the more rigid and dug-in it is, the more secure they are. Whatever their stated politics or personal temperament, most faculty members are invested in a bureaucratic system whose inefficiencies sponsor their academic freedom. Veysey is especially eloquent on this subject:

> The bureaucratic apparatus . . . became a buffer which protected the isolation of the individuals and the small factions on each campus. Thus if the maze of officials and committees grew sufficiently com-plex, the whole machinery might screen the faculty member from the administration. Surrounded by politely affirmative deans and committees, the university president gradually lost touch with what

was going on in "his" classrooms. This could mean that the professor, as long as he avoided sensationalism, became in practice relatively free of intrusion. One speculates that a large measure of academic freedom came about in just such an unintended way.

Freedom from intrusion required a certain refusal of intervention:

> The university throve, as it were, on ignorance. Or, if this way of stating it seems unnecessarily paradoxical, the university throve on the patterned isolation of its component parts, and this isolation required that people continually talk past each other, failing to listen to what others were actually saying. This lack of comprehension, which safeguards one's privacy and one's illusions, doubtless occurs in many groups, but it may be of special importance in explaining the otherwise unfathomable behavior of a society's most intelligent members.[43]

Academic bureaucracy preserves freedom by offering places to hide. This freedom is generally thought to outweigh the ignorance, the errors, even the tacit hostility that circulate in a system predicated on internal exile.

Veysey is describing the situation in 1910, but the next half-century did little but consolidate this management system. Writing at its high point in 1963, President Clark Kerr of UC focused on the power this system had on even its radical members:

> The individual faculty member, and particularly the political liberal of the faculty, is often torn between the "guild" and the "socialist" views of the university. The guild view stands for self-determination, and for resistance against the administration and the trustees; the socialist view, for service to society which the administration and the trustees often represent. The guild view is elitist toward the external environment, conservative toward internal change, conformist in relation to the opinion of colleagues. The socialist view is democratic toward society, radical towards change, and nonconformist. And the political liberal is drawn toward both views. Here is a paradox. Few institutions are so conservative as the universities about their own affairs while their members are so liberal about the affairs of others; and sometimes the most liberal faculty member in one context is the most conservative in another. . . . When change comes it is rarely at the instigation of [the faculty] as a collective body. The group is more likely to accept or reject or comment, than

to devise and propose. The group serves a purpose as a balance wheel. . . . The individual faculty member seeking something new has, in turn, often found his greatest encouragement and leverage coming from the outside; the individual scholar is the inventor, the outside agency the force for innovation. . . . Change comes more through spawning the new than reforming the old.[44]

Faculty express their allegiance to bureaucracy through guild conservatism. The freedom of individual faculty becomes dependent on institutional inertia. In contrast, democratic activity threatens freedom by disrupting protective procedure. After 1980 this situation began to change, as individual faculty members, mostly in science and engineering, became increasingly interested in industry partnerships and start-up companies. But this later assault on a formerly protective university bureaucracy did not fly the flag of faculty democracy, but the flag of individual freedom of contract with commercial sponsors. Over time, academic democracy became the implied enemy of academic freedom.

### · · · *Commercial Vulnerability* · · ·

The second cost of divided governance appears when we ask this question: if academic freedom depends on withdrawal from general management, what happens when external forces attempt to exert influence?

Most academic fields long ago agreed to remain outsiders on the business side. The active faculty who had administrative power held it through the daily grind in their official positions. The faculty majority lacked detailed information and expertise, and would get involved only by playing one of the roles that bureaucracy is least likely to respect: that of protestor or individual exception. This might not have been such a bad thing if managers and academics had equal status. But managers and academics were not equals. The business environment had the upper hand exactly where faculty had no hand at all.

The university's business side has always appealed to the market power of the consumer. Burton Clark has nicely summarized the problem this poses for universities:

Sociologists have observed that the social control of expert services may primarily center in professional self-control, governmental-bureaucratic control, or client-consumer control. In American academia, with its pushing back of governmental control and its localization of bureaucrats, the contest comes down primarily to peer-based versus client-based authority, with the latter expressed through organizational management. As they interpret and implement "demand," and sometimes actively shape it, administrators become the active proxies of consumers. In certain institutional locales, their immediate interpretations of service to clientele become controlling: faculty labor trails along, more other- than inner-driven. But in other major settings, the faculty clearly lead, field by field, taking cues from peers and converting administrators to the fiction that "the faculty is the institution." What we find in academic authority in America depends on where we look in the institutional hierarchy.[45]

Although faculty have possessed much "professional self-control," they could be overridden by the administration's built-in power to trump professional concerns with customer needs.

We can make this point in somewhat different terms. Faculty seemed most free to define their work in élite and research contexts where the student customer was subordinate. Where responding to the student customer was primary, it was clear that faculty were not the lead interpreters and definers of customer needs. Research faculty did not control their customers either. They just attended more to one group of customers, external funders, than to the other, their students. Faculty had ceded most institutional governance of self-government to agencies and administrators who were in fact not their democratic proxies. In doing so, the faculty lost most of their control of their markets by World War I. Markets were controlled (defined and interpreted) by agencies and administrators, especially in large public universities, and the faculty were only one among their many constituents.

### · · · Corporate Individualism · · ·

A third and related cost of divided governance was the restriction of individual agency. By 1900, Veysey writes, "most professors were too contented and the structure of the university had already become too firmly established for basic changes in the distribution of power to be made. The movement for faculty control, unlike the main effort toward academic freedom, became a dated curiosity of the Progressive period. Except for producing some unwieldy academic 'senates' and for encouraging somewhat greater departmental autonomy in the area of appointments, it bore little substantial fruit."[46] In the absence of collective control, individual faculty pursued a prudential care of the self. Hannah Arendt identifies this tendency with Epictetus, who shows that "a man is free if he limits himself to what is in his power, if he does not reach into a realm where he can be hindered. The 'science of living' consists in knowing how to distinguish between the alien world over which man has no power and the self of which he may dispose as he sees fit."[47] There is of course practical wisdom in this: avoid hindrance by ruling in the classroom but not the department, or in the English department but not in the humanities division, or in the humanities but not in the college and so on. This kind of individualism is suited to a republic of scattered estates, where each protects his independence by refusing to interfere with that of others. The fragmented university had a superficial resemblance to exactly that kind of country, with departments ruling themselves but not their neighbors, each on its own freehold.

The psychological impact of this system must also be acknowledged. One of the best studies of white-collar consciousness in bureaucratic systems is that of Charles Heckscher, whose work on downsized corporations in the 1980s and 1990s offers some parallels with faculty reactions in earlier periods. He describes the initial reaction to crisis of middle-class, mid-level employees as "schizophrenia," in which "people alternately and almost in the same breath would express anger at management, hope that the leadership would rescue them, frustration at change, and willingness to suspend judgment." When the intensity of the crisis began to fade, people withdrew "into a cautious individualism. . . . People merely gave up trying to make immediate sense of the situation or to save the company, and focused instead on doing their own jobs well." Often this would be resolved with a "retreat to autonomy." At no point, even when enlisted by upper management, did employees translate their autonomy into an ability to exert leadership in groups.[48]

A similar pattern marked university crises from the start. Faculty members' participation drastically increased in crises, but was rarely sustained. Their participation often lacked the skill, informal knowledge, and determined patience that comes only with daily experience. The faculty tacitly assumed its own belated or secondary status, and except in extreme cases deferred to administrators. Such interventions for the most part confirmed the hierarchical nature of university authority and the rank-and-file faculty member's outsider status within his own institutional politics.

Such interventions did not endow faculty members with a sense that their individual perspectives have relevance to the governing of the larger system. Freedom continued to depend on withdrawal from conflict rather than on exerting one's will through it. Freedom did not mean the freedom to revise the social processes in which one's university life was passing. It did not mean opening up Epictetus's boundary between one's freedom and hindrance into democratic participation. Individual agency instead depended on maintaining a détente with bureaucratic inertia.

An autonomy that depends on a routine powerlessness forms what I've elsewhere called "submissive individualism." Public areas of personal action and sovereignty were often abandoned, and this loss of sovereignty had a direct payoff in personal liberty. But this wasn't simply a reasonable liberty, a liberty that knew its own limits. It was a liberty mixed with frustration at its ineffectuality in local as well as large organizational matters. Autonomy was not translating into self-determination over general administrative matters, which were part of a separate and parallel governing system, one that could steer the professional and academic activities that claimed to be beyond its reach.

The university has helped to define professional life in the terms of a somewhat demoralizing compromise. The university agreed that brain work required individual autonomy: Taylorization would not work. At the same time, the university would not support the brain worker's institutional agency. As in industry, the care of the organization would remain in the hands of upper management. Individual conditions were a private matter: freedom was pursued in private (the study, the classroom, the laboratory); collective placement derived not from collective life but from individual performance. The goal of craft work was not a public life based on the principles of freedom, experience, and other aspects of individuality cherished by both liberal humanist and free labor traditions. The goal of craft work was increasingly privatized self-development, motives housed in the structure of individual upward mobility for which the university stood. Upward mobility, in turn, allowed more effective opting out of collective life, defining freedom as a retreat from the collective and tying craft labor to this diminished version. Free labor, that is, became contingent on the shrinking of the individual's agency to his or her sphere of direct influence. Faculty members were Romanized, resembling not so much republican citizens as landowning stoics living under a benign despotism that they could afford to ignore.

··· *Downsizing Individual Agency* ···

The research university "solved" the contradiction in managerial systems between the retaining and the giving up of top-down sovereignty, but did so by splitting its system in two. Faculty members continued to insist on freedom of intellectual inquiry, but preserved it by separating from management rather than by making management their own.

This was convenient to both sides, which has helped the arrangement to endure. But divided governance also helped to reduce the professional middle class's interest in democratic governance. Faculty long ago grew accustomed to the absence of a rewarding democratic experience in their professional life, and to see this absence as protective. Faculty autonomy, in short, became equivalent to a classical, negative form of freedom — freedom from overt coercion — in the very period during which system management, ruling with muted coercion, was making this kind of freedom less effective. Craft labor was central to professional life. At the same time, it was not part of the university's institutional life. The availability of autonomy and craft labor, particularly in the humanities, continued to be associated with a retreat from active management of the commercial forces that support the university. Faculty free labor had come to depend, practically speaking, on the eclipse of democratic processes by a hierarchical bureaucracy abundantly furnished with hiding places.

Faculty members were unable to associate knowledge with democracy. They were equally unable to associate knowledge with their own free agency. The public regarded academic freedom as a workplace perquisite, a reward for having valid knowledge rather than knowledge's cause: good working conditions were a benefit for faculty who produced a unique kind of bankable productivity.[49] The faculty did not, by and large, proclaim autonomous craft labor to be the fountainhead of creativity and progress. They couldn't make the strong case, in the face of regular public doubts, that technological and cultural advantage depended on radical imaginative freedom, wild speculation, unfettered experimentation, the capacity to think about anything, the ability to dream awake. Academic freedom was espoused as the university's special creed, a kind of cultural value that pluralists should respect, but it was not made the source of the university's capacity to fulfill its public missions.

As the university became increasingly well managed, it felt less need for these two traditional virtues of emancipated societies. It sidestepped democratic governance, and it downplayed individual agency. The research university was not a holdout from the "administered world." Its social effect, instead, was to reconcile such a world with the humanist self-image of the professional-managerial class.

Humanist ideals endured nonetheless. The humanities were still associated with the knowledge that taught freedom as well as tradition. It housed knowledges of oneself, and of oneself in formation, and of oneself moving through various social worlds. The humanities were tied to the experience of unfettered interest, and with free labor expressed (partially concealed) as artistic creation. They sustained feelings of enjoyment, by which I mean the *experience* of freedom. The humanities sustained an enjoyment that could exist *within* the collective systems that we call the corporation, culture, and history. The humanities meant historical knowledge and traditional values. They also meant the possibility of free agency and free labor in spite of or because of everything that is known about the constraints of social life.

In this context, would the humanities disciplines "humanize" and transform management? Would they be managed in turn? Would they create some hybrids of freedom in group life that had not been known before? It is to the response of humanists to the managed university that we now turn.

# CHAPTER 5

. . . . . . . . . . . . . . . . . . . . . . . .

*Babbitry and Meritocracy*

## A Labor Question

In the last two chapters, I have discussed the research university's permanent dependence on both business and humanism. These two ingredients have much in common, but they have often refused to blend. There was divergence between commerce's desire for profitable knowledge and those humanist notions that saw commerce as secondary, irrelevant, or dangerous to human development. The university evolved within an industrial capitalism that was ponderously, aggressively, even anxiously instrumental. The American university lacked the intellectual and cultural resources that had protected the university in Germany. It would need to make its own way in the midst of the revolutionary transition from market to corporate capitalism.

The corporate development of industry made solo artisanship seem obsolete. The same was true of self-directed technical work, which by World War I had been largely absorbed into firms and industrial networks that included partnerships between academia and business. Business spoke plainly to universities about its requirements for technical and managerial employees. The corporate-university alliances that caused much concern in the 1990s had been, as we have seen, developed more than a century earlier.

This system of university-industry partnering sponsored research of the highest quality. It enabled research that individuals could never have accomplished alone, or with small-scale resources. It also raised some fundamental issues about creative work. Would creativity still rest largely on self-direction, hunches, unmanaged desire, and the like? What would happen to the autonomy of self and work in this kind of system? Would creativity be preserved under management, or suffocated? Would technical, professional, critical, and artistic work become regimented and Taylorized as had industrial labor?

Any effective response to these questions would require that humanism articulate individual autonomy *within* increasingly intricate social systems. It could no longer insist simply on the isolated soul's solitary labor, but would need to explain how corporate capitalism's widespread socialization of labor could be shaped, revised, or transformed into a new stage in the advancement of human freedom. Humanism was one of the guardians of autonomous work, of the generative power of the developed self. But would it guard autonomy by protecting self-development from instrumental forms of capitalist socialization? Would it protect the developed self by consolidating its power over organizations, or through a nostalgic celebration of pre-organizational solitude?

Humanism, and its soloist traditions, met business, the great socializer, in the research university. The encounter took place in classrooms and laboratories and under the supervision of university administration. Administrators were generally not business people, and leading administrators could talk about efficiency and personal growth in the same paragraph. But administrators needed to synthesize their educational humanism with institutional needs and the explicit demands of their industrial sponsors. These sponsors wanted workers who combined technical skill with the capacity to work cooperatively in organizations. These workers needed to be manageable, but they also needed to be autonomous. They needed to be autonomous enough to solve problems, create new processes and products, and supervise other workers. They needed to be manageable enough to work well with others and mind their bosses. The university needed to produce a hybrid graduate, and humanists could have a role in shaping the product. But what kind of hybrid would this graduate be?

The old college answer had been relatively clear: the Christian man, the "whole man," the wise citizen — an intellectually, ethically, and spiritually developed self. It's important to remember why this answer could be so clear. The college mission was simplified by narrow boundaries of gender, race, and class: lacking a basic high school feeder system and standards of social inclusion, the college drew its students largely from a narrow class range. Its students were not facing industrial bureaucracy and labor management. The later research university's graduates were. Universities retained the old college's claim that its graduates would avoid the "level of a mere labourer at task-work," and yet they would avoid being laborers not by avoiding organizations but by becoming managers in them.[1] Graduates were preparing for a relatively protected but still managerial work environment, and thus the university had a different model for them.[2]

In keeping with this general project, university leaders usually described the whole or moral or free self as the collegiate preliminary to a university training in production skills. In the university, the moral self was prologue to the social self, the self that could be integrated into production's social process. In practice, the graduate's qualifications could rest in large part on his class standing, on the assumed authority of the white, middle- to upper-class masculinity that predominated in student populations, especially at top schools, until well after World War II. But in principle, the university graduate was a self-reliant employee of the kind we now call the *knowledge worker*. Again, the crucial feature of such a worker was a blending of the apparent opposites of autonomy and manageability, a blend that would be achieved through technical expertise. By 1900 universities had created the organizational atmosphere in which students and teachers learned to manage their own creative processes *and* to submit them to external management.

What role would the humanities disciplines play in producing this socializing personal autonomy? To simplify, would humanism produce the successful manager, or hold out for something closer to the unmanageable artisan or artist?

··· *The Promise of Practical Humanism* ···

One part of the answer appears in the work of yet another university president who married liberal culture to practical goals. Benjamin Ide Wheeler was president of the University of California during the twenty-year period (1899–1919) when the research university formalized the major elements of its current form. Wheeler was a financial mover and shaker, a partisan of research, a tireless fundraiser, and an intimate of the Hearst family who was comfortable in the upper levels of the business world. "Wheeler's arrival," one historian writes, "initiated a new era that would transform the Berkeley campus from a relatively weak and poorly funded state university to one of the nation's premier research universities."[3]

As is true for all university presidents, Wheeler's job was to please most of the people most of the time. Many of his views were especially pleasing to an audience of conservative donors. He was preoccupied with physical health and hygiene and the Teddy Roosevelt vision of the vigorous life. He criticized Charles Eliot's elective system, sometimes repudiating the personal freedom that Eliot and others associated with it.[4] Laurence Veysey puts Wheeler squarely at the center of the "new" conservatism of 1900, of a moderate "defense of order and stability":

> Wheeler applauded military drill as an antidote to the spirit of doing as one pleased; he urged students to cheer the team; he declared that professors must exemplify "sane, normal living," and that the "ascetic, teetotaler, radical, reformer, [or] agitator" was unfit for such a post. . . . [Similarly,] racial prejudice was wrong, but the Japanese ought to be excluded from the country; Grover Cleveland, Theodore Roosevelt, and Porfirio Díaz were all to be admired. . . . "The drift of the times," Wheeler said in a speech on Theodore Roosevelt, "is away from . . . the theories of the doctrinaire toward the capacity for correct and effective action."[5]

Effective action was compatible with conservative politics but had a harder time with democracy, which Wheeler tended to avoid in theory and practice alike.[6]

And yet Wheeler produced some of the period's most passionate defenses of liberal education. Describing "What the University Aims to Give the Student," Wheeler declared,

> It proposes to rescue men from slavery and make them free, in case they want to be free. It proposes in the first place to make them free from the bondage of ignorance. It proposes in the second place to make them free from the bondage of prejudice, routine, and the rule of thumb. A freeman is a man who can initiate, who has sufficient control over his walks and ways to do as his reason and outlook tell him is right and best. A man who acts on a prejudice, or drives his wagon in any other ruts is a slave, no matter how much he may pride himself on his prejudices and loyal adherences. The whole purpose of the university is to provide men with the means of seeing into things themselves, so that they shall not be dependent, but independent. . . . Thirdly, the university aims to give the student the highest and best form of control of himself. . . . The method by which the university proposes to give these things to its students is

in substance the one simple old-fashioned method of the trans-
ference of life.[7]

Wheeler advocated service and discipline and yet the self comes before
these: the self's freedom precedes the self's effectiveness. The goal of
university teaching was the student's self-development, whose goal was
self-determination.

Wheeler also insisted that liberal education be practical. It is a "freeman's training," but not for freemen whose work, as in ancient Athens, will
be done by slaves or bureaucrats.[8] Wheeler didn't mention American
slavery, but the parallel would have been hard to avoid. The American
personality "must vindicate itself . . . through power to act, to shape, to
create." American freedom means the freedom to express the self through
work, creation, "winning bread and doing good."[9] Breadwinning involves
lots of vigorous masculinity — being "of good health, deep-chested, sane-
minded, clean-souled," not hesitating to "plunge into the cold bath of
action when once the clothes are off."

Breadwinning also requires practical skills, and these skills are embed-
ded in a certain kind of self. Math and science teach the graduate to "think
consecutively" and "heroically face the facts," while social science teaches
"the unfolding experience of human society." Most remarkably, Wheeler
defined the practical world as existing in a permanent state of partial and
unstable information. The humanities contributed a fundamental ability
— "contingent reasoning," which means being "able to reason, as life
reasons, in incomplete syllogisms."[10] The outcome of this is "good sense"
and "good taste," which are "priceless gems." Though he used the language of conservative idealism, Wheeler was trying to describe a practical
power rooted in experience rather than pure reason. This power exists
when reasoning skills, taught by math and science, do not unilaterally rule
the self. Wheeler gave this power the conventional name of "good sense,"
but he was talking about a kind of reason that creates because it does not
follow the existing rules of reason so much as it follows the rule of its own
freedom.

But here we encounter the limit of applied humanism. Wheeler, like
most other educators in his position, continued to define self-development as the building of individual character. "Good judgment demands
first sanity, good health of mind and body." Wheeler ignored the con-
stitutively social quality of judgment. Though judgment is "quickened by
dealing with men," these dealings produce lessons for individual con-

sumption rather than any kind of social field. Wheeler's attitude toward social movements was dismissive. He rejected "the shabby judgment of the crank, the agitator, the extremist," without being able to imagine the social basis for dissident views, which he instead attributed to "a false confidence in objective tests and . . . the logician's syllogism."[11] The university finally must produce "all-round men," "men of sanity, men of intellectual grasp and intellectual self-control, men of moral purpose . . . men of character."[12]

Practical humanists like Wheeler wanted university graduates to lead useful and productive lives. They invoked humanist values in praise of the training that would allow for success in management and the professions. But they also invoked humanist values to describe the individual features that would refuse to adapt to the industrial order. It's especially important to recognize the awkward, contradictory status of this humanism: it was instrumental and independent, corporate and noncorporate at the same time. Humanism offered university students a dream in which success and freedom could be reconciled within the industrial order. They would adapt to managerial systems while experiencing no limit on their own liberty.

With hindsight, it's easy to remember how this kind of pragmatic humanism became a corporate apologetics. In this mode, we know that it created a professional-managerial class for capitalism, a class whose special privileges made it unlikely to seek free labor for all. While humanism rested on a vision of human freedom, it did not systematically oppose the industrial labor conditions, nor did it oppose the gender- and race- and nationality-based discriminations that placed clear limits on that freedom. Such opposition arose from overtly Marxist or socialist or African American or women's or "workingman's" criticisms of the economic and social system, and though these movements were humanistic in important ways, humanism was not their determinant ingredient.

But we cannot assume that humanism was inherently procapitalist, that it was an idealism of the middle classes who necessarily submitted to the dominant classes. When we assume this, we succumb to a kind of functionalism of self-interest, one in which pragmatic humanism, through its aestheticism, individualism, ambiguity, or contradictions, becomes the enabling ideology of the upper classes and their supereducated servants. No necessity was at work. The contradictions of pragmatic humanism made it as likely to reject corporate service as to accept it. Nothing in the call for autonomy, for example, meant that it would best be found through employment as a corporate lawyer or accountant or engineer rather than through a rejection of such roles. Nothing necessitated its application to the collegiate few. Most importantly, nothing prevented corporate lawyers and accountants from using humanism, broadly construed, to become management's internal opposition. Back in the university, literary academics could have used humanism to reconceive the individual subject as capable of self-management within complex organizations, capable, to start with, of experiencing her own freedom as the principle by which management would be judged. In such a theory, the standard of freedom would in some sense be self-given, not from pre-social consciousness but from personal experience within organizations.

Academic humanism was not damaged by its aestheticism, classicism, or excessive individualism *as such* but by its *managerialism*. Academic managerialism possessed the features that I noted in the last chapter. These acquired their distinctive mission through the university's reaction to the group differences signified by race.

· · · *The Rise of Meritocracy* · · ·

The research university developed in tandem with corporate industry, and both arose in the post-slavery racial environment of the later nineteenth century. The basic story is well known. The legal abolition of slavery was followed after the war by a period of complex and ambiguous Reconstruction, which itself formally ended in 1877 when the federal government, as the result of a political bargain that resolved the contested presidential election of 1876, withdrew its remaining troops from the South and ceased to take direct responsibility for the conditions that would enable multiracial democracy to develop there. During the 1890s, a decade of major university growth, the Jim Crow system of racial segregation spread throughout the South, and would remain largely unmodified for another seventy years.

Was there a direct connection between Jim Crow and the research university? The latter was largely although not entirely segregated. It was generally supportive of the social stratification that seemed natural to the economic and social leaders it served. Many of its faculty produced the scientific and social theories that justified racial hierarchy, although these views were rejected by some other scholars. The university was also involved in developing an apparently "color-blind" mechanism of stratification, one that to a surprising extent arose from the history of color in the United States.

In the nineteenth century, this system was sometimes called "natural aristocracy." Aristocracy of birth never had any real support in the United States, but most of its leaders had approved of an aristocracy of talent, the rule of the best and the brightest. For example, in 1807, Ralph Waldo Emerson's father, William Emerson, compared democracy to an ocean tempest likely to destroy the fleet unless the course was charted by a wise captain.[13]

This kind of élitism was repeatedly and consistently attacked, and yet it remained quite common. American democrats never managed to convince the vast majority that democracy must mean universal suffrage and, more to the point, full popular sovereignty.[14] They never managed to convince them that popular democracy would lead to efficiency and wealth. One reason for this failure was that leading American democrats did not believe this themselves.

A case in point is Thomas Jefferson, who became the patron saint of meritocracy rather than democracy for James Bryant Conant, a towering figure in higher education policy after World War I. While contemplating the future of the research university, Conant encountered a letter that Jefferson had written to John Adams in 1813. Jefferson had written, "I agree with you that there is a natural aristocracy among men. The grounds of this are virtue and talents. . . . May we not even say that that form of government is the best which provides the most effectually for a pure selection of these natural aristoi into the offices of government?"[15] Conant considered this evidence for the all-American idea that democracy could and indeed should lead to an aristocracy of talent.

In this framework, university graduates could be trusted to manage the national economy only if they were *not* part of the national masses. Independence was crucial to the development of professional expertise, but the expert would not be joining the populace to share equally in decision-making. The university in effect offered society a form of individual autonomy that would not lead to egalitarian democracy.

Conant's view had strong precedents at Harvard, the foremost being that set by the towering liberal humanist and long-time president Charles W. Eliot. As we have seen, Eliot promoted an elective system and called for the creation of free citizens through university training. He also advocated admissions testing as a leader of the College Entrance Examination Board, and belonged to the Eugenics Research Association. For Eliot, opening higher education did not mean replacing aristocracy with democracy but grounding aristocracy in merit.

In his inaugural address as Harvard's president in 1869, Eliot explained his position. He rejected aristocracy in the form of "a stupid and pretentious caste, founded on wealth, and birth, and an affectation of European manners." But he embraced that "aristocracy to which the sons of Harvard have belonged, and, let us hope, will ever aspire to belong — the aristocracy which excels in manly sports, carries off the honors and prizes of the learned professions, and bears itself with distinction in all fields of intellectual labor and combat."[16] Eliot celebrated aristocracy where that meant the rule of the excellent or the victorious over the also-rans.[17] He celebrated aristocracy as the outcome of competitive excellence. Excellence did not represent individual qualities or the substance of the achievement but a measurable rank or position.

A similar interest in ranking appeared in surprising form in the work of Eliot's friend and ally Ralph Waldo Emerson. Born in 1803, Emerson attended Harvard College, became a minister, rebelled against ministerial constraints, and quit the ministry. He gave an important address at the Harvard Divinity School, from which he had graduated and then did not return for the thirty years during which he got famous as a writer and lecturer on the strength of what we would now call his empowerment agenda for those who felt unfulfilled by material success. He was a reliable enemy of slavery and welcomed black emancipation. By the war's end in 1865, he had become a member of New England's cultural establishment. He was readmitted to the Harvard fold in the 1860s, becoming a lecturer and elected overseer, and was a strong supporter of Eliot's appointment as president. During these post–Civil War years, Emerson's lectures paid less attention to personal awakening and more to "social aims." These lectures included a little-known but revealing piece on the nature of aristocracy.

It's worth remembering the context for Emerson's address. Reconstruction was hesitantly moving forward throughout the 1860s. Though aspects of the radical program had been defeated by the time of President Eliot's inauguration, and though Reconstructionists were ambiguous and limited in their notion of equality, white progressive opinion continued to insist on the importance of *legal* equality between blacks and whites. Legal equality raised the specter of other forms of equality that were less palatable to all but the most radical Reconstructionists. There was the possibility of *political* equality between black and white, not to mention *social* equality, which the Congressional leadership of Reconstruction had rejected.[18] After the Civil War, discussions of American democracy raised the prospect of *multiracial* democracy — of a nation-state in which blacks and whites would govern themselves together. Such discussions inspired fear and loathing as well.

As a leading figure of cultural liberalism, Emerson was inclined toward halfway compromises between democracy and merit aristocracy. "The existence of an upper class is not injurious," he wrote, "as long as it is dependent on merit. For so long it is provocation to the bold and generous."[19] Sustaining the rich would reduce a big problem in postbellum America, as Emerson saw it, which was that Americans "venture to put any man in any place."[20] Emerson paralleled Eliot's theme of the rule of the best but took it further:

> It will be agreed everywhere that society must have the benefit of the best leaders. How to obtain them? Birth has been tried and failed. Caste in India has no good result. Ennobling of one family is good for one generation; not sure beyond. Slavery had mischief enough to answer for, but it had this good in it, — the pricing of men. In the South a slave was bluntly but accurately valued at five hundred to a thousand dollars, if a good field-hand; if a mechanic, a carpenter or smith, twelve hundred or two thousand. In Rome or Greece what sums would not be paid for a superior slave, a confidential secretary and manager, an educated slave; a man of genius, a Moses educated in Egypt? I don't know how much Epictetus was sold for, or Aesop, or Toussaint l'Ouverture, and perhaps it was not a good market-day. Time was, in England, when the state stipulated beforehand what price should be paid for each citizen's life, if he was killed. Now, if it were possible, I should like to see that appraisal applied to every man, and every man made acquainted with the true number and weight of every adult citizen, and that he be placed where he belongs, with [only] so much power confided to him as he could carry and use.[21]

Emerson was objecting once again to slavery and yet supporting the "pricing of men."[22] The obsession with black skin color wasn't smart, he implies, nor was the literal ownership of African people. Still, he suggests, why throw out the ranking baby with the slavery bath? Ranking "appraisal" can be improved through general application, one not confined to one race or national origin. What Emerson calls anthropometer and we'd call meritocracy is not the repudiation but the expansion of slavery's human pricing. The new human price system will keep most Africans down, but in this new system only as the result of a general mechanism for putting everyone in his place.

This perspective was applied in 1868 by the founding editor of *The Nation*, E. L. Godkin, another prominent liberal. "The negro race," he said, "must . . . win a good social position in the way other races have won it; and when it has its roll of poets, orators, scholars, soldiers, and statesmen to show, people will greatly respect it; but not till then."[23] Social position would not follow so much from the actual political rights and powers of full citizenship but from testable merit. Much of the liberal writing of this period helped replace the ideal of equal and of shared political powers with merit as a prior allocator of social influence. This was the logic behind literacy tests as a requirement for voting in the South, but it was a common enough attitude in the North as well.

At Chicago, William Rainey Harper advocated the "scientific study of the student" in order to maintain the accomplishments of "individualism, in education, as distinguished from collectivism." The freedoms of the elective system were all to the good. But the next step, the scientific study of each student, would enhance the university's individualism. This involved "a general diagnosis" of the kind that would be applied to a human body. The diagnosis would be a version of Emerson's anthropometer, and would identify the student's individual "character," "intellectual capacity," and "special intellectual characteristics," such as whether "he has control of his mind, or is given to mind wandering." The measurement of the student should include a picture of his overall habits, not unlike those that Henry Ford pursued in investigating the home lives of his employees: Harper wanted the university to know "the social side of [the student's] nature — to judge whether he is fond of companionship, whether he is a leader or follower among his fellows," and so on. These data, Harper wrote, "will determine in large measure the career of the student." In general, Harper wanted institutions to adapt to individuals, and his kind of assessment was broader and more complex than the standardized aptitude tests that would start playing a major sorting role in the 1920s. But in a move that conflicted with his interest in student development, Harper called for sorting and ranking students according to innate qualities.[24]

Harper's dubious move is of course not toward the evaluation of performance — the estimation of individual merit at a given time and in a given context. The dubious move is toward *meritocratic* evaluation. Individual merit need not be measured meritocratically. To the contrary, meritocratic measurement generally ignores or falsifies the group context and individual singularities from which performance obtains its meaning. Leading academic humanists might have spread non-meritocratic, qualitative narratives of merit throughout higher education, but in fact they did not.

These university leaders instead assured society that they provided general principles of selecting and sorting the population. In 1907 Nicholas Murray Butler, the president of Columbia University, linked the developing research university to " 'The progress of all thru all, under the leadership of the best and the wisest.' True democracy will carry on an insistent search for these wisest and best, and will elevate them to posts of leadership and command. . . . It will exactly reverse the communistic formula . . . and will uphold the principle, 'From each according to his needs, to each according to his abilities.' . . . The United States is in sore need today of an aristocracy of intellect and service."[25] The university was the place where the best would be identified and then trained to rule the majority.

Humanism never lost its interest in developing selves that had real autonomy in an industrial society. This interest was not corrupted simply by attempting to apply it to industrial or professional life, where it might have built on the free labor standards of industrial workers. This interest was damaged when leading liberal humanists associated the vision of autonomous self-development with meritocracy. From the standpoint of strong humanism, meritocracy had several major flaws.

First, meritocracy ignored the individual's power to estimate his own processes of self-development. Second, meritocracy created an abstract monoculture in which every citizen could be ranked on one uniform scale. Cultural, national, linguistic, and every other type of difference — the heart and soul of literary and cultural study — were now relegated to the status of subjective features irrelevant to rating a person's quality. Third, meritocracy claimed to translate qualities into quantities, which held a fixed value across social and cultural variations.

Fourth, meritocracy asserted that individual qualities could be accurately expressed as a fixed, innate quantum of merit. This meant that the performing self was not seen as being in a continuous process of unfolding. The self's potential would be defined and measured by an educational system that was increasingly influenced by measures of quantitative output. The idea of the developed self in its autonomy and enjoyment, its sheer singularity, its ongoing change declined into a model essential capacity. The measurement was individualized, but without the directive agency that strong humanism had envisioned. Finally, meritocracy would always express itself as a hierarchy in which everyone had a place, a place by birth as measured by inborn talent.

When it accepted these features, humanism became increasingly wedded not simply to the cultivation of merit, which was central to its ideal of self-development, but to the rank-order hierarchy of meritocracy. Meritocracy had established itself as an *alternative* to mass democracy, and a meritocratic humanism was similarly opposed to it. The development of the individual's powers was simultaneously submitted to general standards of productive efficiency *and* "scientifically" linked to existing patterns of racial exclusion. It is a bitter fact that the research university's great leap forward came in the decades, 1890–1910, during which Jim Crow segregation was being systematically installed in American life. Having cloaked stratification in the languages of nature and science, meritocracy insured that future attempts to value individual difference and diversify higher education would appear not to expand merit but to compromise it.[26]

In general, meritocracy expressed the managerial governance of human development in universities. I repeat their parallel features. Individual merit was to be assessed at a distance from the individual, through the application of general rules. Meritocratic evaluation would treat individual idiosyncrasies as anomalous, and would ignore or even dismiss personal qualities that could not be quantified, that is, standardized across a whole population. The mechanism of assessment would be decentralized and apparently impersonal, and would in later decades become officially blind to color and culture. At the same time, this mechanism would be malfunctioning if it did not generate a social hierarchy, one which solidified existing social stratifications. While merit evaluation could express both the current status of an individual performance and the moving process of its development, meritocracy suppressed these particularities and established a general system for managing performance.

### · · · *The Pluralist Road Not Taken* · · ·

It's tempting to dismiss these reflections as 20/20 hindsight and see the development of meritocracy as a necessary component of organizational life. But in fact academic humanism had other options, the most important being an early version of what we now call cultural pluralism. Pluralism had responded to the plentiful exclusionist legislation of the latter part of the nineteenth century by trying to normalize relations between cultures possessed of their own distinct merits. Such discussions also arose from opponents of assimilationist legislation such as the Dawes Act (1887), which allowed the federal government to convert the tribal land of indigenous peoples to private property, thus encouraging, it was hoped, the tribes to "dissolve, their reservations [to] disappear, and individual Indians [to] be absorbed into the larger community of white settlers."[27] Some held that cultures were at least partially incommensurable — that they should interact without having one culture expect to evaluate the other culture entirely on its own terms.

A version of pluralism appeared as W. E. B. Du Bois's notion of African American double consciousness. In *The Souls of Black Folk* (1903), he advocated "the ideal of fostering and developing the traits and talents of the Negro, not in opposition to or contempt for other races, but rather in large conformity to the greater ideals of the American Republic, in order that some day on American soil two world-races may give each to each those characteristics both so sadly lack."[28] Du Bois imagined an interaction between two races on the common ground of American ideals, but imagined this as an exchange between two distinguishable cultural entities. The country's intercultural relations would not be governed by something like a monoculture of merit emerging from only one of the country's cultures.

The term "cultural pluralism" first appeared in an article by Horace Kallen, writing in *The Nation* in 1915, where he defined it as "multiplicity in unity."[29] But in Kallen's usage, cultural pluralism was something more precise than this. He defined cultural pluralism in opposition to assimilationism — in opposition to the claim that the United States was a "melting-pot" where a multitude of cultures were finally reducible to a single standard. Kallen pointed out that ordinary "Americanization" sought "cultural monism" as its outcome: "Any immigrant on whom difference from the natives lays a burden of inferiority will take Americanization for identification, for digesting differences from them into sameness with them. From this point of view equality *is* identity."[30] By this Kallen means that no actual equality between different groups exists because American society teaches the immigrant that her ways are inferior, which causes the immigrant to replace cultural difference with emulation and replication. Kallen periodically recurs to phrases like "the union of the diverse" and the "American Idea" in distinguishing pluralism from monism, which of course raises the prospect that a subtler kind of assimilationism is happening all over again.[31] But he labored to draw a line between his version of pluralism, always flirting with unity, and the kind of unity denoted by traditional assimilationism.

Three features of Kallen's thinking were particularly important. First, cultural pluralism opposed the idea of a core culture, one that defines a true national identity. Kallen traces this notion to what he calls "cultural racism":

> A new sort of racism emerged [in the late nineteenth century] to segregate and account for the American past and to rationalize present claims. This has its analogies with the racism of Kipling's "white man's burden." But it was not a racism of color as in imperial Britain and America's Southern states. It was a racism of culture. It claimed that the American Idea and the American Way were hereditary to the Anglo-Saxon stock and to that stock only; that other stocks were incapable of producing them, learning them and living them. If, then, America is to survive as a culture of creed and code, it can do so only so long as the chosen Anglo-Saxon race retains its integrity of flesh and spirit and freely sustains and defends their American expression against alien contamination. Universal suffrage, for example, *is* such a contamination [in this view].[32]

Biological racism was bad, but so was a "racism of culture" which assumed that Anglo-Saxon persons, institutions, or ideas should stand for American society. Kallen rejected the claim that "Anglo-Saxon" honesty, and so on, arise from Anglo-Saxon "stock." He rejected the identification of the American Way with one particular group. He thought an institution could be American only when it was *not* Anglo-Saxon or any other monocultural type. Whatever Kallen meant by the unity of diversity, this unity could not have any one cultural center. The grounding of the American in an Anglo-Saxon or other core was not only a monoculturalism; it was cultural racism.

Second, Kallen's cultural pluralism insisted on the irreducible social reality of group life. He rejected the idea that one's group identity must finally dissolve into a larger whole or that one's "individuality" is separate from one's membership in a group. A "group-life prolongs and redirects the lives of the individuals whose association generates, sustains and impels the formations of the group. Individuals not only live and move and nourish their being amid traditions, they are themselves traditions."[33] Kallen is not what we would now call an essentialist on groups: they overlap, move, and mix, and even the word tradition itself, he says, means "a carrying on, a continuous ongoing — but a carrying on, or ongoing, as any person's life goes on, not changelessly, but as a process of changing."[34] Nor is he a determinist: "In freedom, commitment and withdrawal are collaborative decisions of the individual, not compulsions of his group or of any of its institutions."[35] Groups are a fundamental feature of American life, and indeed of culture itself. A cultural group cannot be dismissed as an artificial political faction or as a corruption of the American Idea because cultural groups are part of the American Idea.

Third, Kallen often demands equality among interactive cultures. Cultural pluralism marks "an orchestration of diverse utterances of diversities . . . each developing freely and characteristically in its own enclave, and somehow so intertwined with the others, as to suggest, even to symbolize, the dynamic of the whole. Each is a cultural reservoir whence flows its own singularity of expression to unite in the concrete intercultural total which is the culture of America."[36]

Kallen retains concepts like the "whole," but its orchestration does not mean the subordination of a supposedly lesser culture to a politically dominant one. "Note the word 'intercultural'. . . . The intent is in the . . . prefix: *inter*, which here postulates the parity of the different and their free and friendly communication with one another as both co-operators and competitors."[37] Any national unity is the "total" outcome of interactions among equal and therefore uncoerced cultures, cultures that interact out of their own freedom. Unity thus does not ground these encounters but follows, if at all, from mutual negotiations.

Toward the end of the period that consolidated the modern research university, Horace Kallen offered analysts of culture three criteria for genuine pluralism: a *multicentered* national culture, which could *not* be identified with the values of a dominant group or groups; the inevitability of cultural *groups;* and *equality* among these different cultural groups, whose difference would be negotiated rather than measured by a preexisting standard.

Cultural pluralism would not have shattered standards of technical competence, nor would it have prevented judgments about individual performance. It did offer an alternative to meritocracy. Its strong versions required that both individuals and groups be evaluated through terms that might be partially untranslatable. Pluralist evaluation entailed both translation and negotiation. Were this kind of merit review to have gained some acceptance, three effects would have stood out. Cultural diversity would have been the basic terms of engagement within the university, not an absence or a problem to be overcome. Such engagement would have prized the changing individual singularities at the heart of the evaluation process. Finally, evaluation would have combined individual and group qualities to reflect the ways they constantly interact. These features would keep managerial forms from taking their usual shape on campus. They would have allowed merit evaluation without its hardening into meritocracy.

··· *Management and the New Humanism* ···

Were humanists to maintain their ideal of enabling self-development for anyone who could wish it, they would have had to reject meritocracy as both excessively monocultural *and* anti-individualist. They would have had to judge meritocracy by its ability to bring each member of a pluralist society to a higher state of both competence and freedom. Instead, leading humanists of the World War I era wrote as though both the free self and a plural culture were impossible to grasp or defend.

Gerald Graff has shown that through the end of World War I, the debate within literary study was dominated by two parties: "investigators," who helped to develop research departments, and "generalists," who resisted specialization. The generalists saw themselves as the party of the humanist tradition and of humanist power. In Graff's terms, "The common bond of the generalists was their belief, in Trilling's words, that 'great works of art and thought have a decisive part in shaping the life of a polity,' and their consequent impatience with the narrow pedantry of research, which in their most pessimistic moods they regarded as a betrayal of everything Matthew Arnold had stood for." While the investigators fit themselves into the university's administrative order, the generalists were suspicious of it. "The same reactionary outlook that scorned the vulgarity of the masses," Graff notes, "scorned also the vulgarity of organized business and the assimilation of higher education by the values of the industrial marketplace."[38]

But in spite of their opposition to the marketplace, the generalist leadership gradually eroded the bases for opposing it. Though they opposed industrial forms of management of research or teaching, they did not advance a concept of the self as social *and* autonomous that would have contradicted managerial forms.

A representative figure was the "arch-generalist" Irving Babbitt, professor of French at Harvard during and after Eliot's tenure as president, and founder of a "New Humanism" whose impulses have an important place in the English departments of our own day. Babbitt introduced his landmark work *Literature and the American College* (1908) with the question, "What is Humanism?" Babbitt defined the humanist in terms that we've seen before. His humanist is "interested in the perfecting of the individual." He aims "at forming the complete man (totus teres atque rotundus)." Humanism creates the complete man only through "a movement of emancipation." Emancipation, whether in ancient Greece or Renaissance Italy, arises from "the full and free play" of the "natural faculties."[39]

But Babbitt rejected any link between self-development and history, that obviously collective phenomenon. He specifically attacked "humanitarianism," which errs by seeking a mass version of self-development. He was disgusted, for example, by the poet Schiller's will to "clasp the millions to his bosom" and to bestow "a kiss upon the whole world." Though humanism had gone through periods of "expansion," Babbitt wrote, the true humanist is "interested in the perfecting of the individual *rather than* in schemes of the elevation of mankind as a whole" (emphasis added). Self-development is in reality for the few. The "gentleman and scholar" is much like the "cultivated man . . . in the intensely aristocratic democracy of Athens." Self-development for all is a contradiction in terms. Babbitt carefully defined individual advancement in opposition to the general welfare.[40]

Babbitt also yoked individual development to a fastidious process of selection. "What is wanted" he wrote, "is not sympathy alone, nor again discipline and selection alone, but a disciplined and selective sympathy." Terence's famous line, "Humani nihil a me alienum puto," failed, as Babbitt saw it, "to define the humanist because of the entire absence of the idea of selection." An excessively sympathetic concern for the development of everyone marks a person as a "humanitarian busybody." The true humanist first weeds out unbalanced or fragmented persons, ideas, and feelings, which are always associated with the many.[41]

Babbitt's claim was simple but crucial. Cultural life was not above, prior to, or superior to the meritocractic sorting process that was creating industrial order. Cultural life, properly speaking, *was* that sorting process. Great literature, in particular, expressed the process of merit ranking that fit perfectly with that demanded by industrial bureaucracy.

We can appreciate the immensity of Babbitt's shift if we remember the basic role of free, mobile "interest" to the individual's survival and development.[42] Babbitt did not define humanism as the expression or expansion of interest in distinct selves and diverse cultures. The first duty of Babbitt's humanist was to find "the discipline of a central standard." His humanist did not focus on those epochs of transformation in which the sheer diversity and power of individuality could no longer be ignored. His humanist was instead society's ally in restricting and governing individual interest with reference to an external and monolithic principle. The principle preexisted individual experience. Its purpose was to manage experience without the undue influence of the individual's own process of unfolding.

The central standard balanced the "extremes" that were an inevitable part of self-development, of any individuality with pieces that remained anomalous. "We have seen that the humanist, as we know him historically, moved between an extreme of sympathy and an extreme of discipline and selection, and became humane in proportion as he mediated between these extremes. . . . Man is a creature who is foredoomed to one-sidedness, yet who becomes humane only in proportion as he triumphs over this fatality of his nature, only as he arrives at that measure which comes from tempering his virtues, each by its opposite."[43] Human development required the elimination of qualities judged disproportionate by external authority.

At one stage in his reflections, Babbitt criticized his Harvard colleague William James. In a passage from "Humanism and Truth," James had asked, "Why may not the advancing front of experience, carrying its imminent satisfaction and dissatisfaction, cut against the black inane, as the luminous orb of the moon cuts against the black abyss?" James's question was a direct challenge to Babbitt's version of humanism, since it asked why interest must be disciplined. James made his answer clear: it needn't be. Unrestrained interest, ever-changing experience, can be painful and yet triumph over ignorance and suffering. The power to triumph, for James, resides in the freedom that interest has from prior restraint.

Babbitt's response was negative. " Like the ancient sophist," he wrote, "the pragmatist would forego the discipline of a central standard, and make of individual man and his thoughts and feelings the measure of all things. . . . To make Professor James's metaphor just, the moon would need to deny its allegiance to the central unity, and wander off by itself on an impressionistic journey of exploration through space."[44] Selves here, when they become autonomous, have lost their orbit; autonomy guarantees imbalance and must therefore be managed. Babbitt flatly rejected James's trust in self-organized experience.[45]

Babbitt's new humanism affirmed the conceptual structure of meritocracy and rejected those of pluralism. An ordered culture is always a monoculture, and it hacks away whatever makes an individual oppositional. Cultural plurality and strong individual agency are equally unacceptable.

· · · *The Triumph of Babbittry* · · ·

"Babbittry" most famously refers to Sinclair Lewis's portrait of the small-town businessman of 1920, George F. Babbitt. We might remember George Babbitt as a booster and philistine, the apparent opposite of a Harvard professor of French literature, a man who felt "the office was his pirate ship" and his "motor car was poetry and tragedy, love and heroism," who "serenely believed that the one purpose of the real-estate business was to make money for George F. Babbitt."[46] But the brilliance of Lewis's portrait owes much to his sense of George's alienation from the career he has eagerly built. George confides to the reader that he longs to run off to the woods, "and loaf all day. . . . And play poker, and cuss as much as I feel like, and drink a hundred and nine-thousand bottles of beer."[47] George Babbitt proceeds to shatter his carefully managed tranquility, has quasi-Dionysian adventures, messes up others' lives and his own, and crawls back home again. There his son tells him that he wants to go to the factory instead of college. George replies, "I've never done a single thing I've wanted to in my whole life! I don't know's I've accomplished anything except just get along . . . But I do get a kind of sneaking pleasure out of the fact that you knew what you wanted to do and did it . . . I'll back you. Take your factory job, if you want to. Don't be scared of the family. No, nor all of Zenith. Nor of yourself, the way I've been."[48] "Babbittry" is not simple middlebrow conformity to consumer society. It is conformity to and rebellion against it, a failed rebellion in which the "grey-flannel rebel" approaches his professional life through his unhappy curtailing of himself.[49]

Irving Babbitt in effect theorized the rationale and method for this hamstrung middle-class psyche. The new humanist held that the unmanaged self was the unbalanced self. The passionate — the "interested" — self required governance through a system of explicit, impersonal procedures. These procedures treated individual exceptions as anomalous and enclosed them in a system of regularity, proportion, and due process. This system was rigorously selective and hierarchical. Official authority derived from recognized positions in a larger system. The individual held legitimate power to the degree to which her expertise fit within this larger system. Power was decentralized enough to require self-regulation, but not enough to eliminate the need for deference to authority. Given this list of features, we can see that the new humanism matched managerial requirements point for point. Whether he meant to or not, Irving Babbitt harmonized humanistic with managerial visions of order.[50]

George F. Babbitt became the most renowned illustration of the likely result. The future professional would learn to monitor his yearning to do as he liked. He would learn to manage it and not simply repress it, for he needed to sublimate it into boosterish productivity. He would learn to disdain his wish for "non-productive" freedom. Self-contempt would insure that his occasional rebellions would be regressive and destructive — fraternity revelry in college; secret, harmful antics as an adult; unhappy affairs with unrepressed women that would temporarily free him from professional life and yet make him miss it. He would above all learn to fear himself. He would treat his desires as dangerous, and would let others treat them in the same way.

The humanities continued to have central responsibility for the university's mission of forming selves. Irving Babbitt and his kin offered to literary studies a plausible version of the profession's new humanist goals. As the ethos of new humanism took hold, the great majority of literary academics were increasingly unable to advance two causes that otherwise might have seemed a logical fit. Generally speaking, they did not advocate the nonsystemic, noneconomic, passionately creative, working self as a middle-class norm. And they did not advocate even rudimentary cultural diversity. Literary studies instead came to supply the psychological forms of meritocracy. It trained graduates who could work independently but who always knew their rank in society. These graduates would be guided by what literature taught them about the fixed truths, about the unity of true culture, about their own lack of greatness.

The new humanism was bad for humanism. Ironically, it was little better for its relations with the sciences. The new humanism rejected scientific methodology in literary studies, and yet did not devise a clear methodological alternative out of the humanities' narrative-based, anti-reductionist, experiential knowledge. Such knowledge came from the unsystematized mingling of private and social experience, and arose from the perpetual unbinding of interest and agency. The new humanism recoiled from this, subjecting the individual's wayward thoughts to a scrutiny that aimed at inhibiting them. At the same time, it could not offer the same payoff as disciplinary knowledge: ever-advancing information and commercial products.

The new humanism effectively served as a youth counselor to university science. It imposed rules on the self's interests, and offered a service that Harper and others had located in the university's lower-division college, where identity formation could be viewed as a disciplinary prologue to professional training. The new humanism in effect agreed that real training could proceed only after the individual had finished developing her self by managing her interests into conformity with external requirements. The new humanism defined the ideal self as that which had adapted to this process. The completed self was an expert whose unorthodox personal knowledge would be denied by his organizational existence. Hence the melancholy of the George F. Babbitts, who felt the loss of their "real" selves. The most general and subtle form of organizational existence was culture itself, in which management took place on the level of personal desire and social identity. Irving Babbitt in effect defined the work of criticism as the management of the self rather than its free development.

In writing up the new humanism, Babbitt repeated one of the saddest tendencies in literary study: the repudiation of one's strongest humanist allies, even a respectable figure like William James, in favor of one's scientistic opponents. As Babbitt was attacking him, James was in the midst of battle with positivistic and behavioristic psychologists who were rapidly moving the field away from philosophical and experiential considerations —ones stemming in part from James's beloved introspection—and toward the more prestigious paradigms of natural science. The outcome of this move was increased determinism, the systematic and yet reductive attempts of psychology to trace psychological phenomena to preexisting natural laws. The whole point of such scientific laws was that they did *not* resemble a polycentric system with the variety of forces, scales, and effects one would find in a multicultural society. They instead resembled Babbitt's "central unity" detected by the constant refinement of diverse cultures to a single canon. Scientific psychology of course holds much of value, but it was already driving out humanistic approaches, reducing intellectual diversity, and narrowing the meaning of the human. Babbitt claimed to defend humanism, and yet where humanism strayed from scientism, he subjected it to attack.

One result of these kinds of attacks, as the twentieth century progressed, was the failure of academic humanism to develop independent, nonscientific methodologies by which to study the cultural and social world. These methods could have started from an existing epistemology — the varieties of person-centered, process-based, noninstrumental pragmatisms that went under the name, to follow James, of humanism. They could have rested on two fundamental insights: individual agency is not reducible to systemic determinants; and systemic determinants are multiple and often incommensurable. The new humanism took the opposite tack. It stigmatized autonomous agency *and* cultural diversity as what literary knowledge must overcome.

As new humanist training reinforced a student's psychological readiness for meritocratic procedure, it produced setbacks on two fronts at once. One front was multiracial inclusion. Lacking an internal push toward inclusion from its cultural fields, the research university remained an intensely Anglo-Saxon institution in a profoundly diverse society.[51] The other setback was for the free agency of the already included. Historically speaking, meritocracy, a powerful form of cultural management, weakened diversity and individuality together. In the new humanism, meritocracy found a pivotal cultural ally.

The new humanism had many enemies. Though its model of canon-based cultivation became a prevailing practice in English and other literature departments, contrary visions of literary study continued to unfurl. We will look at these developments in later chapters. In the meantime, we need to keep in mind the source of literary retrenchment. It was not aestheticism as such. It was not an excessive individualism. The weakness of literary studies instead flowed from the *weakness* of its individualism. This was in turn part and parcel of its social, political, and ethnic narrowness. The danger that literary studies posed to its own strength and health flowed from its withdrawal from its own ideals of liberty and multiplicity. The new humanism offered to the university its own version of corporate individualism, which fit well with the managerial features of modern life that humanism had wished to oppose.

# CHAPTER 6

. . . . . . . . . . . . . . . . . . . . . . . . .

## Managerial Protection and Scientific Success

### Prometheus Bound

For the research university, the fifty years between 1910 and 1960 were ones of steady evolution in the knowledge management system.[1] The overall economic story was the expansion of "Fordist" mass production under the direction of large-scale multidivisional corporations. The major financial story for higher education began during World War II, which added massive and permanent federal government patronage to existing sources in private firms and foundations. By the 1950s the research university had become a major partner of what Dwight D. Eisenhower called the military-industrial complex.[2] The university steadily evolved an industrial management structure that it applied equally to federal contracts and industry partnerships. The university was industry's junior partner, receiving only 10 percent of the federal government's research and development budget, but it became increasingly dependent on this funding from its junior position. Federal research money in 1960 "accounted for 75 percent of all university expenditures on research and 15 percent of total university budgets."[3] Federal money also increased the uneven development among the country's universities, since "six universities received 57 percent of the funds" around that time, "and twenty universities received 79 percent."[4]

The postwar period's major student story was the GI Bill and the enormous expansion of enrollments, especially at public universities. In the five years after World War II, higher education enrollments in California tripled, from 26,400 to 79,500; enrollments passed 300,000 by 1960.[5] Nationally, higher education enrollments increased 78 percent in the 1940s, 31 percent in the 1950s, and 120 percent in the 1960s.[6] Public institutions had about half of total higher education enrollments in 1950; by 1995 they had 80 percent.

The major political story was ethnocentric progressivism: political and educational leaders routinely praised universities as the engine of growth and prosperity, but racialized communities were largely excluded from this version of economic democracy. In 1940 the college and university population was 97 percent white. It was still about 80 percent white in 1995, and most of this change occurred because of aggressive admissions policies and affirmative action after 1965.[7] In situations of economic dependency, organizations "take on the characteristics of their resource providers."[8] It's not surprising, then, that postwar research universities looked like science agencies and corporations rather than like America — until political movements forced the issue.

Those fifty years also completed the university's loss of its *sense* of autonomy from the surrounding society. Writing in 1963, President Clark Kerr of the University of California noted that Cardinal Newman's vision of a bastion of liberal knowledge devoted to mapping "the territory of the intellect" had been built over by institutions devoted to the competing, Baconian vision of useful knowledge, where "useful" was effectively defined by government and industry. Kerr claimed that liberal knowledge was already being eclipsed by German industrial research even as Newman wrote in 1852. The liberal arts vision of self-development lived on in the colleges, which sustained every kind of progressive experimentalism. Antioch, Reed, Goddard, Oberlin, Berea, Black Mountain, Bennington, and a hundred others maintained intimate and everyday contact with the subjective conditions of academic freedom and creativity.[9] The same vision lived on in the broader society, particularly during the interwar years, when modernist and popular arts were animated by a confidence in the masses' history-changing agency among people — working classes, ethnic and racial communities — who had minimal access to universities.[10] Creativity and transformation were also valued in universities, but the dimension of self-development was considered preliminary or secondary or adolescent in relation to the production and delivery of useful knowledge to the military and industrial sponsors representing the nation at large.

I'm especially struck by the tone of "Prometheus bound" emitted by the era's educational leaders. Kerr is a good example: one of the most successful university presidents of the twentieth century, head of the largest and most prestigious state university system in the world, its guide through California's golden age of public sector provisioning, overseen

by Gov. Pat Brown and stoked by the Pentagon, Kerr was a major archi-
tect of the state's Master Plan for Higher Education, which had given UC
a special and highly fundable mission.[11] He was presiding over ever-
increasing revenues, and was in the midst of a near-doubling of the system's number of general research campuses and student enrollments. At
the same time, he was expressing reservations about the entire enterprise.

At one point, Kerr entertained the claim of the prominent sociologist
David Riesman that major universities had lost their way, that they were
"directionless . . . as far as major innovations are concerned." Kerr ob-
jected, but in a melancholy tone. Universities, he wrote,

> are not directionless; they have been moving in clear directions and
> with considerable speed; there has been no "stalemate." But these
> directions have not been set as much by the university's visions of its
> destiny as by the external environment, including the federal gov-
> ernment, the foundations, the surrounding and sometimes engulf-
> ing industry.
>
> The university has been embraced and led down the garden path
> by its environmental suitors; it has been so attractive and so accom-
> modating; who could resist it and why would it, in turn, want to
> resist?[12]

Kerr went on to say that the external environment might not be able to
solve society's growing problems: "The university may now again need to
find out whether it has a brain as well as a body."[13] And yet his brilliant
analysis of the state of the "multiversity" is riddled with the peaceful
bitterness of one who oversees the thriving plantation of a domineering
landlord. The wealthy university of the postwar period had lost its agency.
It was thriving, but at the cost of its independence.[14]

The postwar research university was dependent on external sponsors
and run through its management systems. Those features were permanent. What would happen to innovative research within this environment? Could management be used to defend innovation rather than con-
fine it?

### · · · The Old New Economy · · ·

If the university's liberal arts vision had been eclipsed by an industrial one,
the reason was not simply the power of industry but the idea of the
knowledge industry. Anticipating Daniel Bell and other observers, Kerr

believed that the United States of 1960 was already becoming "postin-dustrial." "The basic reality, for the university," he wrote, "is the wide-spread recognition that new knowledge is the most important factor in economic and social growth. We are just now perceiving that the univer-sity's invisible product, knowledge, may be the most powerful single ele-ment in our culture, affecting the rise and fall of professions and even of social classes, of regions and even of nations."[15]

Kerr was himself a liberal arts graduate (Swarthmore) and was ambiva-lent about industrial knowledge. "Universities have become 'bait' to be dangled in front of industry" by states and communities, since they now have "drawing power greater than low taxes or cheap labor."[16] Kerr men-tioned Route 128 near Boston as an example of a business-university complex, along with "the great developing industrial complexes in the San Francisco Bay Area and Southern California." He observed the military foundation of these technological alliances: "41 percent of defense con-tracts for research in the fiscal year 1961 were concentrated in California."

Industry was sharing university ground by the time Kerr produced his somewhat alarmed account. "Sometimes," he warned, "industry will reach into a university laboratory to extract the newest ideas almost before they are born. Instead of waiting outside the gates, agents are working the corridors. They also work the placement offices."[17] It was not an ordinary relationship that provoked the usually implacable Kerr to conjure images of abortion, espionage, and child stealing in the space of three sentences. He went on to note that industry had generated a new competitiveness among universities, who were driven by a new fear that "the university center of each industrial complex shall not be 'second best.'"[18]

The university-industrial complex was so far along by 1960 that the connection could be taken for granted. "The university and segments of industry," Kerr noted, "are becoming more alike." The linchpin figure was the professor who "becomes tied into the world of work," and who "takes on the characteristics of an entrepreneur." Faculty entrepreneurs were likely more loyal to the source of their funding than to their university. Whether the money came from government or industry, it changed the university's culture. The faculty entrepreneur's "concern with the general welfare of the university is eroded and they become tenants rather than owners."

Although Kerr didn't mention it, the university's welfare rested on a range of vital caretaking activities — teaching first and foremost — that in-creasingly seemed in conflict with the research that brought in the money.

Federal grants were polarizing university activities into paying and non-paying, into those which advanced one's career and those which advanced others'. Extramural grants, whether from government or industry, reinforced a division between research and teaching, personal advantage and collective welfare, brilliance and nurture, knowledge and relationships. The ever-increasing flood of outside money also increased the gap between the university's twin missions of economic and personal development, which generally required different processes and skills.

This gap was not bridged by the influence of extramural funders, whether public or private. To the contrary, we find the sober Kerr calling his faculty entrepreneur "a euphoric schizophrenic."[19] When the student movements of the 1960s arose on campus, their participants were correct to sense divisions between educational and commercial missions, humanistic and technological assumptions, basic and applied research, personal and economic priorities. Their most famous administrative nemesis, Clark Kerr, felt them too.

· · · *The Non-Market Entrepreneur* · · ·

In its efforts to manage these conflicts, the research university often created a wonderful environment for teaching and research. Out of fraught mixtures emerged a unique attempt to synthesize creative autonomy and bureaucratic protection.

As heirs of the 1990s, we are accustomed to define the entrepreneur as the free agent who has broken the chains of bureaucracy. But this assumption reflects our own neoliberal moment in the history of economic ideology rather than any essential features of entrepreneurship. Other periods have tied entrepreneurship to collaboration, and in the postwar university many believed that modern scientific research required broad social support.

The biologist R. C. Lewontin lived through much of this period and nicely captures its core assumptions; I quote him at some length. Earlier stages of technological innovation could rely on individual entrepreneurs, he writes. But by World War II,

> innovation became increasingly dependent on a very high level of scientific and technological expertise, and on a corresponding investment in an extremely expensive capital plant to carry out research and development so that only very large enterprises could undertake such programs. . . . Although the aggregate resources in

the hands of corporations are more than sufficient, those resources cannot be mobilized by the usual anarchic and competitive mechanisms of capitalism. . . .

Some method must be found to pool the individually limited resources of private producers while resolving the contradiction between the individual competitive demands for immediate profit and market advantage on the one hand, and the long-term cooperative nature of research on the other. That is, both the cost *and the conduct* of research and technological education must be socialized. To produce the spreading effect of innovation on the economy, both the patrons and the performers of research must initially be outside the system of proprietary interest. Only when an innovation comes close to taking a concrete form, as an actual commodity, can an individual firm be allowed to appropriate it as property. Before that point, the process of innovation must be socialized. It is obvious that only the state can be the instrument of that socialization.[20]

Postwar science depended on a socialization of its massive cost. Its academic entrepreneurs were subsidized entrepreneurs whose work depended on large-scale collective investment.[21]

Innovation did not need socialization for funding alone. Complex research depended on intellectual collaboration and a supportive, inspiring group psychology. Its key feature was security. Kerr, for example, had argued that the basis of faculty "inventiveness" is "the protection and solidity of the surrounding institutional structure":

The university . . . needs to create an environment that gives to its faculty members:

a sense of stability — they should not fear constant change that distracts them from their work;

a sense of security — they should not need to worry about the attacks against them from outside the gate;

a sense of continuity — they should not be concerned that their work and the structure of their lives will be greatly disrupted;

a sense of equity — they should not be suspicious that others are being treated better than they are.[22]

This vision could lose its paternalism while retaining the core conviction that innovation does *not* flow primarily from the market and its ethos of competition and wealth. Innovation depends on replacing the market with a stable organization. The institution would do much of the funding and support, leaving the inventor the time and autonomy to create. Technological invention required *liberation from business*. It meant liberation from the market that fragmented or abandoned discovery. Stability, security, continuity, and equity — creative genius requires a kind of socialism, or guild protection, or social security, or distributive justice, or stable bureaucracy, always cast in neutral and technocratic terms.

### · · · *Bureaucratic Genius* · · ·

The leading sponsors of the huge federal role for military-industrial research certainly saw themselves as working solidly within the capitalist system. They linked military and industrial health, and felt that scientific research could promote both at once. Although we now tend to contrast business and government influence, academic leaders have always courted both and faculty have used them simultaneously as patrons.[23] Postwar administrators sought a system that could funnel federal and private funds through university laboratories, boosting both national security and economic growth. It's all the more remarkable, then, that they tried to protect research from market forces.

In July 1945 Vannevar Bush, the director of the Office of Scientific Research and Development, published *Science: The Endless Frontier,* an influential report that called for the creation of a National Research Foundation. After five years of wrangling, including President Truman's veto of the first congressional legislation, Congress created the National Science Foundation largely in accord with Bush's vision.[24]

In *Science,* Bush justified federal science funding as a matter of national security. "The bitter and dangerous battle against the U-boat was a battle of scientific techniques — and our margin of success was dangerously small. . . . V-2 was countered only by capture of the launching sites. We cannot again rely on our allies to hold off the enemy while we struggle to catch up. There must be more — and more adequate military research in peacetime."[25] This is of course evidence for the claim of Lewontin and others that the American political system springs big government funding only under the threat of war. But Bush was also making a subtler claim: when the war began, American industry had not done enough basic research to insure Allied victory. We were in the embarrassing position of relying on Europe, for market-based enterprise had not kept American science in front. Advanced science required government funding.

Bush certainly didn't come right out and say this, which would have caused him political damage. But he was writing at a time when the status of market and government were almost the reverse of what they are now. The market had most recently delivered the Great Depression. The government had just won World War II.

Having noted the national security argument for a National Research Foundation, Bush also claimed that it would benefit the public welfare:

> One of our hopes is that after the war there will be full employment. To reach that goal the full creative and productive energies of the American people must be released. To create more jobs we must make new and better and cheaper products. We want plenty of new, vigorous enterprises. But new products and processes are not born full-grown. They are founded on new principles and new conceptions which in turn result from basic scientific research. Basic scientific research is scientific capital. Moreover, we cannot any longer depend on Europe as a major source of this scientific capital. Clearly, more and better scientific research is one essential to the achievement of our goal of full employment.

Scientific capital will increase only if the country has "plenty of men and women trained in science," and strengthened "centers of basic research which are principally the colleges, universities, and research institutes." Bush acknowledged the importance of applied research, but said that the government could best promote that by increasing "the flow of new scientific knowledge through support of basic research, and to aid in the development of scientific talent."

Given industry's majority share of research and development, why did basic research require government support? Because "with some notable exceptions, most research in industry and in Government involves application of existing scientific knowledge to practical problems. It is only the colleges, universities, and a few research institutes that devote most of their research efforts to expanding the frontiers of knowledge."[26] Bush's discretion doesn't conceal his view that the market regularly fails to support basic research *and* the human development on which research depends. Since the public welfare in turn depends on basic research, the public welfare depends on research that is shielded from market forces.[27]

We are confronted with an interesting complexity at the heart of the postwar university. Its scientific research was a cornerstone of the military-industrial complex; military need was always its strongest advocate.[28] And yet research had to be protected from the industrial logic of market capitalism. The university and its increasingly corporate-styled administration was an anti-market protection device.

Strange as it may now seem, mid-century analysts were quite capable of advocating both private enterprise and market regulation. Perhaps the most famous example of a defense of both was Joseph A. Schumpeter's landmark reinterpretation of the capitalist process of value creation, *Capitalism, Socialism, and Democracy* (1942). This work has acquired biblical status for advocates of deregulated market mechanisms and their powers of "creative destruction." In fact, Schumpeter was as strongly opposed to the theory of perfect competition in deregulated markets as he was to the theory of state socialism. He took the essential feature of capitalism to be continuous innovation, but saw innovation as damaged by the enormous "social waste" of competition, which forces business to squander capital on "advertising campaigns, the suppression of new methods of production (buying up of patents in order not to use them) and so on."[29] Schumpeter found his evidence in the relatively high increases of total output that he traced to periods of relative monopoly. When we "inquire into the individual items in which progress was most conspicuous, the trail leads not to the doors of those firms that work under conditions of comparatively free competition but precisely to the doors of the large concerns."[30] These are precisely those concerns whose wealth and size allows them to suppress market mechanisms in the internal allocation of resources for research and development, among other things. This passage, which appears in Schumpeter's famous chapter "The Process of Creative Destruction," shows how creativity could be seen as dependent on the *containment* of market forces.

The link between creativity and nonmarket procedures helps to explain Vannevar Bush's interest in government funding. "Research," he declared, "is the exploration of the unknown and is necessarily speculative. It is inhibited by conventional approaches, traditions, and standards. It cannot be satisfactorily conducted in an atmosphere where it is gauged and tested by operating or production standards." Market speculation is not the friend of intellectual speculation, certainly not as good a friend as a government agency could be. Accordingly, Bush invoked five founding principles for his science foundation. The first of these was "stability of funds over a period of years so that long-range programs may be undertaken." The second was that the funding agency should be administered by citizens selected for their interest and capacity in science, which implied a system of peer review. These peers were above all those who lacked financial interests in the research.

Bush's third and fourth principles granted autonomy to the colleges, universities, and institutes that conducted the research for the government. The local units should have "complete independence and freedom for the nature, scope, and methodology of research." Finally, the foundation should be accountable to the public through the president and Congress. The ultimate supervisor of the autonomous researchers would be society, but only indirectly. The market would exist for product development and revenues, but would not determine the shape of scientific thought. Bush assumed that basic research meant what we would now call "bottom-up" management — peer review, intellectual freedom, and self-determination around the work itself.[31]

## · · · Unbusinesslike Breakthroughs · · ·

Bush's ideal postwar foundation was not a creature of his imagination. It rested on his personal experience with stable multiyear funding at MIT, funding that came from both government and business sources. His ideal was confirmed by the success of wartime research enterprises such as the Manhattan Project, which had massively accelerated both scientific and technological development in producing the atomic bomb. Wartime research in highly sheltered conditions had apparently incubated legendary feats of individual brilliance. Though few scientists directly praised the dull grey edifice of the federal granting agency and its local supervisors, many had tacitly concluded that personal genius depended on the surprisingly open, often unaccountable structure of the sleepy quadrangle and the government lab. This system for "blue sky" research encouraged self-directed concentration.

One good illustration comes from the prominent physicist and science generalist Freeman Dyson. One day, he writes,

> I happened to walk into a basement workshop in the physics building at Cornell University. There I saw two students, dressed in the customary style, with bare feet and long unkempt hair. They were working with intense concentration, building a cryostat, a super-refrigerator for low-temperature experiments using liquid helium. This was not an ordinary helium cryostat that would take you down to one degree above absolute zero. This was a new type of cryostat,

working with the rare isotope of helium, that would take you down to a few millidegrees above absolute zero. The students were exploring a new world and a new technology. . . . Their brains and hands were stretched to the limit. . . . At the time when I saw them as students putting the apparatus together, they were not dreaming of Nobel prizes. They were driven by the same passion that drove my [boilermaker] grandfather, the joy of a skilled craftsman in a job well done. Science gave them their chance to build things that opened new horizons, just as their ancestors built ships to explore new continents. They had found a creative middle way, between the hierarchical world of big business and the utopian dreams of student rebellion.[32]

The students' adventure rests on two features. The first is their withdrawal from every aspect of the system except the task at hand. Their success depends on total abandonment to the task, on nearly perfect concentration. Their concentration depends on the university's structure's willingness to let go of them. They exist in a world of their own, looking and acting exactly as they think necessary.

This freedom from structure leads directly to a second feature, which is the fusion of big science with craft labor. Dyson's likening of a cryostat to a boiler makes physics a craft, a practice that joins brains and hands. In a craft, no one with the possible exception of a unique master knows the job better than the artisan on the job, whose mind and body are directly and intimately bound to the work. Physics, like boilermaking, is at bottom unsupervisable. The genius of the university is to see this and to leave its artisans alone. It provides a structure which supports good working conditions and which recedes when the work begins. The work is directed solely and exclusively by the workers.

Abstract discovery processes enjoyed a similar freedom. Richard Feynman used to tell a story about the origins of his Nobel Prize. He was teaching at Cornell after the war, and was, for lack of a better word, depressed:

> I had another thought: Physics disgusts me a little bit now, but I used to *enjoy* doing physics. Why did I enjoy it? I used to *play* with it. I used to do whatever I felt like doing — it didn't have to do with whether it was important for the development of nuclear physics, but whether it was interesting and amusing for me to play with. . . . So I got this new attitude. Now that I *am* burned out and I'll never

accomplish anything, I've got this nice position at the university teaching classes which I rather enjoy, and just like I read the *Arabian Nights* for pleasure, I'm going to *play* with physics, whenever I want to, without worrying about any importance whatsoever.

Within a week I was in the cafeteria and some guy, fooling around, throws a plate in the air. As the plate went up in the air I saw it wobble, and I noticed the red medallion of Cornell on the plate going around. It was pretty obvious to me that the medallion went around faster than the wobbling.

I had nothing to do, so I start to figure out the motion of the rotating plate. I discover that when the angle is very slight, the medallion rotates twice as fast as the wobble rate — two to one. It came out of a complicated equation! Then I thought, "Is there some way I can see in a more fundamental way, by looking at the forces or the dynamics, why it's two to one?"

Feynman showed his equations to Hans Bethe, who asked about their importance. Feynman replied, "'There's no importance whatsoever. I'm just doing it for the fun of it.' His reaction didn't discourage me; I had made up my mind I was going to enjoy physics and do whatever I liked."

Feynman gradually links his wobbling-plate equations to "all those old-fashioned, wonderful" problems in physics: "It was effortless. It was easy to play with these things. It was like uncorking a bottle: Everything flowed out effortlessly. I almost tried to resist it! There was no importance to what I was doing, but ultimately there was. The diagrams and the whole business that I got the Nobel Prize for came from that piddling around with the wobbling plate."[33] This tale has all the earmarks of folklore, and an aristocratic kind at that. But big science folklore reflects a vision of the creative process that has remained remarkably consistent.[34] Instrumental goals and institutional authority weigh down Feynman's mind and heart. To make himself feel better, he decides to take advantage of his cushy job and mess around. Messing around further decouples him from the need to produce, which allows him to waste time and thereby pay attention to small and ordinary things. These forms of attention involve him in a series of observations and calculations ruled by his own sense of enjoyment. Enjoyment leads to discoveries that seem to "flow out effortlessly."

The folklore of postwar science represented breakthroughs arising from periods of "not trying." They were a kind of not-trying that depended on the suspension of determinate forces — the various demands to be productive — enabled by the university barrier to the market.[35] In this period, scientists were not noticing the university's bureaucratic apparatus and yet it protected them all the same. As they worked they were profoundly unbusinesslike, and more creative as a result.

· · · *Labor Humanism* · · ·

The assumptions of scientists like Feynman reflected both of the university's two founding legacies of economic and personal development. The first appeared as the continuous pressure to produce technologies of value to either industry or government. The second, broadly speaking, appeared as humanism, including its core tenet of the open, change-making nature of ordinary experience. A version of this tenet propelled the American version of existentialism: Norman Mailer, for example, defined the "existential moment" as that "when we do not know how things will turn out."[36] Uncertainty, fluidity, risk, chance, and the casting of the self into everyday chaos: these have since been appropriated by market discourse, but at mid-century they were the unstable center of the personal experience through which one constructed one's identity and one's power of will. Outside the domain of "new humanism," broadly conceived, humanism endorsed the practical activity that insulated Feynman — and Feynman's experience — from the technocratic forces that funded and shaped his work. The key was a refusal to manage experience with an eye on production. This refusal was often supported by academic bureaucracy.

Faculty members like Feynman could assume that academic freedom would be at least partially protected from economic determinants by the university's administration. Successful administrators did whatever they could to expand external patronage, of course, and this often meant moving reluctant departments toward the market or the military. Stanford University, for example, went from a regional college to an international leader in science and engineering through a federal funding boom orchestrated by administrators like its long-time provost Frederick Terman, who manhandled departments and their personnel decisions into conformance with his revenue vision.[37] Academic freedom was under constant pressure in the postwar period, which brought classified research and intelligence agencies to campus, created the loyalty oath controversy at UC in the 1940s, and at various universities inspired purges of faculty members for their political views.[38] Yet faculty remained privileged and protected by comparison with industrial workers who were directly exposed to market pressures.

What would humanist notions of freedom do when directly exposed to the market? One option was to adapt to financial needs. This was a common white-collar solution. Another was to insist even more radically on the priority of emancipation. This was more common on the pro-labor American left. For example, the cultural critic Kenneth Burke wrote in 1935 that "the only coherent and organized movement making for the subjection of the technological genius to humane ends is that of Communism, by whatever name it may finally prevail."[39] Some Marxists, notably the younger Sidney Hook, tried to wrest communism away from the technological determinism of the "American engineer." Hook's larger motives included a preference for Marxism's vision of social justice, but he also attacked technocratic communism in the name of personal experience. "The starting point of perception," he wrote, is "an *interacting process*" rather than a disembodied idea. Marxism "appears in the main as a huge judgment on practice, in Dewey's sense of the phrase, and its truth or falsity (instrument adequacy) is an experimental matter. Believing it and acting upon it helps make it true or false."[40] Truth was decided by reference to experience and action (both individual and systemic). It was not to be decided by reference to scientific method as such.

Experience was so important because it signified both freedom and free labor. The reverence for craft links an otherwise disparate group that includes Marx, Ruskin, Cardinal Newman, William Morris, William James, Albert Einstein, W. E. B. Du Bois, Freeman Dyson, Richard Feynman, Hook, and Burke, along with C. L. R. James, who wrote eloquently about machinery under the control of the hands-on, experienced worker: "The immense majority of the American workers want to work and love handling the intricate scientific masses of machinery more than anything else in the world. A worker who has been on strike, fought the speed of the assembly line, denounced scientific improvements which have given him more work and has behaved for a whole year like a convinced anarchist, this same worker takes a delight in seeing the finished Buick, Dodge or whatever it is." This desire to work with machines leads to the "fundamental conflict" of industrial capitalism: "There is on the one hand the need, the desire, created in him by the whole mighty mechanism of American industry, to work, to learn, to master the machine, to cooperate with others, in guiding glittering miracles that would achieve wonders, to work out ways and means to do in two hours what ordinarily takes four, to organize the plant as only workers know how. And on the other hand, the endless frustration of being merely a cog in a great machine, a piece of production as is a bolt of steel, a pot of paint or a mule which drags a load of corn."[41] The labor problem is not technology but technology without craft labor. The labor problem is technology without the priority to management of worker experience and human relations *and* the desire to work miracles. The solution, James writes, "is that somehow the creative energies of modern man, the sense of personality of hundreds of millions of modern men must be made to function in their daily work. Utopian maybe. But if not, then the fate of Rome and of medieval Europe will be our fate."[42]

The crux for James is the sovereignty of the *masses'* "sense of personality." Creative energy could transform human and productive relations, and it emerged from the locus of individual identity and experience (always in contact with social processes). The personality and its creative capacity were equally important to the Marxist and liberal versions of humanism. Their common interest appeared in a range of institutions that included union locals and federally funded scientific labs. Marxists and liberals shared this hope for the personality in common opposition to scientific management. That is why the Marxist James could cite approvingly the liberal corporatist Peter Drucker's claim that "only if the power in the plant is based on the responsibility and decision of the members can industrial society be free."[43] Their common interest drew on the radical insight of humanism, on a radical humanism where the belief in open experience met a vision of free labor. Radical humanism underwrote much research science and many labor struggles. In both cases it offered a vision of creativity that rejected the market faith in competition and commercialization. Visions of industrial free labor, of scientific craft labor, of creativity at everyday work all hinged on implicit understandings of something like unmanaged personal experience, buoyed by its developed skills, caught in rapt attachment to everyday life.

### · · · *The Managed and the Unmanaged* · · ·

For all their differences, radical labor and academic scientists had at least two things in common. Managerial systems framed the doors they entered when they went to work and pumped the air they breathed there. The general features I've previously ascribed to management could be found in postwar industries and universities alike. At the same time, parts of big science and radical labor rejected a principal tenet of management theory from within their managed environments. They rejected the belief that externally managed work was the most efficient work. Taylorized mass production reduced quantifiable labor costs, but it also reduced the efficiencies that came from craft knowledge and basic research. "Efficiency" was in fact a mixture of rationalized production and unmanaged creativity. Industry elevated the former without really understanding the latter, and without studying the relationship between them. Various figures in labor and science sought to protect anomalous individuals as the source of innovation and value. Housed in the university, science had an easier time making its case.

It's crucial to remember that rejection of the managed personality took place within management systems. Organization was not oppressive in itself, nor was administration. The value of academic management depended on its respect for individual agency *and* group self-organization. If it left these alone, management could at the same time protect any kind of worker from immediate market pressure. Doing so was sometimes a way of cementing the status quo, since markets might be in the process of forcing innovation by changing demand. More likely, especially during the period of stable, Fordist mass production, markets forced the undeviating applications of existing routines. But university bureaucracy *could* support free innovation by keeping markets at bay.

Innovators fought economic determinism on two fronts. They carved out freedom for aberration, drift, idleness, play, and the misdirection of funds within *and* against management systems. Such efforts became slightly more common in industry after the extraordinary production successes of Lockheed's "skunkworks" during World War II. But they were already common in universities, where the faculty retained their historic ability to hide in the bureaucratic maze. At the same time, individuals looked to management for shelter from the normalizing forces of markets themselves. Management was the potentially smothering buffer, simultaneously an enemy and a friend. Individuals could negotiate this tricky relationship only by keeping a practical and psychological distance between themselves and this valuable shield from market forces.

An investigator or worker could preserve this distance only if she could feel the difference between managed and unmanaged work experience. When I put the point this way, the contrast may seem too stark and polarized to be plausible. And yet the postwar period abounds in reverence for the not-yet-manageable experience that doesn't quite fit with what is known. This experience was preserved — though partly sanitized — by creativity folklore like Feynman's, which broadcast Alice in Wonderland images of radiant, Promethean frolic. The folklore downplayed the negative effects, the rivalry, hostility, contempt, and disappointment that goaded many into wasteful, destructive attacks on their colleagues. Nonetheless, the folklore accurately captured the dependence of innovative research on the investigator's belief that these effects, positive and negative, had real distinctness from the existing conceptual structure and could guide their thought beyond it. She had to believe in the continuous possibility and value of creativity *and* in its dependence on anomalous, deviant, twisted, fleeting, stubborn, or perverse experience. Creativity depended on unmanaged experience in this sense. The experience used management to avoid market reductions while avoiding management too.

It was clear to many in higher education that progress and safety depended on genius. Genius, however, depended on unforeseen, unpredictable, partially unhinged eruptions of personal agency. This agency wasn't optional, something you could replace with efficient teamwork. Though many types of labor had to be collaborative, the trick was always to maximize the freedom of individual laborers. In other words, economic development (and national security) depended on continuing personal development, and some of the most militarized academic spaces in history produced some of the most interesting combinations of aesthetic and craft labor ideas, brought together in the context of big science and in the spirit of play. Many educational leaders realized that one need not choose between individual autonomy and group coordination, that basic research depended on their conjunction, that basic research depended on their insulation from markets.[44] The benefactor of their partial synthesis was university management when it blocked market instrumentality while allowing employees to dodge its own.

The cold war system had negative outcomes that have been widely discussed, but these should not obscure the mid-century university's achievement in combining nonmarket management and free agency and self-organization. If there was an intellectual as well as a fiscal golden age on campus, this combination was its source.

# CHAPTER 7

. . . . . . . . . . . . . . . . . . . . . . . . .

## Grey Flannel Radicals

Academic science offered the country one model of labor's world-making power. It revealed the centrality of craft labor traditions to successful professional life, and was the privileged emblem of craft "elevated" to a white-collar pinnacle of social authority. Last but not least, it exemplified the glory of innovation explicitly sheltered from market forces.

Yet these were not the dominant images of academic science. Science was the partner of the military and of industry, two of the most powerful forces in society. Science was also more popularly associated with innate mental superiority than with craft, and was the province not of the people but of special genius. Top scientists were seen as the finest fruit of American meritocracy. During the Sputnik era, science was confirmed as the thing that the great majority of Americans could not understand.

There was nothing inevitable about having the general culture see science as an expression of special intelligence rather than of free labor. Though science could not be expected to provide itself with the philosophical justification of high-technology craft work in nonmarket conditions, such a justification might have come from philosophy or literary criticism or some other humanities discipline. The humanities had traditionally provided the standard language about the university's noneconomic missions. Furthermore, influential literary critics like T. S. Eliot, F. R. Leavis, William Empson, Allen Tate, Kenneth Burke, and John Crowe Ransom opposed major features of industrial society, including what Cardinal Newman had long before denounced as "servile labor." Humanists had an interest in seeing their students thrive in a business-led society without succumbing to its assorted barbarisms. Professors of art, history, language, literature, music, and philosophy would need to equip their students to sustain lives of thought and feeling, and to do this for more than just the brilliant few. No university or English department marched to a slogan like "building a nation of geniuses." But wasn't general genius the goal of cultural development? And wasn't "following one's own genius" the basis of civilized, not to mention democratic, life? Humanism's ties to the professional version of craft labor suggested that the humanities disciplines, alongside science, might harbor the preconditions of a fully democratic higher learning.

In retrospect, it is easy to see these possibilities as nonexistent. As a group, academic humanists seem to have been too ethnocentric or racist, and too élitist, and too insecure about their social value, and too phobic about politics and science. These kinds of criticisms are frequently true. But they may also rest on the kind of Whig history that stresses features of the past most closely related to prevailing conditions today. The humanities disciplines were defined by their conflicting currents, and the humanities outside academia were even more diverse. They contained forms of thought that could readily elaborate and explain the psychological and cultural bases of craft labor and inventive genius. Major strains of this thought developed during the interwar period, in the characteristic ideas of two major figures in the twentieth-century humanities — and two of its suited radicals — John Dewey in philosophy and Kenneth Burke in criticism.

· · · *Dewey and Democratic Humanism* · · ·

Although Dewey's thought has been revived in literary criticism in the past twenty years, he remains best known as the leading philosopher of twentieth-century progressive education, whose base he began to develop at the University of Chicago during William Rainey Harper's tenure as president. There were humanists who took up more radical positions than Dewey, particularly the many nonacademics associated with labor and anti-segregationist struggles, and later with Popular Front cultural organizations. Dewey did not offer the last word on radical humanism, but he offered a highly respectable, university-based word: he was an influential and prestigious thinker who had the kind of mainstream academic influence that might have allowed literary academics to adopt him. Dewey favored revision over revolution, and generally accepted the inevitability of the managerial systems that he tried to democratize. At the same time, he spent several decades elaborating a nonmanagerial theory of education, experience, and consciousness itself.

By 1890 Dewey had become a key exponent of the strong form of liberal humanism that I discussed in chapter 3. In essays like "Self-Realization as the Moral Ideal" (1893), we can already find the five interlocking features of liberal humanism: a focus on the free self, the primacy of experiential knowledge, self-development as a process, and the individual agency and enjoyment that were part of these. It's worth remembering that these features were in conflict with the basic elements of bureaucratic management which governed individual agency with uniform, impersonal procedures, predefined functions, codified expertise, and hierarchical authority.

One way of stating Dewey's most basic observation is that external management damages the individual's capacity to learn. Self-realization, Dewey claimed, "cannot lie in the subordination of self to any law outside itself."[1] He argued often that the self could not be seen as a fixed "schema or outline," that the self was a capacity, that capacity manifested itself as action and was experienced not as passive consciousness but as agency.[2] The self consisted of its experiences and its activities, which had no ultimate motive other than their sheer existence. "The aim of experience (like any educational aim) must be included within the process of experience." Experience is misconceived, Dewey continued, "when it is measured by tangible external products, and not by the achieving of a distinctively valuable experience."[3] Valuable experience was that which was not codified in advance. Development required that the self be able to take itself on its own terms.

In spite of his passion for self-development, Dewey refused to define the undeveloped self as deficient. He wrote that we must "surrender our habit of thinking of instruction as a method of supplying this lack by pouring knowledge into a mental and moral hole which awaits filling. Since life means growth, a living creature lives as truly and positively at one stage as at another, with the same intrinsic fullness and the same absolute claims."[4] The living self, in Dewey's terms, was the self that did not identify with its lacks and losses, that was not melancholic about something that was missing. The living self was the self that experienced "interest," in Silvan Tomkins's sense that I've described before. The living self was the self that identified with its simultaneous and interwoven interests in the world and in itself. "Life as growth" was, in our terms, a way for Dewey to describe every self's capacity for building a coherent reality out of its unmanaged experience. Unmanaged experience was that which was primarily influenced by the individual and her immediate relationships rather than by "laws outside itself." The crucial capacity was the ability to have more interest in one's own experience — whether inexpressible or intersubjective — than in these conventions. Though these conventions were always operating on the self, the self, educated or not, could and should pay more attention to the "something incommensurable about" itself and gain leverage over conventions that way. Dewey wanted to reconnect developed subjectivity to the production of knowledge. Humanists like Harper tended to praise the process of self-formation while separating it from science. Dewey held that the self's development was always part of creating any kind of knowledge.

This was partly an epistemological point, for Dewey did not believe that science achieved context-free forms of objective knowledge. He was a central player in the overwhelmingly important "interpretative turn" in twentieth-century Western thought, which claimed that even those entities we call scientific facts take their meaning as much from the system of signs and meanings in which they occur as from the objects to which they refer.[5] Knowledge was always mediated by an interpretive context, making the crucial choice not between objective and subjective interpretation, impersonal and personal knowledge, truth and opinion, but between better and worse forms of interpretative knowledge (more or less functional, more or less beautiful).

But Dewey was also making a psychological point: creative discovery depends on selves that remain aware of and untraumatized by change and dissonance. The self's creative capacity rests on its "incommensurability" with the surrounding world. More accurately, it rests on its comfort with — its untraumatized interest in — this incommensurability. Innovative selves found oddities fascinating, starting with their own oddity, and were on good terms with anomalies of various kinds. Though communication did depend on similarity and sharing, on understanding, "imaginatively, something of another's experience," it also depended on the integrity, the distinction, the difference of the individual's experience.[6] The experimental method that Dewey loved for leading to scientific knowledge rested on this attachment to anomaly and distinction. Maintaining the sense of incommensurability involved an evasion of external laws.

This is where the arts and letters made themselves indispensable. A major function of art, Dewey wrote in 1916, was "enhancement of the qualities which make any ordinary experience appealing, appropriable — capable of full assimilation — and enjoyable."[7] Enjoyment was the basis of change, and the capacity for enjoyment was the same as the capacity for individuality. Art made interest more unmanageable in part by making pleasure more intense. The individual always operated within enormously complex systems of education and socialization, and yet the advancement of knowledge depended on her sustained incommensurability with these, which in turn required her enjoyment of incommensurability itself.

By World War I, Dewey had taken up liberal humanism and radicalized it as a simultaneously psychological and social philosophy. Much of his thinking was in place by the time he published *Democracy and Education* (1916), and my account of Dewey's thinking draws on this work especially. But Dewey remained prolific in the decades leading up to World War II, and in books like *The Public and Its Problems* (1927), *Individualism Old and New* (1929), *Art and Experience* (1934), and *Liberalism and Social Action* (1935), he evolved an influential public philosophy that might have encouraged academics to see self-development as the centerpiece of the discovery process and of collective life.

Throughout this period, technological and professional fields continued to find allegedly natural, impersonal, and objective bases for social conditions. The academic disciplines specialized in articulating "external" laws. One of Dewey's purposes was to reconnect these laws to their subjective and social dimensions. A key example was the notion of efficiency, which was driving much economic and social policy — Taylorism was only the most famous of its various forms. To this day, efficiency is generally defined as an objective measure of output to input, one that has little to do with individual desires and needs. Taylorism and its intellectual kin generally see these desires as obstacles to efficiency: the personal comes very close to efficiency's opposite. Individual desire, artisanal skill, personal choice, and self-direction are all inferior to scientific or systemic management as a means to efficiency. Dewey's response was to turn the concept of social efficiency inside out.

> Social efficiency means neither more nor less than capacity to share in a give and take of experience. It covers all that makes one's own experience more worth while to others, and all that enables one to participate more richly in the worthwhile experiences of others. Ability to produce and enjoy art, capacity for recreation, the significant utilization of leisure, are more important elements in it than elements conventionally associated oftentimes with citizenship. In the broadest sense, social efficiency is nothing less than that socialization

of *mind* which is actively concerned in making experiences more communicable; in breaking down the barriers of social stratification which make individuals impervious to the interests of others.[8]

For Dewey, social efficiency is nothing more than freer individual experience more freely committed. Communication and production go hand in hand with art, leisure, and recreation, and express one and the same kind of activity. Mind is not private and separate but socialized; at the same time, socialization cannot be allowed to degenerate into a form of external management. External management, in fact, reduces efficiency rather than enhances it.

In case this sounds like romantic individualism struggling uselessly against organizations, and a falsification of what some Dewey readers see as his democratic *anti*-individualism, this would be a good time to remember how completely social the self was in his view.[9] Dewey believed that defining individualism through "inner" experience was a mistake: "What is called inner is simply that which does not connect with others — which is not capable of free and full communication. What is termed spiritual culture has usually been futile, with something rotten about it, just because it has been conceived as a thing which a man might have internally — and therefore exclusively. What one is as a person is what one is as associated with others, in a free give and take of intercourse. This transcends both efficiency which consists in supplying products to others and the culture which is an exclusive refinement and polish."[10] The conventional concept of inner life rested on a proprietary secrecy that for Dewey signaled entrapment rather than freedom. Genuine inner life occurred in constant and often communicable interaction with society. The trick of escaping the limits of an "old liberalism," an "old individualism," and an "old humanism" was to reject the dichotomy of public and private in describing the formation of the active self.[11] That dualism was simply untenable. Education, for example, was "a freeing of individual capacity in a progressive growth directed to social ends."[12] Personal growth isn't socially directed but self-directed, and yet its processes and outcomes are inevitably social. Dewey retains humanism's privileging of free individual experience while rejecting liberal humanism's claim that the self is other than or prior to social life.[13]

Finally, Dewey rejected the dichotomy between "liberal" and "useful" knowledge. Liberal humanism had always privileged freedom of thought and mind, and Dewey made this point with unusual force. "Knowledge is humanistic in quality," he wrote, "not because it is *about* human products in the past, but because of what it *does* in liberating human intelligence and human sympathy. Any subject matter which accomplishes this result is humane, and any subject matter which does not accomplish it is not even educational."[14] Dewey transferred humanistic authority from its transmission of a great tradition to its effects on the people that encounter it. He rejected the boundary between the humanities and other fields: science and engineering could be as humanistic as art history, or even more so—it depended on their power of liberation. Education, Dewey concluded, "should aim not at keeping science as a study of nature apart from literature as a record of human interests, but at cross-fertilizing both the natural sciences and the various human disciplines such as history, literature, economics, and politics."[15]

Science could be just as good as the humanities at offering "emancipation from local and temporary incidents of experience, and the opening of intellectual vistas unobscured by the accidents of personal habit and predilection."[16] In this sense it had the same wonderful effect on individual and collective consciousness as Plato and Milton did. "The logical traits of abstraction, generalization, and definite formulation," sometimes seen as nonhumanist, were humanist in "emancipating an idea from the particular context in which it originated and giving it a wider reference," which in turn allowed it to feed general social betterment.[17] The value of ideas had less to do with the field or method from which they came and everything to do with their practical effect. If they opened possibilities, they were useful and liberal at the same time.

It was one thing to extend the privilege of humanism from art to science. Dewey took a more drastic step in offering the same mantle to industry. "The idea still prevails," he complained, "that a truly cultural or liberal education cannot have anything in common, directly at least, with industrial affairs." The idea helped to reduce mass education to "a useful or practical education in a sense which opposes useful and practical to nurture of appreciation and liberation of thought." The result, he lamented, "is a system in which both 'cultural' and 'utilitarian' subjects exist in an inorganic composite where the former are not by dominant purpose socially serviceable and the latter not liberative of imagination or thinking power."[18] This split had produced a "one-sided" and "aristocratic" humanism which assumed that work and industry were irrelevant to a humane knowledge obtained in leisure, and which had lost proportionate influence in education.

But Dewey's point was not that humanism should be assimilated to managerial needs, however often that happened in practice. His point was that separating them had made managerial solutions more rather than less likely. Craft labor ideals had assumed that the worker was both hands and brains, both individual creator and citizen of the trade and the community. *This* humanism had been purged from industry; guarding it in the humanities, and keeping the humanities away from industry, simply made the purgation complete. "While the intellectual *possibilities* of industry have multiplied," Dewey wrote, "industrial conditions tend to make industry, for great masses, less of an educative resource than it was in the days of hand production for local markets."[19] The artificial split between liberal and useful knowledge had only made it easier for scientific management to separate hands and brains, reducing workers to hands that required the manager's brain to run them. "The great majority of workers have no insight into the social aims of their pursuits and no personal interest in them. The results actually achieved are not the ends of their actions, but only of their employers. They do what they do, not freely and intelligently, but for the sake of the wage earned."[20] This system was exploitative, but what Dewey called it here was "illiberal": the work activity "is not free because not freely participated in." The split between liberal and useful knowledge supported a managerial in place of a democratic society.

This system was also completely unnecessary, and technological progress was already making it obsolete. In an early attempt to see industrial workers as what we would now call "knowledge workers," Dewey believed that industry would be forced to "acquaint workers with the scientific and social bases and bearings of their pursuits." Such workers would no longer be willing to "sink to the role of appendages to the machines they operate."[21] They might not own the machines that were useless without them, but their industrial labor would recover some of the elements of craft labor that managers had driven out. This recovery would be much easier if the educational system would reintegrate liberal and useful knowledge. When the university divided liberal from useful knowledge it failed to teach the personal valuation of one's own worth, thus weakening the individual's power of self-direction. And in so doing, it made external management more rather than less necessary. The university could play an especially useful role in the reversal of this trend.

Dewey, in short, transformed the individuality of brilliant eccentrics like Feynman into the precondition of a democratic society. He radicalized each of liberal humanism's core elements. He stressed that free-dom involved meaningful autonomy from the external management that was a ubiquitous feature of modern economies. He argued that subjec-tivity and scientific knowledge were both experiential, which entailed the experience of one's partial incommensurability with its environment. He defined self-development as social. He insisted that agency and enjoyment were the measures of efficiency, and not the other way around, and that they were actually enhanced through contact with the entire problematic of production. Not only could humanism be redefined as an alternative to managerial systems of control, humanism *had* to be so redefined, precisely so it could move through managerial life to some higher and more open set of relations between selves and systems. Dewey's psychology would not be the simple negation of management, for it would need to include some negation of this negation in a higher sense of organizational life. Though Dewey never imagined a modern United States without organi-zations, he did imagine a radical, that is, a democratic humanism that could subsume scientific management.

· · · *The Burkean Language Agents* · · ·

Transformation was also on Kenneth Burke's mind in the 1930s. He had thought of literature primarily in aesthetic terms in the previous decade, became dissatisfied with "otherworldly art" even when it was anti-author-itarian, emerged as a socialist in response to the crises of the Depression, and then scrubbed his political conclusions from the 1950s editions of his earlier work.[22] But from about 1930 on, Burke tried systematically to see art and society in relation to each other. He lived much more in Dewey's intellectual world than in Irving Babbitt's, but did not lose his interest in art as an aesthetic and symbolic phenomenon. The title of his famous essay "Literature as Equipment for Living" captured much of his sen-sibility during the years leading up to World War II. He sought a "*so-ciological* criticism of literature" that was simultaneously a "rhetorical form of cultural criticism."[23] In most of his work, Burke sidestepped the per-petual conflict between formal and historical approaches to literature. This in itself was a large contribution to a profession that had been debili-tated by the conflict. It also allowed him to see the private and psychologi-cal processes of art as simultaneously public and social.

Burke produced a complex, changing lifetime of work that has re-ceived voluminous attention; I will focus on a few aspects of his thought in writings of the 1930s that appeared in *The Philosophy of Literary Form* (1941). In that collection, Burke defined sociological criticism as seeking "to codify the various strategies which artists have developed with relation to the naming of situations."[24] Sociological classification not only refers to the social situations to which art reacts, but "would derive its relevance from the fact that it should apply both to works of art and to social situations outside of art."[25] The point was not simply to break down the barrier between aesthetic and social considerations, though Burke did consider this barrier artificial. Sociological criticism's purpose was to see art and literature as modes of *action*, "strategies" whereby the subject represents or symbolizes the world in order to *do* something in it.[26]

In general, our motive for doing something in or to the world is to sustain ourselves: art is first and foremost a form of action that defends the self. In the title essay, Burke said that "poetry is produced for purposes of comfort, as part of the *consolatio philosophiae*. It is undertaken as *equipment for living*, as a ritualistic way of arming us to confront perplexities and risks. It would *protect* us."[27] Burke closed his "Equipment" essay with a testament to this kind of action: Sociological categories, he says, "would consider works of art . . . as strategies for selecting enemies and allies, for socializing losses, for warding off evil eye, for purification, propitiation, and desanctification, consolation and vengeance, admonition and exhortation, implicit commands or instructions of one sort or another."[28] Burke by this point has completely broken with Babbitt, for where Babbitt saw true culture requiring protection from the ungoverned self, and wanted to govern the self to that end, Burke held that the self needed protection from culture, especially its "base" of economic determinants, and saw art as part of that care of the self.

Care of the self was required not so much by social life as such, which taught us to exist in society by playing roles, as by the enormous governing role of "symbols of authority." Authority ruled the domains of psychology and economics and their interrelations. "Relations to symbols of authority" were covered by the concept of "identity," which Burke saw as multiple, conflictual, and always acquired in relation to one's membership in various groups. Symbolization—including that found in art—was routinely involved in negotiating relations with authority. "Power" was not an add-on issue, as it has often been treated in literary criticism, but lay at the heart of symbolic action.

Burke further believed that attitudes toward authority consisted of ratios of acceptance and rejection, and that these ratios were a major component of one's identity. When the symbols of authority become inadequate to express or "operate" a person's experienced reality, the person would move toward rejecting them. The state of rejecting the symbols of authority, Burke held, "is synonymous with 'alienation.'" Alienation was the undesirable condition in which one's identity could no longer be constituted by existing systems of authority, in which one no longer felt a part of his or her social world. In a state of alienation, the world sees the unfamiliar and often dangerous effect of laws that one does not and cannot control. In "highly transitional eras," a large number of people reject the idea that these laws, the ones that do not belong to them, are natural and inevitable. The symbols of authority cease to function, and identities based on them experience a state of crisis. Alienation becomes widespread, many people shift their allegiances, and the interpretation of art becomes especially urgent since in art "all the implicit social processes become explicit." For Burke, knowledge about the sociocultural world could never be separated from symbols of authority, and both were always bound up in knowledge about personal identity.[29]

In conceiving of art as symbolic action, Burke's self, like Dewey's, could not be conceived as exclusively private. Art's "situations are real," he wrote; "the strategies for handling them have public content."[30] Selves equipped themselves en masse, and in fact the collective equipping was the true source of culture and of language itself:

> Mencken's book on *The American Language,* I hate to say, is splendid. I console myself with the reminder that Mencken didn't write it. Many millions of people wrote it, and Mencken was merely the amanuensis who took it down from their dictation. . . . He gets the royalties, but the job was done by collectivity. As you read that book, you see a people who were up against a new set of typical recurrent situations, situations typical of their business, their politics, their criminal organizations, their sports. Either there were no words for these in standard English, or people didn't know them, or they didn't "sound right." So a new vocabulary arose, to "give us a word for it. . . . American slang . . . was developed [because people] had to "size things up." They had to console and strike, to promise and admonish.[31]

Language doesn't come from a handful of geniuses but from mass genius. The genius in the masses appears through its endless efforts to "size things up," which both defend and express the individuals who are creating new forms to deal with the world. Burke's sociological criticism retains the romantic sense of language and symbols as self-expressive, arising from personal enjoyment, while at the same time building culture and its world.

Art responds to the facts of psychology and society, in the company of science, and yet when it works right it is a form of magic. Its magic consists of the power of representation, and appears "in the mere act of naming an object or situation" that is "implicit in all language." It is important, Burke insisted, that we seek an accurate magic, "a *correct* magic, magic whose decrees about the naming of real situations is the closest possible approximation to the situation named." Art's magic does not reject empirical realism but presumes it. At times, this magic seems to borrow the power of the thing that it represents. "Men share in the magical resources of some power," Burke wrote, "by speaking 'in the name of' that power."[32]

But given the logic of his argument, it would be more accurate for Burke to say that art is a form of magic when it speaks in the name of our *own* power, when it expresses our power to represent the world and through this to handle it. The magic is the magic of our own agency, one not finally dominated by the world's situations. This is an agency that exists through no special material force of our own, but through our ability to make symbols for the world. Agency exists through the symbol-ization process, and reveals more the closer we come to the advanced forms that we associate with literature. Even in our alienated state, we can at least always represent the world, and in representing it we experience our own capacity to confront it. The magic of art is its power to diminish our alienation from a world that seems made by others, the ones who seem to mean to harm us. Symbolic action is the means by which we create identities that are not powerless in a world of organizations.

Burke shared the features of Dewey's democratic humanism. He valued unmanaged experience, the incommensurate self that he called (among other things) alienated, the group-based sources of identity, the measuring of social functioning by popular, passionate reactions. Burke brought to literary criticism a crucial means by which highly managed societies might be changed by their own members, and means that could work *within* those systems rather than require transcendence of them. If literary criticism could accept the corporate sources of identity, and the interconnection of sociology and aesthetics, the collaborative nature of culture, the world-making power of symbolic action, it could be a leading

source of knowledge about how personal experience creates new principles of authority and social life. That power was proper to literary criticism, for it inhered in symbolization itself. In our terms, Burke saw
symbolic action as a mode of self-management, a mode as determinate as
any of the laws of production.

### ··· New Managerial Criticism ···

I see Dewey and Burke as the heirs and radicalizers of the humanism I described in chapter 3, but they seem to have had few enough academic heirs
of their own. They worked toward a democratic culture steered by the
demands of human development, and economic production rooted in the
standards of craft and art. Their professional successors appeared quite the
opposite — would-be mandarins who replaced sociological with formalist
criticism and banished politics from literary journals and classrooms.
Burke was not acknowledged as a precursor or member of the New Criticism which came to dominate literary academia: apparently he was too
leftist, too behavioral, too sociological, too soft on mass culture, too
friendly toward the masses in general.[33] Burke's ostracism certainly fits
with our established view of New Criticism as a conservative professionalization that consolidated the status of literature departments in research
universities at the cost of engagement with the outside world. As for offering a thorough schooling in a non-managerial vision of personal experience, sociological aesthetics, and self-development — forget about it.

But what really explains the rise of New Criticism, especially its turn
toward formalism, which consolidated an entire academic field through
the close analysis of a work's formal features, through a tendency to practice criticism by "explicating texts in a vacuum"?[34] This question has
produced an enormous amount of commentary over the years, and three
factors have led the way. The first was the general cold war crackdown on
left-wing political thought and on political controversy of any kind. Literary studies found some peace and safety by functioning as a "pastoral
retreat within the university," considering academic issues about which
the broader culture decreasingly cared.[35] Formalism was thought the logical corollary of depoliticization, to the extent that there had been any
serious political dissent within literature departments in the first place.
Parallel changes occurred in literary taste: the literary historian Morris
Dickstein has noted, "After the war, as America assumed its position on
the world stage, the old rebels and naturalists, who were still reacting

against a bygone Victorian America, gave way to the growing influence of the great modernists, to Hemingway, Faulkner, and Fitzgerald, to Kafka, Joyce, and Proust. Problems of style, along with the brooding concerns of the inner life, became more important to the younger writers than the social documentation of a Farrell or a Dos Passos, or the grandiose, inchoate yearnings of a Thomas Wolfe."[36] Conflict continued, of course, but the rise of New Critical formalism owed something to an intensified academic aversion to political controversy.

A second factor in the rise of New Criticism is described by the literary historian John Guillory, who has linked New Criticism to a strengthened professionalization of literary study. New Critics, he writes, insisted that "the language of poetry, and of literature in general, was intrinsically *difficult*. This was . . . a difficulty which did not disappear in the process of interpretation so much as it was confirmed."[37] The difficulty of "real" literature insured the importance of professionals specially trained to overcome that difficulty. Literary studies thus obeyed the logic of all professions, which assert special access to expertise based on laborious training and results that are hard for the general public to understand.

Difficulty ties in to a third factor in New Criticism's rise. If real literature was hard to understand, then accessible literature was inferior literature, was in fact not real literature at all. Many observers have noted that the New Critics were avid canonizers of demanding writers like the metaphysical poets of the seventeenth century and the high modernists of the twentieth.[38] Guillory notes that the New Critics gradually expelled "popular" modernists (Vachel Lindsay, Amy Lowell, Edgar Lee Masters, and Carl Sandburg) from the college classroom.[39] Truly literary language was not the common language that typified mass culture. The result was not only a certain arduous, even pleasureless tone in criticism, but also the creation of a professional firewall between the definable set of literary master texts worthy of professional study and the kind of shallow entertainments favored by the folk. Literary criticism came to ground itself on the barrier between "high" and "popular" culture that Dewey and Burke had sought to overcome.

New Criticism was assisted by a fourth factor. Its high culture bias was not only a sign that a middle-class profession was trying to empower itself by identifying with the culture of leisured élites, but was also able to furnish an immigrant and multinational United States with a common culture. Mass culture was not so much low culture as it was multiple cultures, which we'd now call multiculturalism, the obvious fact of the unrelenting diversity of American cultures. American society managed these differences through political, economic, and legal means, such as ethnic as well as racial segregation, economic stratification, immigration restrictions, racial "sciences," and intellectual and admissions exams, but it also used cultural methods, enabling competing claims to be handled by subordinating their (sub)cultures of origin to an Anglo-Saxon core.

Cultural assimilation aroused dissent from African American and Native American intellectual traditions, as well as many Jewish intellectuals and not-quite-white ethnics.[40] But the remarkable fact is that virtually none of this dissent took place in university literature departments. Language departments like French and German largely devoted themselves to the canonical masterpieces of their national traditions; Spanish focused on the Iberian peninsula and especially on Spain's Golden Age. Departments of English did parallel nationalist work by defining a British canon that it taught as the great tradition of the United States. More critical, self-reflexive versions of these projects continue to this day, as English departments retain a size and wealth that departments of foreign languages, American studies, and ethnic studies can only dream about. (The only competitors of English departments in size among humanities disciplines, the departments of history, try to cover the history of the world.) English's acculturation project was explicitly mandated during the 1930s and 1940s. At Chicago, Robert Hutchins instituted "humanities" courses that were to teach "the elements of our common human nature," and furnish "a common stock of ideas and common methods of dealing with them."[41] As World War II was ending, the influential Harvard report *General Education in a Free Society* (1945) described the United States as a "centrifugal culture in extreme need of unifying forces." A prominent unifying force, it noted, was literary study: "It is through the poetry, the imaginative understanding of things in common, that minds most deeply and essentially meet." The report called for the teaching of books that have been mankind's "common possessions," the "great meeting points."[42] If the university could unify society, it would be at that society's center. If the humanities could offer a unified culture, it would put itself at the center of the university. If New Criticism could offer a means to this unity, English would lead the humanities.

The provision for a common culture helps explain a major feature of the New Criticism: it defined genuine aesthetic experience as unified experience, which it opposed to ordinary experience. Richard Ohmann, an analyst of literary academia, made the point quite well:

One should ask why the selection and ordering that any of us performs just in the course of being awake, or that science offers, are inferior to the selection and ordering achieved by art. The answer is clear in the reasons the New Critics give for setting such extraordinary value as they do on irony, ambiguity, tension, and paradox, in critical practice: these devices are important for their "resolution of apparently antithetical attitudes," which both daily life and science leave in dissonance. . . . [Cleanth] Brooks says that the good poems manage a "unification of attitudes into a hierarchy subordinated to a total and governing attitude. In a unified poem the poet has 'come to terms' with his experience."[43]

If the humanities was to offer the university a way of unifying culture, New Criticism offered to the humanities the unifying methodology.

Figures like Brooks, for all their love of art and beauty, in effect cast the good poem as a Weberian manager of experience. The various factors behind the rise of New Criticism — the political chill of the 1950s, professionalism, canonicity, and cultural assimilationism — met at this point. New Criticism subordinated the culturally diverse knowledge of the general public to that of the (English) poet. It would not produce knowledge about the contemporary cultures that graduates would enter, but teach a capacity for critical unification. While training in critical reading was extremely valuable, the outcome brought about by New Criticism was unduly narrow: to reveal a formal unity expressing a unity of experience, which would produce graduates who had an interest in a unified society and who would find popular culture inadequate, even unpleasant. New Criticism's basic outlook remained close to Irving Babbitt's: literary study made itself useful by instilling a yearning for unity without inciting a too-explicit individual will. The unity would be the managerial kind that professionals favored, acting not through imposed sovereignty but through the higher faculties of the mind. It offered refuge from the violence and coercion of industrial life, while encouraging, through poetic unity, a feeling for managed experience. Management could be detached from commerce, and be part of the civilizing mission itself.

··· *Declarations of Independence* ···

It's tempting to leave the subject of New Criticism's rise with that set of interests and results, the management of too-democratic society being first among them. But that story is incomplete. Literary study continued to attract romantics and aesthetes, poets and renegades whose interest in managerial elements was nil. There are two crucial elements missing from the story thus far, to which I will devote this section and the next: the autonomous ego that literary academics continued to counterpose to the determinations of history, and the institutional and class identity in which this ego dwelt.

Some New Critics contrasted literature to science because of literature's special relation to personal experience. The tendency is clear in Allen Tate's influential essay "Literature as Knowledge." Poetry, he writes, "is neither the world of verifiable science nor a projection of ourselves; yet it is *complete*. . . . The order of completeness that it achieves in the great works of the imagination is not the order of experimental completeness aimed at by the positivist sciences, whose responsibility is directed towards the verification of limited techniques. The completeness of science is an abstraction covering an ideal of cooperation among specialized methods. No one can have an experience of science, or of a single science. For the completeness of *Hamlet* is not of the experimental order, but of the experienced order."[44]

The poem does not offer literally "complete" knowledge — by "complete," Tate means something more like "concrete," or something he can think of as belonging to the *relationship* between the subject and the objects of experience. The relationship consists of perception and projection and of a range of contents all in continuous motion. This is what F. R. Leavis meant by literature's power to represent "life," another inaccurate word that tries to see literature as knowledge of the irreducible. The result, for Tate, would be to devote literary criticism to rhetoric, where rhetoric is "the study and the use of the figurative language of experience as the discipline by means of which men govern their relations with one another in the light of truth."[45] Tate here holds that rhetoric enacts both self-knowledge and collective self-organization.

As the years passed, and New Criticism became a school, the school attracted adherents who crystallized its core assumptions. One of these, William Handy of the University of Texas, grounded New Criticism in neo-Kantianism. The New Critics, Handy wrote, believed that "we give meaning to the world of our experience in two distinct ways. Either we formulate experience through a process of reduction in an attempt to understand its determining principles, or we formulate it through a process of concretion in an attempt to comprehend its unabstracted particularity." Literature avoids reduction in favor of concretion. Handy traced this distinction back through Ransom to Kant, where Kant "called for a distinction to be made between the understanding, the faculty which reduces its object to a concept in order to classify it, and the imagination, the faculty which maintains its object in a presentation in order to know it as it is, undistorted by logical reduction."[46]

Literature had various means of avoiding reduction. In particular, it stuck close to conflict and inconsistency. In fact, it specialized in paradox. Handy cites Tate's claim that "in poetry all things are possible . . . They are possible because in poetry the disparate elements are not combined in logic, which can join things only under certain categories and under the laws of contradiction; they are combined in poetry rather as experience, and experience has decided to ignore logic, except perhaps as another field of experience."[47] Literary language, unlike scientific forms, grasps an experience that is always prior to logic. At least some New Critics sought to establish the literary imagination as a basis for nonreductive knowledge, which would reveal aspects of the world that science could not.

Experience was conflicted and paradoxical in part because it included the not-yet-present. It expressed intuition and intimation, it manifested the unconscious and the emergent, it projected interest beyond the real. A more complex psychology entered mainstream criticism through the efforts of critics such as Lionel Trilling, who were writing about Freud's relevance to literature in the 1930s and 1940s. In "Freud and Literature," Trilling wrote that society might foolishly "turn away from Blake struggling to expound a psychology which would include the forces beneath the priority of social man in general, but the idea of the hidden thing went forward" anyway.[48] Literature was the territory of the hidden thing, mixed with the apparently familiar.

Trilling castigated liberalism, the dominant American ethos, for tending "to select the emotions and qualities that are most susceptible of organization."[49] Beyond socially induced order lay the dynamics of psychic life. Literary scholars, free of Freud's sometimes crippling positivism, could see that "reality is malleable and subject to creation; it is not static but is rather a series of situations which are dealt with in their own terms."[50] Literature offered a reality no less "true" than that of science, for it knew the psychological depths that both controlled humanity and gave it power.

Trilling rejected the suggestion that these depths were a sign of neurosis. The writer was not neurotic, or at least no more neurotic than a lawyer or scientist. Unlike the neurotic, he wrote, "the poet is in command of his fantasy."[51] The writer is a willful though of course a never-fully-conscious agent who brings psychic reality into view alongside the realities of idioms like science and politics; the writer works in continuous touch with these. If the artist is ill, so too is any conscious being. Trilling's paradox is psychological: "we are all ill, but we are ill in the service of health, or ill in the service of life, or, at the very least, ill in the service of life-in-culture."[52] Once again, it is literary form that can best cut through technocratic reductions that had shrunk the valuable to the efficient and the real to the known. Literature knew the named river, but also its subterranean tributaries.

Critics as different as Tate, Handy, and Trilling gave to their professional object of literature a role that nothing else could play, a role that was among the most important on earth: to represent and thus preserve human consciousness in its trans-scientific entirety from technological and other forms of determinism. Some of these critics saw this preservation as important to democracy as well. John Crowe Ransom has a militant moment like this: "A poem is, so to speak, a democratic state, whereas a prose discourse — mathematical, scientific, ethical, or practical and vernacular — is a totalitarian state. The intention of a democratic state is to perform the work of state as effectively as it can perform it, subject to one reservation of conscience; that it will not despoil its members, the citizens, of the free exercise of their own private and independent characters."[53] The literal claim is bizarre, but the desire is clear: that poetry model a higher efficiency, one based on the kingdom of free thinking in an administered world.

Postwar criticism tried to establish literature as a third way between the rule-governed discourses of science and ethics. Literature included the two other dominant modes of rational and normative discourse but was not limited to these. Literature allowed the fulfillment of the faculties described in Kant's third critique, the critique of aesthetic judgment. Modernity made the aesthetic more rather than less urgent, for it promised that the common sensation of being crushed by an overwhelming external power — as in technological, war-ridden, market-driven industrial life — would lead to an experience of the self's countervailing power.

The romantic revival that followed New Criticism only intensified this vision of the self evading an omnipotent determinism. Scholars like M. H. Abrams and Harold Bloom, and, quite differently, Raymond Williams, revived a poetics which, though in many ways opposed to New Critical modernism, sustained its half-veiled image of an expressive self that superseded technocracy. Literature had a not-entirely-secular form of a redemptive mission. It restored unaided power. It conveyed self-determination. It enabled world making on personal grounds. It built an alternative modernity where the forces of production would be no more than a partner of the needs of the perceiving and expressive self. This was my own impression of literary study when I first encountered it at Reed College in the late 1970s. It suggested that though literature had little direct influence on history, it filled its readers with the sense that they could make history through the unmanaged exploration of experience.

### · · · Acts of Self-Interruption · · ·

Did this vision of the poet as agent and the poem as nonreductionist truth successfully resist the managerial forces and outcomes that I've described in previous sections? Literary criticism hung on to a crucial feature of radical humanism — the self's irreducible experience — and yet literary critics were interpreting the poetic hero through their own institutional and class positions. Embracing professional status also involved embracing professional consciousness. John Crowe Ransom articulated the mission in his well-known essay "Criticism, Inc." (1937):

> It is from the professors of literature, in this country the professors of English for the most part, that I should hope eventually for the erection of intelligent standards of criticism. It is their business.
>
> Criticism must become more scientific, or precise and systematic, and this means that it must be developed by the collective and sustained effort of learned persons — which means that its proper seat is in the universities. . . .
>
> Rather than occasional criticism by amateurs, I should think the whole enterprise might be seriously taken in hand by professionals. Perhaps I use a distasteful figure, but I have the idea that what we need is Criticism, Inc., or Criticism, Ltd.[54]

Critics could not professionalize simply by becoming more learned, collaborative, and systematic and stopping there. Professionalization also required adaptation to its institutional and, most crucially, its psychological norms. The professional-managerial class activity of critics left its fingerprints all over critical consciousness, segregating them from the poets they revered.

The template was established, I've noted earlier, by Irving Babbitt's new humanism, which saw the self as blind and dangerous in the absence of external restraint. Babbitt kept up this refrain for most of his life. He kicked off the interwar period with *Rousseau and Romanticism,* which criticized both for their equation of Western civilization with the "eccentric individualist." Like Rousseauistic loneliness, he complained, "Rousseauistic love is also unlimited, whether one understands by love either passion or a diffusive sympathy for mankind at large. . . . Wordsworth cultivated a love for the lowly that quite overflowed the bounds of neo-classic selection." And so Babbitt wound his way through his repeated call for "some center or principle of control set above the ordinary self," rendering personnel management as the process of cultivated selection.[55]

A more explicit influence came from T. S. Eliot. His enormous impact on American literary study flowed in large part from a single essay, "Tradition and the Individual Talent" (1917). While claiming the existence of a romantic artistry that must be controlled, Eliot argued that romantic subjectivity cannot really exist in the first place. The poet undoes himself in the act of writing: "What happens is a continual surrender of himself as he is at the moment to something which is more valuable. The progress of an artist is a continual self-sacrifice, a continual extinction of personality."

There was little in Eliot's essay that was not a variation on this theme of self-negation. The poet has "not a 'personality' to express, but a particular medium, which is only a medium and not a personality." "Poetry," he wrote a bit later, "is not a turning loose of emotion, but an escape from emotion; it is not the expression of personality, but an escape from personality." Science made an appearance, to allow Eliot to liken the poet to a catalyst. A certain reaction depends on the presence of a "filament of platinum." "Nevertheless the newly formed acid contains no trace of platinum, and the platinum itself is apparently unaffected." Poem and poet meet and part, personality not touching art. The poem emerges not from the poet's symbolic action, but from the withholding of that action.

It's easy to chalk up this view to Eliot's transcendental Christianity and other features of unusual conservatism. But in fact it becomes a default position in criticism, influencing even his antagonists. Eliot's anti-humanism mingled with Babbitt's new humanism and produced a weak humanism — its central if silent axiom being the self's weak agency. The situation changed little in the postwar years. Northrop Frye offered one of the period's major literary alternatives to New Criticism, and yet, as Frank Lentricchia has shown, he defines literature as other to the "descriptive or assertive writing which derives from the active will and the conscious mind." Creation, "whether of god, man, or nature, seems to be an activity whose only intention is to abolish intention, to eliminate final dependence on a relation to something else."[56] Frye was obsessed with freedom, which involves avoiding "dependence" on external determinants, and yet simultaneously abolished intention. Though intention is an inadequate explanation for literary and virtually every other human process, a larger explanation requires linking intention to other forces rather than abolishing intention as such. Again and again, mid-century critics declared the humanist self to be free, and defined freedom as giving up the self.

Many of New Criticism's major position papers exhorted critics to replace agency with technique. W. K. Wimsatt and Monroe Beardsley together wrote two such essays: "The Intentional Fallacy" (1946) warned against focusing on the author's intention, "The Affective Fallacy" (1949) against focusing on the reader' reception. The basic idea was anti-reductionist: in "The Intentional Fallacy," for example, the authors insist that the literary object be interpreted in its own right, and its meaning not be reduced to imputed authorial designs or effects on the audience. But Wimsatt and Beardsley went to great lengths to sever the object from its source in poetic activity. "The poem is not the critic's own," they wrote, "and not the author's (it is detached from the author at the birth and goes about the world beyond his power to intend it or control it). The poem belongs to the public." It's odd to imagine university critics defining poetry as a form of public property, but they seemed willing if it removed the agent from view. The authors further noted, "There is criticism of poetry and there is author psychology," the twain preferably not meeting in interpretive acts. In general, they cast "expression" as the false coin of "aesthetic achievement," which led to some industrial toughness: "Judging a poem is like judging a pudding or a machine. One demands that it works."[57]

A similar separation of person from object occurred in "The Affective Fallacy," where the person was associated with affect, with emotive language. Wimsatt and Beardsley drew various distinctions between affective and referential language, and recommended that affect be examined through the descriptive analysis of its sources in language.[58] The authors discussed affects in terms that aligned them with neurosis, mass psychology, and the distortion of truth.[59] Though "poetry is characteristically a discourse about both emotions and objects, or about the emotive quality of objects," poetic emotions are "not communicated to the reader like an infection or disease, not inflicted mechanically like a bullet or knife wound, not administered like a poison, not simply expressed as by expletives or grimaces or rhythms, presented in their objects and contemplated as a pattern of knowledge. Poetry is a way of fixing emotions or making them more permanently perceptible."[60] Wimsatt and Beardsley associated unmediated affect with violence and destruction. Poetry was valuable precisely for the management it provides, and therefore had to be protected from the will of author and critic alike. Without this kind of self-denial, and denial of other selves, interpretation could not be professional.

This drift did not go entirely unnoticed. Writing in *Partisan Review* in 1947, J. F. Wolpert noted the difficult position of the American intellectual, who tended to be paralyzed by the psychological conflict "engendered by the contradiction between his style of life and his critical attitude toward the prevailing norms." Interestingly, Wolpert traced the problem to a managerial condition. "There is an unconscious and conscious pull on the academic to produce toward the existing bureaucratic order." As a result, "the imaginative and/or adventurous thinker . . . finds himself gradually moving into a pattern not of his own making."[61]

But this kind of insight was not the norm. In 1944 Arthur Koestler claimed that "there never was an intelligentsia without a guilt-complex: it is the income tax one has to pay for wanting to make others richer." In the early 1950s Sidney Hook channeled Irving Babbitt long enough to claim that "the cardinal attribute of the life of thought — its proper virtue — is the capacity to discriminate, to make relevant distinctions." Irving Howe remarked that "negativism in our age is not a whim, it is a necessity of hygiene." And Allen Tate, though still advocating the language of experience, was also advocating limits. "Literary criticism," he wrote, "like the Kingdom of God on earth, is perpetually necessary and, in the very nature of its middle position between imagination and philosophy, perpetually impossible. Like man, literary criticism is nothing in itself."[62] The symposium critics felt stuck in the middle. But rather than critique their own managerial state, they oscillated between attacking the dangerous power of the masses and lamenting the inevitable weakness of themselves.

We can see a similar fading of the critic's agency in Trilling, that great

champion of the artistic will. In *The Liberal Imagination,* Trilling invoked
Charles Lamb as a model of the poetic actor. The true poet, Lamb wrote,
"dreams being awake. He is not possessed by his subject but has domin-
ion over it." To create "implies shaping and consistency." It means being
*active,* "for to be active is to call something into act and form." So far so
good — the individual in all its agency and yet its dreaming too, conscious
and unconscious, experience and contradiction. But Lamb is defining the
artist against the ordinary man, the "little wit" behind the poet's great
one. These small men "finding in the raptures of the higher poetry a
condition of exaltation, to which they have no parallel in their own experience, besides the spurious resemblance of it in dreams and fevers, im-
pute a state of dreaminess and fever to the poet." Rather than seeing the
little wits as lesser poets, Lamb denies them access to the waking dream,
that is, to the *being active* that is creation as such. The nonartist is not
creative, but "passive as men in sick dreams." Trilling endorsed this. Neurotic people may imitate the artist, but they lack the shaping power.
"What marks the artist," Trilling wrote, "is his power to shape the material
of pain we all have."[63]

What marked the critic is his sense of exclusion from this. The rare
renegade like Harold Bloom may have insisted that poetry is criticism in
verse, and that both genres have the power of creation. Even this position, whose limits I will note later, was not common. Trilling's was more
typical, as he defended the artist without counting himself or others as
one. Does the academic critic feel the "condition of exaltation" in which
all determinations disappear? Trilling said nothing like this. The point of
his essay was to deny neurosis. The artist is normal; the critic who sees
this, even more so.

As time passed, Trilling became increasingly aware of the problem, but
without an increased sense of solution. This can be seen in the capstone
essay "The Two Environments," delivered as the Henry Sidgwick lecture at
Cambridge University in 1965. Trilling noted that the study of literature
continues to require justification, while the study of science and social
science does not. "The classic defense of literary study," he said, lies in its
power of "making the mind free and active." This enables moral intelligence, for Trilling, which means that literature makes "the whole man" —
the purpose of the old college living on in the modern research university.[64] The university, Trilling claimed, will submit America's business-
minded students "to certain humanizing and liberalizing disciplines,
among which literature is pre-eminent." Humanism involves "the making

of whole men or the construction of people," which ultimately concerns "the state and with the quality of the persons who shall control the state" or at least criticize it.[65] Humanism continues to draw on Matthew Arnold's definition of literature as "a criticism of life" — the humanist making of selves centers on the making of "critical intelligence."[66]

But Trilling was questioning whether this defense of literary study still held up. Students were studying modern more than classical literature. They did so in a modern culture in which it seemed that society was "being released from the old bondage to Necessity and [had] actually got one foot into the realm of Freedom, where the faculty of conscientious reason is no longer needed." People sought "a true relation to the sources of life," and expressed this relation not through rational doctrine but through "the style of life" the society fosters — "in short, by its *culture*, which we judge as a whole, rather as if it were a work of art."[67]

At first this sounded like good news — a society inches closer to the realm of freedom and its culture offers more open contact with the "sources of life." As Trilling continued, it still sounded good: "The fact is that the student today is at liberty to choose between two cultural environments." One is "Philistine and dull, satisfied with its unexamined, unpromising beliefs." The other is the one committed to the "sources of life" — "by its adherence to the imagination of fullness, freedom, and potency of life, and to what goes with this imagination, the concern with moralized taste and with the styles which indicate that one has successfully gained control of the sources of life."[68] The study of literature enforces the power of the second environment, and seems to be winning on a scale Arnold never imagined. But Trilling wasn't sure that the critics were up to the task.

> Modern criticism's achievement has been . . . of an elementary sort. It has taught us how to read certain books; it has not taught us how to engage them. Modern literature . . . is directed toward moral and spiritual renovation; its subject is damnation and salvation. It is a literature of doctrine which, although often concealed, is very aggressive. The occasions are few when criticism has met this doctrine on its own fierce terms. Of modern criticism it can be said that it has instructed us in an intelligent passivity before the beneficent aggression of literature. Attributing to literature virtually angelic powers, it has passed the word to the readers of literature that the one thing you do not do when you meet an angel is wrestle with him.[69]

The result is dire: where literature liberates the self from "the idols of the Marketplace," criticism actually undermines this power. It becomes a kind of "Criticism, Inc." without even trying.

Trilling's was an extraordinary condemnation of academic criticism from a leading critic. It suggested criticism's sense of its own marginality in relation not only to science but to literature as well. It suggested criticism's lack of confidence, and Trilling's lack of confidence in criticism, signaled indirectly by the failure of this greatest of academic stylists to maintain, in this essay, the "style" that shows the critic's freedom. The critic is in fact not free, but bounded by science, by literature, by the masses of Philistines who lay claim to freedom and "potency of life," who manifestly *have* potency, *have* culture, *make* culture, *make* popular culture on their own. Trilling did not say that the masses are insufficiently critical to make true culture. He instead said that *critics* are insufficiently critical, which I take to mean insufficiently sure of their own independent authority by which they might criticize society. Authority, independence, agency, "life" — these belong to the poets *and* to the masses, neither of whom needs the mediation of the critic.[70]

The subjectivity that Trilling expressed can be partly explained by the cold war and the other factors I mentioned earlier. But its closest match, and best institutional fit, was with the subjectivity of the middle manager. The middle manager was, academically, Clark Kerr's guild conservative: the critic was, in varying ratios, receptive to cues from superiors, respectful of established authorities, skeptical about systematic change, hostile to collective movements, devoted to the prerogatives of position, doubtful about the public's cultural capacities, and contented with the administered university life. The academic critic was a knowledge manager, handling, distributing, sorting, and allocating knowledge more than creating it. Teaching involved the classic bureaucratic functions of supervising, monitoring, correcting, disciplining, evaluating, motivating, and reporting. Ever mindful of being above and below (students and masses, poets and administrators), the critic managed the middle realms, and helped shape the middle classes to occupy them. What made all of this work — all of it sufficiently agreeable, sufficiently compatible with a limited sense of freedom — was the modest personal agency theorized by the period's leading critics.

··· *Where the Sixties Made No Difference* ···

We usually see the 1960s as a breaking point in the history of criticism. Criticism in the 1970s was clearly "after the new criticism": formalism gave way to analysis that drew on radical European philosophy, as with deconstruction, as well as on social movements, as with feminist and ethnic studies. Research universities began the slow journey toward some form of racial integration, and some élite schools began admitting women for the first time. Many of the upheavals of the period were motivated by a pervasive distrust of the managerial and corporate systems that had seemed so permanent even to sophisticated observers like John Kenneth Galbraith as late as 1967.[71] Literary studies came to house its own dissidents, including the Radical Caucus that formed in the context of a rebellion at the annual convention of the Modern Language Association in 1968.[72]

I will focus on these changes in another volume on the university's more recent history. I do not at all want to minimize the significance of the academic movements, as they have decisively enlarged and transformed the profession of literary studies. But here I will stress an extraordinary continuity in the mainstream discipline before and after the 1960s. In the midst of widespread doubts about managerial authority, influential criticism sustained key elements of a managerial tradition.

We can see this if we turn to the least melancholic of major postwar critics, Stanley Fish, the incarnation of Eliot's dreaded "personality," and a candidate for literature's most entrepreneurial postwar critic. Fish's career is a model of self-fashioning, apparently steered by a conscious will and rational deliberation from one major job and paradigm to the next. Fifteen years after Trilling's Cambridge meditation, Fish published one of the most self-reflexive introductions in recent critical history, one in which he marched the reader through the ever-evolving changes in his analytical positions.

No critic ever seemed more endowed with life. Fish presented his thought as a continuous unfolding, a course of intellectual development in which apparent truth is repeatedly overturned by the power of symbolic action. The content of the development appears to affirm the critic's agency, for Fish repudiated criticism as the description of formal features in favor of criticism as the reader's active response. Criticism is a process of continuous change, and requires a confident awareness of change's inevitability. Criticism is an act and an activity: Fish noted that he held himself back at one point because of his "unthinking acceptance of [the] formalist assumption . . . that subjectivity is an ever present danger and that any critical procedure must include a mechanism for holding it in check."[73] Fish showed how he learned to love interpretation, which meant learning to love its subjective basis.

But here is the strange part: Fish no sooner arrived at this conclusion than he blocked it. His real concern about the work he was attacking (stylistics) was that "it can be done all too easily and in any direction one likes." He feared that "in the absence of impersonal and universal constraints, interpreters will be free to impose their idiosyncratic meanings on texts." Fish decided to deal with this fear by "reconceiving . . . the reader in such a way as to eliminate the category of 'the subjective' altogether."[74]

By this phrase, Fish meant that he would see the reader's individual subjectivity as constituted by the assumptions of the "interpretive community" to which he belongs. "The reader is identified not as a free agent, making literature any old way, but as a member of a community whose assumptions about literature determine the kind of attention he pays and thus the kind of literature 'he' makes."[75] The quotation marks aren't ironizing the male gender but the idea of autonomous subjectivity. Perhaps affected by Arnoldian fears of "doing as one likes," or by memories of Wimsatt and Beardsley, Fish did not simply condition subjectivity on its inevitable context, but rejected the subjective as such.

The rest of the introduction, like the book's final chapter, ends his worrying about subjectivity by making it entirely dependent on its interpretive context. "The crucial step will be to see that the claims of neither the text nor the reader can be upheld, because neither has the independent status that would make its claim possible."[76] Or again, interpretive strategies "are not [the critics'] in the sense that would make him an independent agent. Rather, they proceed not from him but from the interpretive community of which he is a member; they are, in effect, community property, and insofar as they at once enable and limit the operations of his consciousness, he is too."[77]

Fish was of course right to say that free will is never absolute or outside interpretive conventions or linguistic structures, and that it works through these. But what's remarkable is that he did not develop a theory of organizational or managed subjectivity in which the subject has some relatively or strategically or calculatedly autonomous agency, agency constructed through a combination of managerial experience and unmanaged impulse.

Instead, he denied the subject any independence. Community property oddly echoes the public property of Wimsatt and Beardsley, as though literary critics remain willing to advocate interpretative corporatism in order to regulate individuals. Fish got into many debates about these issues in subsequent years, and offered versions of qualified conceptual independence. But the dominant theme of his criticism remained the sovereignty of the interpretive system.

If Fish has been a leading institutionalist of the period since the 1960s, Harold Bloom has been a leading romantic. Bloom insisted on placing the romantic imagination at the center of literature itself, and described it as freedom without compromise. "The creative Eros of the Romantics," he wrote, "is not renunciatory though it is self-transcendent. It is, to use Shelley's phrasing, a total going-out from our own natures, total because the force moving out is not only the Promethean libido, but rather a fusion between the libido and the active or imaginative element in the ego; or, simply, desire wholly taken up into the imagination."[78] The imagination evacuates the reality principle; there is no necessary sacrifice, no compromise, no required loss of life to the self. "The movement to the reality of Eden is one of re-creation, or better, of knowledge not purchased by the loss of power, and so of power and freedom gained *through* a going-out of our nature."[79] The promise of literary creation has rarely been more powerfully described. "What is called real," Bloom claimed, "is too often an exhausted phantasmagoria, and the reality principle can too easily be debased into a principle of surrender, an accommodation with death-in-life."[80] To be creative is never to surrender; criticism, itself creative, must refuse surrender as well.

A high romantic argument is exhausting to sustain, for Bloom as for any other academic critic. In the 1970s he both Oedipalized and theologized his system. The poet's struggle became less about his own projective vision than about wrestling with his dominant precursors and approaching some deeper form of being than his own. The fury remained the same, but we can get at some of the conceptual slippage in a couple of misreadings in *Agon* (1982), which marked the end of an era. In a chapter on Emerson, Bloom quoted one of Emerson's journal entries: "In the highest moments, we are a vision. There is nothing that can be called gratitude nor properly joy. The soul is raised over passion. It seeth nothing so much as Identity. It is a Perceiving that Truth and Right ARE. Hence it becomes a perfect Peace out of the *knowing* that all things will go well. Vast spaces of nature the Atlantic Ocean, the South Sea; vast intervals of time years, centuries, are annihilated to it; this which I think and feel underlay that former state of life and circumstances, as it does underlie my present, and will always all circumstance, and what is called life and what is called death."[81] Bloom read the excerpt as a description of the moments when "we know the identity between ourselves and our knowledge of ourselves. Space, time, and mortality flee away, to be replaced by 'the knowing.' . . . This passage . . . achieves persuasion by the trick of affirming identity with a wholly discontinuous self, one which *knows* only the highest moments in which it *is* a vision."[82]

Unfortunately for this reading, Emerson is quite explicitly annihilating the self along with space and time. The self achieves a state in which all dissolves into one Identity, the self along with it; peace and destiny reside there. This may be blissful, but it is not a moment in which libido fuses with imagination and the poet "lives" in thought and, ultimately, revolutionizes history. Bloom confused the dissolved ego with the revolutionary ego. It's as though academic Babbittry spoke from the grave: Bloom celebrated a moment of Eliotian loss of personality as though it were the justifiable kind of romantic fulfillment.

The fragility of literary agency showed up in another way. Bloom cited Gershom Scholem defining the *zelem,* or image, as "the principle of individuality with which every single human being is endowed. . . . Two notions are combined in this concept, one relating to the idea of human individuation and the other to man's ethereal garment or ethereal (subtle) body which serves as an intermediary between his material body and his soul. . . . An ancient belief concerning such an ethereal body . . . was that the *zelem* was actually a man's true self."[83] Bloom commented: "Like Benjamin's *aura,* the *zelem* is final evidence of an authentic individuality, and its image of a luminous envelope suits Benjamin's curiously visionary materialism, his sense that the *aura* is a final defense of the soul against the shock or catastrophe of multiplicity, against masses of objects or multitudes of people in the streets. . . . Emerson, in his essay, *The Poet,* had invoked the Cambridge Platonist Cudworth's image of *aura* for what he regarded as the authentic mark of creativity: 'The condition of true naming, on the poet's part, is his resigning himself to the divine *aura* which breathes through forms, and accompanying that.' "[84] Bloom doesn't cite Scholem or Benjamin contrasting individuality to the masses: that is his importation, speaking eloquently of his own conviction that the masses are a catastrophe for the self. Yet it is not the self of the revolutionary ego;

to the contrary, it is the self that dissolves before the divine aura. Like Dewey, Benjamin was obsessed with a radical individualism that was simultaneously social, and could thrive in society. Bloom rejected this, and again I am struck by the inability of a charismatic literary critic to imagine a self that could remain autonomous among the poets, and that instead renounced freedom as long as that means bondage to a higher power, here not the interpretive community but the divine. The secret voice remained that of T. S. Eliot.

Literary criticism had sociological and political sources for its humility and marginality. Its abandonment of the general public — of mass democracy — was unmistakable, as was its nationalist mission of cultural unification in the postwar university. Its leaders did not generally imagine intelligent agency in those brought up on mass culture, and criticism largely turned its back on them. But more surprisingly, many dominant critics felt their *own* agency to be a shadowy thing. They too sensed their lack of influence over history; they felt no means of shaping "useful" knowledge. They seemed to feel remote from artists and from popular culture, from makers and consumers alike. They drained the imagination of personality. The treated their own agency as a fictional thing, a function of discursive and historical forces that no analysis could affect. When poststructuralism arrived to critique the conceptual bases of the subject and its representations, the critiques were necessary intellectually but superfluous institutionally. The self that willed itself into authority through language was already missing, already marginal, already a ghost in the house of criticism.

Without arguments for strong individual *or* collective agency, literary critics were likely to be managed by prevailing conditions. Without confidence in the value of critical agency *or* social movements, their thinking became inadvertently managerial as I have defined it. The success that democratic humanism did enjoy after the 1960s came less from the critical mainstream than from ethnic studies, feminist studies, and other fields that had not been important to English. Since literary humanism had not so much led the charge for these fields as it had tolerated those who did, the changes in English advanced not in the name of literary humanism but in opposition to it.

To top it off, literature and history after the 1960s were steadily losing enrollments to technological, vocational, and professional fields, most of which traded on their access to industry. The university wanted to support these growth-producing industry relations while maintaining its unique identity. It could maintain that identity only by defining academic freedom, basic research, open publication, and other standards as indispensable and inviolate. It is to this effort to maintain the specialness of the university that I now turn, where the management of relations with industry fell largely to science and engineering.

PART III    *The Market Revival*

. . . . . . . . . . . . . . . . . . . . . . . . . . .

· · · · · · · · · · · · · · · · · · · · · · · · · ·

## CHAPTER 8

## The Industry-Science Alliance

### The Second Corporate Revolution

The two preceding chapters, juxtaposed, suggest that the humanities suffered more than the sciences from the managerial conditions I've described. This may at first seem peculiar, since scientists were so deeply involved in the everyday management of complex grants, laboratory operations, and varied personnel, and since they had so much contact with industry. But scientists occupied a different place in the university's culture. Their place wasn't inherently closer to the top—though they had greater political and economic power—but their place was closer to external forces. Some of these forces represented government funders, and others represented industry and the marketplace. By the 1970s scientists and humanists were heading for different positions in the professional-managerial class. To generalize, humanists were headed for service and supervisory categories. Scientists were moving toward a hybrid position then emerging in the corporate world: that of the PMC-entrepreneur.

The entrepreneur represented a significant mutation in the corporation's Weberian bureaucracy. The bureaucratic tradition offered many negative responses to the downturn of the early 1970s. Under its guidance, industry cut its workforce, starting with the "routine production" workers whose predecessors had been systematically routinized by Taylorism two or three generations before. Industry also sold or closed unprofitable sectors, moved some production to lower-wage countries, and intensified every kind of financial pressure on its own operations. But industry also had a positive response, which was *cultural*. It resurrected the entrepreneur as the lifegiver of profits and products.[1] Foremost among entrepreneurs was the entrepreneur of technology, who could use science to generate entirely new sources of profit.

Entrepreneurship looked like a highway out of the university's managerial doldrums. There were other escape routes as well, but they were generally less well traveled. In this chapter, I will tell the story of how science enterprise became the main route. The story is partly about the pressure that business exerted on universities, a pressure as old as universities themselves. But it is mainly a story of the university's active role — and of the activism of the university's technology faculty. One outcome was intensified stratification within the PMC between technological and nontechnological professionals or, to simplify, between science and the humanities. This increasing division within a formerly coherent social class began, in important ways, on university campuses. In the process, it changed the social status of the university and the production of its knowledge.

· · · *Clarifying the Research Mission* · · ·

At the close of World War II, Vannevar Bush and other science leaders had identified basic research as a special activity of enormous national importance (see chapter 6). Bush influentially defined basic research as distinct from applied or commercial research. Ultimately, the two kinds of research were partners, but effective funding structures would have to respect their differences. Industry could not and should not be expected to satisfy the nation's great need for basic research. Since basic research must be governed by rigorously intellectual criteria, and since the university was the institution where intellectual standards prevailed over all others, the university would be the primary setting for basic research.

As we have seen, the University of California took early advantage of government funding and has remained a leader in developing advanced and complex industry ties.[2] In the 1950s the University of California, like many others, moved to specify and regulate its distinctive mission. The cornerstone of this effort was University Regulation no. 4. Established in June 1958 and widely viewed as "the major policy framework for UC industry relations," it affirmed a clear distinction between basic and applied research, and defined the university as the privileged setting for the former.[3] Although in reality basic and applied research continuously interacted, the conceptual barrier continues to govern science policy.[4]

Regulation no. 4 reiterated that the university serves society in a range of ways and defined the kind of services that university personnel could provide to "individuals and organizations outside the University."[5] It acknowledged that the university must let "the discretion of the individual" faculty member decide how to allocate time to various activities, but also declared that faculty activities must be consistent with the university's missions. The "Principles Underlying Regulation No. 4" stated that outside service "may be justified if it does not interfere with University commitments and if 1) it gives the individual experience and knowledge of value to his teaching or research; 2) it is suitable research through which the individual may make worthy contributions to knowledge; or 3) it is appropriate public service."[6]

The university did not classify direct service to industry as a public service. While helping general economic development was a public service, as Bush had noted, helping an industry with production and other business problems was not. Partnership with industry had to respect the university's primary commitment to basic research by contributing directly to basic research. Regulation no. 4 called this a "worthy contribution to knowledge." The phrase "worthy contribution to knowledge" was subject to interpretation, and Regulation no. 4 described two of its necessary features, features that would recur in many later regulations and reports.

The first feature appeared in the following language of the regulation: "University participation in tests and investigations shall be limited to activities which lead to the extension of knowledge or to increased effectiveness in teaching. Routine tasks of a commonplace type will not be undertaken." Routine tasks include "tests, studies or investigations of purely commercial character, such as mineral assays" among many examples.[7] In a general way, the regulation divided research into that which creates new knowledge and that which applies existing knowledge. New knowledge was the terrain of the university and applied knowledge was not. The first necessary feature of a "worthy contribution to knowledge" was that it created *new* knowledge.

The second feature was the open publication of results. "All such research shall be conducted so as to be as generally useful as possible. To this end, the right of publication is reserved by the university."[8] The Office of the President's Contract and Grant Manual amplified this requirement: "It is longstanding University policy that freedom to publish or disseminate results is a major criterion of the appropriateness of a sponsored project, and particularly of a research project."[9] The manual offered examples of commercial restrictions on publication that would ordinarily be unacceptable, such as "assigning the final decision as to what may be published to the extramural fund source." Although limited exceptions were granted (as when "the sponsor reserves first right of publication" for a "reasonable interval of time"), university research led to public rather than proprietary knowledge.

These two features rested on a further general principle that was more often implied than stated. The principle was that the university would remain independent of all particular interests, be they financial, political, familial, or personal. The university could only perform research and public service if it could offer impartial evidence and analysis on all the subjects with which it was concerned. Its staff and faculty could not remain impartial if they had the wrong kind of self-interest, including financial self-interest, in the matter at hand. As conflicts of interest continued to arise, university officials tried to make this principle more explicit. In the late 1970s President Saxon noted that "universities serve all kinds and manners of interests, but the central truth is that, by serving each of these interests, the University serves the interest of all and is the handmaiden of none."[10]

The University of California's *Report of the University-Industry Relations Project* (1982) affirmed this principle with a crucial instance of it: "University research . . . will contribute to technological change and also provide a critique of it."[11] Throughout most of the postwar period, the university's leaders held that it could perform its special role only in freedom from economic and political interests: "In this tradition, social scientists and others offer objective analyses to government and private groups about matters that require dispassionate judgment."[12] Impartiality went hand in hand with the emphasis on new knowledge and open publication.

The postwar university sought connections with industry as it had in the past. It also sought to limit these connections to those that reflected the distinctive research role of the university. The university had defined its distinctive research role through the general principles of new knowledge and open publication. Although university officials were well aware that industry engaged in large amounts of research, much of it on scientific frontiers, university policy cast industry as concerned primarily with applying existing knowledge and developing proprietary techniques. The university expected its negotiations with industry to maintain its detachment from direct self-interest in research results, financial interests included. Although university faculty would be allowed to contract their services to industry, these services would need to comply with university expectations for impartiality, breakthrough knowledge, and the open dissemination of results.

## · · · A Changing Economy · · ·

There is no evidence that university administrators and faculty ever changed their minds that the university's core function was the production and dissemination of new knowledge. But in the 1970s, the university's external environment changed dramatically, as did the interests of many students and faculty.

The most relevant environmental change was economic. The 1970s are rightly remembered for recession and "stagflation," which to many at the time seemed the temporary results of oil price shocks, bad monetary policy, corporate mismanagement, and other reversible factors. In retrospect, most historians think that the decade marked an epochal change in the history of capitalism.

At the close of World War II, the United States was the largest and virtually the only undamaged economy in the world. It centered on "Fordist" mass production, which generated large profits through economies of scale, assembly-line manufacturing, and large markets that accepted standardized, inexpensive goods. The American economy was also "Taylorist" in that it relied on a relatively regimented form of "scientific management" that attributed efficiency to the carefully calibrated and complete supervision of work and workers. Postwar profits and productivity increases flowed largely from the successful engineering of large and technical labor systems in a world economy where the United States enjoyed a unique economic preeminence.

The slump of the 1970s made clear that American preeminence had been declining for years. The nation's share of world trade had suffered from the steadily strengthening competition of rebuilt industrial countries such as Germany, Japan, and France, and of the newly industrialized countries, particularly those in Asia. Competition was often fiercest for the mass-produced consumer goods sold to the huge, stable markets that were the Fordist system's bread and butter: Sony's very first product was a cheap electric blanket. In addition, these markets became more unstable and segmented as consumers increasingly sought specialized and continuously changing products.

Other factors also made a difference, although there was little agreement about these. Some argued that the government's regulatory apparatus was rigid and outmoded and deserved major cuts. Others pointed to excessive wage increases granted because of wage union pressure. Still others noted the inefficiency of regimented, dehumanizing production work (this group included the Nixon administration's Department of Labor).[13] Some influential analysts claimed that American business had been spending enormous time and resources on financial and marketing activities that achieved short-term profits at the expense of long-term product development and productivity gains.[14] Perhaps most importantly, many observers, including parts of the science establishment, pointed to industry's weakening record of developing innovative technology.[15] It appeared that Fordist mass production's components — production design, corporate management, consumer markets, state regulation, economic and social supports, and technological development — were all failing at the same time.

As business's confidence in large-scale routine production declined, it began to shed or export its industrial base and look for new sources of profit. One new source — and certainly the most exciting — were new products based on new technologies that would form entirely new markets.[16] These products would be difficult to design and produce, and they would require a highly educated and highly motivated workforce. Research and development would take on a renewed importance, and so would liberal management techniques that inspired and networked rather than confined and directed its innovative employees. The advanced nature of such products would provide American business with a new competitive advantage in the world economy.[17] In other words, the best counter to a weak economy would be a new economy, and the new economy would rest on a larger and faster supply of breakthroughs in biotechnology, for example, and information technology.

Industry's intensified interest in new technology meant an intensified interest in the research university. The feeling was mutual. Congress chimed in as well, and had authorized the NSF to undertake "applied research" in 1968; several pilot programs in the early 1970s funded partnerships between industry and higher education.[18] Universities presented themselves as housing sophisticated knowledge, expert faculty, and students with the latest training. University personnel, they said, valued independence and innovation and could work on their own in areas too advanced to be supervised. They would show the same "entrepreneurial" impulses they had used to raise extramural funding for their research. The *Report of the University-Industry Relations Project* summarized the idea in

1982: "Industry faces shortages of skilled employees in critical high technology areas and wants access to the fundamental research base of universities."[19] Industries and universities might cooperate in streamlining the process of technology transfer whereby basic science yielded important new commodities. Government also supported industry-university partnerships, the UC report claimed. Government "looks upon closer ties as a way of improving economic performance through more rapid and effective translation of basic science to useful products and processes."[20]

The university was also suffering from financial pressures. The recessions of the 1970s had cut federal and state support and put the future of public funding in doubt. Basic research was becoming more complex and more expensive every year, and general education was following suit. High tuition increases were damaging popular support for higher education without actually covering steadily increasing costs. The university's ties with government were lucrative but also cumbersome and restrictive; industry ties often appeared straightforward and manageable by comparison. As administrators lost confidence in traditional funding sources, and felt less able to pass on increased costs by increasing fees, they tended to see industry as an underused resource.

Revenue figures suggest that universities had already intensified their industry links by the early 1980s. At UC, "funding from industrial sources grew from $24 million in 1978/1979 to $42 million in 1980/1981." In the latter fiscal year, industry sources accounted for "between 4% and 5% of total funds available for research."[21] In the late 1970s, in other words, industry support of UC research nearly doubled in the course of two years. It would double again over the course of another fifteen to twenty years, reaching about 9 percent of total research funding in 2000.[22] The UC figure for industry funding in the late 1990s was similar to the national average.[23]

··· *Industry's Claims to Research* ···

The changing economy of the 1970s put universities under financial pressure that continues into the present, and also introduced another lasting change. In the most exciting, lucrative sectors of the struggling economy, such as biotechnology, the advanced research was coming from industry as much as from the university. The view that universities had a monopoly on basic research was weakened by the advances taking place outside it.

The dichotomy between basic and applied, nonprofit and for-profit research had always been more ideal than fact. The postwar *growth* in the universities' share of overall R&D in the United States attracted much attention, as it doubled from 7.4 percent in 1960 to nearly 16 percent in 1995. But industry accounted for at least 70 percent of R&D throughout the period and sometimes considerably more. Some significant portion of that R&D was long term and could be defined as "basic." The NSF estimated that universities accounted for about 62 percent of the basic research performed within the United States in 1995.[24] This is a high proportion, but it still leaves industry in the position of providing over one-third even of basic research.[25] The inverse was also true: even after federal funding came to eclipse industry funding on university campuses, "much university research . . . retained an applied character, reflecting the importance of research support from such federal 'mission agencies' as the Defense Department."[26] The university had a special focus on basic research, but it did not have an exclusive franchise.[27] Industry could say not only that it was doing much of the basic research, but that it was doing much of the best.

By the late 1970s administrators had reaffirmed the university's fundamental dependence on industry, a dependence that had been veiled by cold war federal funding. They acknowledged that industry contacts enhanced job prospects for students at a time when finding employment was becoming increasingly difficult.[28] They heard top faculty threatening to leave either for industry or for a university with more flexible corporate connections. UC's University-Industry Relations Project was motivated in part by a concern that the university could lose its best professors and graduate students to industry, and miss major opportunities along the way.

Industry did not respond to its economic problems by imposing itself on the university. The university actively pursued closer relations with industry. Nor did university administrators impose industry sponsorship on reluctant faculty. Faculty actively pursued this sponsorship. There were a number of reasons for the interest shown by universities, but one was the longstanding overlap between basic and applied research, an overlap that the elevation of basic research had distorted. Basic and applied research both involved figuring out how things work. Motives were similar among astronomers and chemical engineers. Basic research might yield more generalizable knowledge, but so might applied work that addressed a production problem. Applied research could be as challenging and exciting as basic research. The craft labor behind each was similar. This is why Freeman Dyson had compared experimental physics to the work of his boilermaker grandfather. The operations and outcomes of university and industrial *systems* were different. The experience and motives of the intellectual craft work were often not.

Industry in general applied Taylorist forms of managerial control to its own frontline employees. Its management structures were of course undemocratic, resting on authority that flowed from top to bottom, and that wielded powers ranging from work organization to penalization and firing. Its dominant model of capacity remained a kind of autocratic decisiveness; it tended to venerate its CEOs as great men along the lines of kings and generals. Given these facts about corporate life, it is natural to assume that industry connections would replace academic freedom with autocratic Taylorism in university work. But there is little evidence of this. To the contrary, industry sponsorship could mean more pragmatism and less paperwork. The emphasis could be on practical problem solving with fewer distractions than in government work and as much autonomy. There is little evidence, in other words, that industry funding damaged the *process* of scientific creativity of university scientists. There were and are instances of corrupt influence, such as the sponsorship by General Motors of the Ketteridge Institute at the University of Cincinnati, which for decades "proved" the safety of lead additives in gasoline. Such cases of bias and other abuses justify continuing and intensive vigilance. They do not necessarily support the broader claim that industry funding compromised the intellectual freedom underlying the process of basic research, or at least that the compromises taking place were new.

The relationship was changing in another way. By 1980 universities were regularly looking to business not only for funding but for advanced science. While there is room to debate the quality, quantity, and ultimate impact of basic research coming from various sources, a psychological and cultural shift had occurred. Commercial research was no longer being classified as "routine." Instead it appeared to show dynamism, innovation, and in some cases conceptual leadership. Thus it was for intellectual as well as financial reasons that fields historically close to industry were deepening their ties, and that areas of science with little previous commercial contact developed subfields with commercial potential. Overall, university faculty and administrators came to believe that industry was doing comparable, exciting, and certainly fundamental research in some of the most important fields of science and technology. Many no longer assumed the university's preeminence at the intellectual cutting edge, and at times worried that industry was leaving the university behind.

The postwar research university had presented itself as society's primary site of basic research. It had defined basic research in contrast to commercial research. That contrast had always been oversimplified, but as the economy and technology entered their "post-Fordist" period, the contrast appeared to many faculty and administrators to be a burden. The university had always worked with industry, but the partnerships had seemed marginal to the university's core mission of basic research. Without a clear contrast between basic and applied research, commercial considerations were free to move toward the center of university activity, and to mix with science in the complex ways that the university now claimed had prevailed all along. If science was becoming more commercial, it was not because the university had shifted from basic to applied research. It was because scientists on and off campus increasingly rejected a clear distinction between basic and applied.

One of the cornerstones of the university's postwar identity was changing. Two others were soon to follow.

### · · · *The Production Partnership: Rediscovering a Tradition* · · ·

Postwar administrators had defined service to industry and public service as two different things. This dichotomy also became less certain in the 1970s. Wasn't the creation of new products — new drugs, new biological and information technologies, new antipollution devices, new pest-resistant crops — a major public service? Didn't industry serve society? Wasn't, therefore, service to industry also service to society?

Considerations like these were part of a gradual but decisive shift in the way some administrators described service to society as a whole. The *Report of the University-Industry Relations Project*, while noting David Saxon's comment that the university must serve all interests, described the "land grant principle" as authorizing universities to serve "the productive sector of society," meaning agriculture and industry. It also interpreted the principle to mean that "American higher education has been a vehicle for government to subsidize research for industry."[29] This is a significant narrowing of the notion of public service embodied in the Morrill Act of 1862. It fails to acknowledge that many activities in society are productive without being profitable or commercial, from child rearing and mass transit to disease control, environmental protection, and "blue sky" research.

The shift here is not of exclusion but of emphasis. The report does not wish to break with the past but to claim it and build on it. It reflects common administrative wisdom in acknowledging the university's non-profit social responsibilities, claiming that these do not "militate against cooperation with industry so long as such cooperation is not to the exclusion of responsiveness to other social interests and needs."[30] Though these "other social interests" are not to be excluded, they are not the university's central and driving social constituency, which is industry. These other social interests must in their turn be aware that industry partnerships were envisioned at the founding of the public research university.[31] The report intended to frame, expand, refine, streamline, and improve existing partnership traditions rather than break with the past or start something new. The report thus saw service to industry as continuing the tradition of serving the public.

The idea that serving commerce meant serving society rested on a venerable, though often contested, equation between industry, production, and productivity. Many administrators and faculty followed the mainstream market view that commercialization and production was the franchise of the private sector. No university leader suggested that the university might form partnerships with foundations or the federal government to bring research to market. The public sector controlled research that bore directly on national security and with social services that lacked profit potential. As with ARPANET, the original internet that emerged from research funded by the Department of Defense, industry would handle any process of commercialization.

Most administrators assumed industrial partnership to be a settled fact with clear social benefits.[32] They assumed that the products to which basic research would lead were for the most part socially useful. Those like napalm that destroyed natural habitats for military purposes were exceptions to the rule. The university could simply avoid partnerships that were likely to lead to worthless or harmful products, and case-by-case rejections did not require a categorical suspicion or rejection of industry partnering. In addition, the misuse of the university's basic research would primarily be industry's responsibility.

Once one accepted that all production would and even should be handled by industry, and, implicitly, that it was the market that stimulated productivity, it was a short step, and a logically unwarranted though understandable one, to define industry as *the* productive sector of society. It became harder to imagine how the university could serve society *without* serving the corporate sector to which society apparently owed its wealth, knowledge, and way of life.

Given most administrators' perception of industry's dynamism, capacity for basic research, and near-monopoly on productivity, they saw a clear choice. The university could partner with industry and see its discoveries turn into popular and useful products that, not incidentally, yielded some return to the university. Or the university could remain on its own, contributing little to the marketplace while losing its research edge.

Those who opposed increased ties with industry pointed out that the second option was certainly compatible with the university's social mission and intellectual greatness. Dozens of fields, from archeology and art history to philosophy and political science, had changed the course of culture and society while yielding little monetary value. Even fields that had paid off commercially produced much additional knowledge that would not lead directly to products or profits. In addition, they said, industry continues to look to the university for the latest work in every technological field.

No less importantly, many researchers across the disciplines felt that a noncommercial atmosphere was crucial to preserving intellectual freedom, to investigating problems according to their internal requirements, without regard to artificial institutional or financial goals. Advocates of industry alliances had to show that these alliances would not impair freedom of inquiry, a freedom which most felt lay behind the greatness of American science.[33]

Advocates did not in fact offer that kind of general assurance. To the contrary, they acknowledged conflicts of interest and other problems with university partnerships. The UC report noted that much of the university community remained skeptical and concerned, and resistant to intensified industry ties; that other social responsibilities needed to be maintained, including the responsibility to criticize industry practices; that problems were raised by the intermingling of public and private funds; that industry might seek to sponsor research inappropriate to a university; that industry might seek not only to delay the publication of research results, as it already sometimes did, but to suppress publication altogether; that licensing and patenting and intellectual property issues were complicated, unresolved, and likely to involve the university in unethical compromises.

We will look at the report's key solutions below. What must be stressed here is that the report did not refute the value of noncommercial sites of free inquiry. It maintained that value, and yet eclipsed it with two competing, though partial, realities. First, it claimed, nonmarket freedom of investigation had never exactly existed, since industry had been on campus from the beginning. Second, nonmarket investigation was not strictly necessary, since commercial research had been yielding such strong "basic" results.

Noncommercial research remained a compelling ideal for many if not most practitioners in the arts and sciences. But defenses of the ideal had rested on contrasts between basic and applied research and between public service and service to industry. By 1980 a significant proportion of administrators and faculty were finding these distinctions obsolete. Applied and basic research were thought to be mingled in practice. And serving industry was thought to be serving society.

Two cornerstones of the postwar university had been modified. The same process was being applied to the third.

#### · · · A Watershed in Patent Law · · ·

The culmination of the 1970s discussions of university-industry relations was a striking change in the proprietorship of federally funded research. Through the 1970s, patentable inventions and processes developed in part through federal funds remained in the possession of the federal government. Universities that had conducted the research could negotiate intellectual property agreements (IPAs) with federal agencies. But title was the federal government's to license or transfer and not the university's or the individual researcher's. Different federal agencies had different patent policies. IPAs were negotiated case by case and with a variety of outcomes. The government held patent rights as the trustee of the public, and research funded by the public would remain in the public domain to be licensed for public benefit. Statutory law also required that the government avoid placing any one contractor in a preferred position.[34]

Industry was not satisfied with this situation, but the same was true of many academics. One of the major participants in the 1970s discussions, Richard C. Atkinson, describes the motive behind changing patent law: "It was clear to us in the late seventies that the process of transforming ideas into applications was not working as well as it should. We assembled a number of working groups at NSF to see what could be done to improve matters. A particularly thorny issue was the federal policy requiring that patents generated from government-supported research at universities reside with the government. This was a clear impediment to transfer. What is the incentive to move ideas into the marketplace if government reaps the rewards? But could the federal government actually give up intellectual property rights? No one knew for sure, but we began to draft legislation in the late seventies. By 1982, Congress had passed the Bayh-Dole Act, which transferred patent rights to universities."[35] Bayh-Dole, formally known as the Patent and Trademark Amendments Act of 1980, established a uniform invention policy for all agencies and universities. It gave the institutions that conducted federally funded research the right to patent and license the results. It explicitly encouraged the commercialization of federally supported university research.[36] As Atkinson and others envisioned, universities now had direct financial incentives to patent and license research findings. In subsequent years, the federal judiciary strengthened the legal position of patent holders and thus the securability of financial returns.[37] In 1983 the Act's provisions were extended, by Ronald Reagan's executive order, from universities and small businesses to large corporations.[38]

Bayh-Dole was passed over vehement objections from some quarters. In his congressional testimony, Ralph Nader argued that easier corporate access to university research would damage academic and democratic values. "The corporate model concentrates power, restricts the production and application of knowledge, and increases uniform behavior, self-censorship and when needed — outright suppression."[39] Interestingly, Admiral Hyman Rickover, spearhead of the nuclear navy and veteran of decades of industry contracting, felt much the same way.[40]

Pro or con, most observers regard the Bayh-Dole Act as the beginning of a new era in university-industry relations. The act did not initiate relations with industry, as we have seen. It did not initiate the research university's interest in industry sponsorship or patent revenues, for the university's experiences with industry, catalyzed by a changing economic climate, were more the cause of the Bayh-Dole Act than its effect. Nonetheless, the act is often credited with greatly expanding university-industry relations, and with shifting the balance of power in favor of industry. We will have to distinguish several simultaneous trends in order to identify Bayh-Dole's actual effects.

The first outcome was intentional. University patent policies began to move toward a common standard of university ownership of intellectual property. In the past, patent policies had been surprisingly diverse. In their study of three university leaders in technology transfer, Mowery et al. found policy convergence gradually replacing policy diversity. The University of California had established commercialization mechanisms in 1943, and began requiring faculty disclosure of inventions and licenses in 1963. Before Bayh-Dole, Columbia University actually discouraged patenting in its medical school, but then declared in 1944 that its non-medical employees were "free to patent any device or discovery resulting from their personal researches." The situation was similar at Stanford, which in 1970 declared that it "shall be the policy of the University to permit employees of the University, both faculty and staff, and students to retain all rights to inventions made by them."[41]

Bayh-Dole encouraged a general reversal of policies that had allowed patents to remain in the hands of the government or the inventor. UC regularized its ownership of patent rights to the research results of all its employees. Columbia's new policy, effective July 1, 1981, the same day Bayh-Dole became effective, retained all rights of patent ownership for research conducted with its resources while sharing some royalties with the individual inventors. Stanford, interestingly, did not retain patent title on its personnel's inventions until 1994, when its policy became similar to those of UC and Columbia.[42]

In short, research that was supported with federal money and by faculty and graduate student labor became the property of the host university. Corporations had long claimed title to their employees' inventions, and state laws usually backed them up.[43] On this point, Bayh-Dole moved universities closer to the corporate model.

A second outcome followed from the first. Universities now had direct financial incentives to see "basic" research overlap with applied, science turn into technology, and the discovery process lead to commercial products. As we have seen, the university in the 1970s had already become more likely to describe industry partnership as public service. With Bayh-Dole, it could justify these partnerships as financial prudence and economic development. Although universities continued to have institutional, intellectual, and cultural stakes in their difference from business, they also had stakes in closer ties with it.

These stakes could not be measured only in dollar revenues. A deeper cultural shift was taking place, one that was changing definitions of administrative foresight, leadership, and prowess. Industry partnership became the measure of all these things. It was slowly but inexorably becoming harder for administrators, even at public universities, to say that they were truly advancing the institution if they were not involved in fundraising and partnering with the private sector. The university had an interest in making money through these partnerships. It also wanted to be seen as interested in making money, as interested in doing whatever it took to become a player.[44]

This second outcome led directly to a third. As we have seen, the postwar research university had distinguished itself through three conceptual contrasts, and we have also seen that the contrast between basic and applied research, and that between service to society and service to industry, became increasingly qualified in the 1970s. The Bayh-Dole Act posed a challenge to the third contrast, that between open and proprietary research results.

This was a supremely sensitive issue. The value of open publication came as close to being a universal belief as any feature of higher education. It was arguably the university's single most important quality for participants that included academics, students, administrators, legislators, industry managers, and the general public. Truth, enlightenment, progress, functionality — however one defined the value of knowledge, open publication of results was the one sure way to achieve it. Virtually all researchers saw it as the heart and soul of scientific knowledge, and virtually all administrators recognized it as a preeminent public virtue.

The university's open publication of impartial research became even more important as industry seemed to respond to the crises of the 1970s by going farther down the other, proprietary road. Technology secrets appeared increasingly to define the margin between success and failure, and secrecy became an even more important part of company policy. Industry also continued a trend which had taken root in the 1960s toward the marketing of everything, which meant selecting, pitching, manipulating, and spinning information that was often presented as independent research ("3 out of 5 doctors recommend Bayer to their patients"). Marketing intensified in socially sensitive industries like pharmaceuticals that required the recovery of high development costs. As advertising for products ranging from Alka-Seltzer to cigarettes became increasingly sophisticated and ubiquitous, the university seemed an increasingly distinctive haven of accurate data and impartial analysis.[45] The stakes were raised further by revelations in the 1970s that industry had distorted or suppressed studies of the negative health effects of pesticides, leaded fuel, automobile gas tanks, and waste disposal, among other products and services. Public skepticism only increased in the 1980s with controversies about AIDS, Bhopal, and similar disasters. In a world of pseudo-research, wall-to-wall product hype, soaring medical costs, and constant economic anxiety, the public could use a university that remained above the fray, uncompromised by financial and other self-interests, beholden to no great power, always ready to tell the truth.

··· *Open Research in Proprietary Markets* ···

The *Report of the University-Industry Relations Project,* UC's major policy statement in the wake of Bayh-Dole, recognized the value of open publication. It noted "the special need of the University of California, a major public research university, to maintain its public trust. Also," it continued, "the University has a social responsibility to assure a diversity of research activities and to continue its tradition of independence from undue influence by a single source."[46] The report's fourth recommendation reads as follows: "Maintaining an open and collegial environment for teaching and research is a fundamental principle of the University. The University's publication policy, i.e., freedom to publish and to disseminate research results, is also fundamental. Limited periods of delaying publication are permissible only to permit filing of patent applications or to enable the sponsor to comment. *Campuses, the Academic Senate or faculty in fields where openness may be strained should take steps to see that norms that assure an environment of openness are upheld. The University should continue its consistent and forceful application of publication policy.*"[47] Openness, the report claimed, must remain central to the university's operation.

But what kind of patenting system was implied by open publication? If unbiased knowledge depended on open publication, then might not the most efficient product development depend on open access to intellectual property? In theory at least, if scientific knowledge rightly belonged in the public domain, then would research results be the property of the public? Did open publication suggest something like a public domain approach to patenting?

The question isn't speculative, for it describes the status of federally funded research that existed in the decades before Bayh-Dole: "Prior to Bayh-Dole, inventions paid for by taxpayer dollars were considered to belong to the public. A license to manufacture the invention could be issued to a corporation, but only on a nonexclusive basis. What this meant in practice was that manufacturers of inventions would have to compete with other companies that could also secure licenses. In this manner, it was thought, the costs to the public would be minimized because market competition protected the public from monopolistic control and pricing."[48] Open market access presumably reduced the cost of new products. We might add that it could reduce obstacles to the advancement of knowledge by allowing more people to try more things with more data than they could were the data privately owned. Proprietary knowledge, in this frame, raised costs *and* slowed discovery. By contrast, public patent ownership might mean the extension of the university's principle of openness to the economy as a whole.

This view could not be dismissed as reflecting, say, the socialist views of critics of private property. It had been implicit in Vannevar Bush's vision of publicly funded research, and was clearly part of Admiral Rickover's thinking. In addition, some mainstream economists who studied the economics of research had come to similar conclusions.

In a remarkable article published in 1959, the economist Richard R. Nelson had argued that profit incentives could never support all scientific research that had social value. A for-profit firm would undertake research only if its returns could be expected to exceed its costs. This meant that a given firm would readily support applied research, where the basic principles were known, the problem was clearly defined, and a successful application was likely. Such calculations did not apply to basic research, for basic research is by definition that in which "the degree of uncertainty about the results of specific research projects increases, and the goals become less clearly defined."[49] If a firm could not calculate with meaningful certainty that research returns would be greater than research costs, it had no rational reason to undertake the work.

Nelson's central insight was that the uncertainty of basic research does not only increase its *risk* but also increases its *value*. That is because the largest long-term value comes from breakthroughs that affect knowledge well beyond the boundaries of a particular application.[50] These discoveries are by their nature unforeseen, and their degree of uncertainty is nearly total. The most successful basic research often yields the most unanticipated results, results that could not possibly be planned and budgeted in advance. The most successful basic research is thus the riskiest research, and also the least "rational" to pursue, and hence the least likely to be pursued by a prudent firm.

This argument had profound implications. Most participants in the American market economy accept the truism that market calculations are compatible with and reinforce social development. This is the essence of claims about the "invisible hand," according to which an untold number of private profit calculations add up to the maximum "profit" for society. Richard Atkinson expressed a version of this idea when he noted that universities require profit incentives to move ideas into the marketplace, which would in turn enrich society: social benefits increase as private profits increase. Nelson, though clearly an advocate of what he calls "our enterprise economy," pointed out that in fact private gain can *decrease* social gain. Sound, rational calculation will tell firms to avoid undertaking the expensive, risky research that produces the greatest long-term social gains, gains that mostly go to other people and other firms. Private ownership of patents can cut those patents' social value, resulting in a loss to society.[51]

The leaders of research universities generally assumed a fit between private and public benefit. They downplayed the possibility that they were damaging the public good by acting, after Bayh-Dole, as brokers for the private ownership of publicly funded patents. They downplayed as well the possibility that the incentive system, which encouraged proprietary knowledge, conflicted with social efficiency, which required open knowledge.[52] To put the point another way, they acted as though open and proprietary knowledge systems had the same eventual outcomes, and were in practice close to the same thing.

The UC report sought a reconciliation of open and proprietary systems. It recommended, first, that "the University community should take a positive stance in expanding involvement with industry."[53] It also recommended that mechanisms be established to maintain "an open and collegial environment," including "freedom to publish and to disseminate research results."[54]

The university's patent policy was front and center in the task of synthesizing diverse priorities. These included achieving "reasonable revenues" for the university, the development of inventions for the marketplace, "maintaining good relations with industry," and "protecting against the use of public funds for private gain."[55] The university founded its attempted harmonization on the belief that none of these goals actually contradicted any others. It assumed, for example, that it *could* prevent public money from subsidizing private profit even as it licensed publicly funded inventions. It assumed that its patent policy could protect open publication while offering firms proprietary knowledge.

How could the university do these competing things at once? First, its patent policy "required every employee to agree to disclose inventions arising from University research and to assign patents to The Regents."[56] The university would act as a trustee for the public by preventing individual employees from arranging side deals for their intellectual property with private companies.

Second, the university would license its inventions nonexclusively. The only exceptions would be "firms that have funded the total cost of research leading to the invention." These firms could expect an exclusive license, but only if they also satisfied a further condition of "due diligence in development and payment of royalties."[57] If the research rested entirely on private money then it could result in private gain. But if public money were involved, then the public's interest would be protected by allowing open access to the patent and blocking strict proprietary use.

Third, the report defined patent application as open publication. "Because patent applications, with some national security exceptions, are public, the University's patent policy contributes to the dissemination of research results."[58] The university would tolerate short delays in publication "that permit a sponsor to comment or to permit filing of patent applications," but it would not allow a private sponsor to obtain a long delay in or suppress publication.[59] While a private firm might own the license to manufacture a product based on an invention, the knowledge, the art, the principles, the science underlying the invention would be public information. In this sense, open publication and proprietary use could be made compatible.

But fourth, and perhaps most crucially, the report diluted the definition and scope of "openness." A central paragraph is worth citing at length:

> One problem of some immediacy is that the licensing of tangible research products may depend on maintaining some degree of secrecy, *i.e.*, not making materials available to all upon request. Tangible research products refer to cell lines, plasmids, mechanical structural drawings, etc., which are either not patentable or have not yet been patented. Firms, in exchange for research support, are often interested in having access to this type of product through licensing arrangements including the expectation of the University protecting the know-how associated with the tangible research product. The position taken by [the Committee on Rights to Intellectual Property], we believe, is a sensible one. It would permit licensing of tangible research products, but only under the condition that such agreements include provisions clearly stating that the results of the research project are publishable and that there are no restraints on publication or exchange of information among those participating in the research process. The assumption of the CRIP recommendation is that a restriction on dissemination of tangible research products is not the same as restricting publication because detailed infor-

mation on the tangible research product is not usually included in scholarly publications nor presented at professional meetings. However, the CRIP committee makes it clear that the University cannot take responsibility to prevent disclosure of such information.[60]

Here the report accepts that proprietary use requires restrictions on open publication. It suggests that the publication of the results of sponsored research is sufficiently open if it occurs "among those participating in the research process," which on its face at least excludes the public. The report champions open publication, while restricting the relevance of openness to the point where it is compatible with secrecy about aspects of research having potential market value. One could imagine cases where the content of publication would be utterly unaffected, and others where it would be affected. At the very least, the university was demonstrating its willingness to trim open publication to fit patenting prospects.

Readers might therefore be forgiven for concluding that the report champions open publication while tacitly endorsing garden-variety commercial secrecy. They might suspect that research results will be open only when the sponsor sees no commercial potential. It's easy to protect public knowledge from the market when that knowledge has no present market value.[61] The real challenge involves research that would be considered basic were it not potentially profitable. The report protects openness from secrecy by limiting openness to those elements that do not detail the research product. It would seem that more distinctive "know-how" could be withheld indefinitely.

There is no doubt that the report's authors wished to keep the university independent of industry. There is also no doubt that this independence rested on three contrasts—basic versus applied research, public versus commercial service, open versus proprietary knowledge—which had been oversimplified in theory and were hard to disentangle in practice. We can fully credit the good intentions of the report's authors, their devotion to the university's special social role, and their belief in public service, and still note that the project of disentangling contrasting modes and functions had ground to a halt. The university community would continue to define itself in terms of these contrasts, and invoke basic research, public service, and open publication as its watchwords. At the interface with industry, a different game was being played, one which accepted that the contrasts were outmoded or untenable. The lines would be drawn case by case. This meant that industry was a partner in defining the functional meaning of terms like "basic" research and "open" publication. Industry was thus a partner in defining the terms of the university's basic identity.

### · · · Sanctioning Financial Incentives · · ·

We are now in a better position to understand the importance of a major preoccupation of the report. The postwar university had implemented policies like Regulation no. 4, which had sought to apply standard principles to all cases. The report moved in another direction by seeking decentralization and enlarged discretion in defining boundaries and limits.

The report concluded that "research activity must be appropriate to the mission and character of the University," but added that "there is no hard and fast definition of appropriateness." This meant that "the regular faculty have a central and continuous role in deciding on the appropriateness of research within an administrative structure that assures review of these decisions" (recommendation 3).[62] In putting decisions in the hands of faculty, the report also claimed that "the major policy framework for UC industry relations," Regulation no. 4, was "in part out of date and needs revising." Twenty years later this revision is still in the offing, as several academic generations continue to wonder whether Regulation no. 4's framework, including the distinction between public and commercial service, may be too restrictive.

Other recommendations in the report also sought greater flexibility. Industry partnerships require speed and responsiveness. Thus patent administration should in part be moved to individual campuses, "and the Chancellor's authority [on each campus] should be expanded to provide for increased flexibility and effectiveness in negotiations with industry sponsors.[63] The university should pursue "innovative organizational approaches to industry," with the proviso that the university, including the chancellors and president, be a "major participant" in designing these approaches. The university should "assist federal, state and local officials in developing the necessary tax incentives," that is, tax flexibility, that would subsidize high-technology research. Each campus should develop ways of supporting faculty efforts to partner with industry that are suited to varying circumstances. The university should develop a "handbook on University-Industry relations," one that describes relevant university policies. The handbook should also "make clear that no bias against cooperation with industrial firms and associations exists." This can be taken to mean that no particular policy should be read as presenting a fixed, *a priori* barrier to partnership.

Discretion was also enlarged around the sensitive issue of financial conflict of interest. A faculty member might be "conducting research which is funded by a firm in which he or she has substantial financial involvement."[64] The question of secrecy emerged again: there was a danger that "as a result of service to the competitive advantage of the firm, the faculty member would suppress information or material normally available to colleagues and students, thereby undermining the integrity of the teaching and research process."[65] A conflict of interest might also lead a faculty member to "improperly remove patentable inventions or licensable tangible research products from the University to the firm." University supplies, equipment, and staff time might be siphoned off to the faculty member's firm, or the faculty member might subordinate his or her university responsibilities to the "needs of the firm."[66]

Any of these would represent a significant loss to the university and to the public for which the university is a trustee. The State of California, faced with similar issues for its employees that handle contracting, vending, and other relations with outside parties, addressed them by prohibiting *any* employee participation "in the making of a decision if there exists for him or her a foreseeable financial gain."[67] The relevant legislation, the California Political Reform Act (1974), required all public officials "to reveal all sources of income that might come in conflict with their responsibilities as elected or appointed government servants." But the act specifically exempted "decisions on the selection of teaching and other program materials and decisions about research (the Academic Freedom exemption)."[68] The report used the exemption to allow faculty members to make university decisions about firms in which they had a financial interest. The university required disclosure of these interests, and management of them by university officials, but did not prohibit them.[69]

When the university rejected a provision prohibiting faculty members from having a financial interest in the outcome of their research, they had a major intellectual reason. The report noted that faculty members with financial interests in a research program may be exactly those "uniquely qualified" to pursue it. But the university had another reason. It was worried that such a prohibition would induce good faculty — and faculty with good industry connections — to jump ship either for a more lenient university or for industry itself. The report warned that if "appropriate modes of relationships that reasonably accommodate the incentives of the situation are not found, academia may lose a generation of people to industry."[70] It advocated the development of university research centers and other means "to accommodate the pressures and incentives."

In lieu of a prohibition on commercial research, the report recommended two mechanisms for regulating the faculty's relations with industry. The first was that industry-sponsored research be peer-reviewed by committees composed of other faculty on each campus.[71] Industry relations would be allowed in every case that did not violate university standards as interpreted by one's colleagues. This was a mechanism of professional self-policing with a rationale similar to that of organizations like the American Medical Association.

The second alternative to prohibition was to classify many relations with industry as consulting arrangements. Various activities — service on corporate boards, off-campus collaboration with industry scientists, and so on — could be placed under this heading as well.[72] Regulation no 4. gave the university a much smaller burden of enforcement concerning the consulting relationships formed by individual faculty. Faculty could not "solicit" employment of their services by outside parties, nor could such employment "interfere with their University duties."[73] But the regulation's core requirements that activities "lead to the extension of knowledge or increased effectiveness in teaching" and that they never be "of a purely commercial character" applied only to activities where the university was an official participant.[74] When the contracting party was an individual faculty member, arranging the disposition of his personal time, commercial activity was allowed.

This opened up leeway for both the university and the researcher. The university could limit itself to enforcing requirements that the individual fulfill his or her university obligations and disclose outside relationships. The university need only, in other words, enforce the contract between the faculty member and itself. The contract between the faculty member and a commercial firm could then be handled as a private matter, where the individual's right to privacy and right to make contracts would have to be weighed against university requirements that the contract might violate.

The report thus noted, "It is the policy of the university to separate an employee's university and private interests."[75] It argued that both intellectual and financial motives are in play, observing in passing that "the perceived opportunities to make money are great and involve not only the sale of products but more likely the speculative returns to an equity investment and the salary possibilities."[76] The report put financial interests in the context of the pressure on the university "to accommodate the pressures and incentives." The ensuing recommendation stated that the university should pursue "innovative organizational approaches to industry funding," ones that would lead to "a framework in which the University as an institution is a major participant." Consulting offers a situation in which the work and the legal responsibilities devolve to the faculty entrepreneur, who is compensated in the form of financial gains, part of which may later flow to the university that has in a sense ridden the faculty's coattails into an industry relationship.

The report wanted both to preserve the university's integrity and to enable a wide range of industry relations. Many of these would be relationships at a distance, with certain boundaries firmly in place. Patent ownership, for example, would almost always be retained by the university and then licensed to a firm under specific conditions. At the same time, the university sought partnerships by promoting the flexibility of these lines. Though easier in theory than in practice, flexibility meant that even those industry partnerships that created conflicts of interest would receive a case-by-case evaluation. Conflicts of interest would usually be managed rather than ruled out in advance, often by apportioning decision making to distinct parties within the university. Financial incentives were now not simply a private benefit to the researcher, to be tolerated if not encouraged, but officially acknowledged by the university as a normal part of university employment and the research process.

· · · *The Familiarity of Commerce* · · ·

We should be precise about what this did and did not mean. Bayh-Dole did not begin or force-feed industry contacts. It did not make the university corporate for the first time. It did not significantly reorient university research away from answering fundamental questions and toward commercial applications. It did not lower academic standards or significantly change the partly intellectual, partly bureaucratic, partly entrepreneurial ways of doing science. It did not mean that university patent and licensing staffs were less vigilant — if anything, they worked harder than ever to hold the line.

Bayh-Dole did mean that the conceptual basis for a general university-industry *distinction* would be harder to use and explain. The act cemented the process in which market forces came to seem the ally of all basic research rather than a frequent obstruction or irrelevance. In the Vannevar Bush era of postwar research, industry and the marketplace were legitimate partners for specific and limited purposes. By 1980 market forces were an appropriate presence in virtually any field that could attract commercial sponsorship, and the process of attracting it would not harm the science. The university, at least in official circles, was losing its ability to articulate two of its historically crucial features. The first was the university as a specifically *non*commercial realm of fundamental investigation. The second was the university as beholden to no interests, able to arbitrate the truth irrespective of which side the money was on.

The Bayh-Dole Act offered the university a renewed centrality to society and the economy. At the same time, the act may have been a symptom of the university's loss of confidence in its own ways. After 1980 it was less likely that university officials would boast about their insulation and remoteness from industrial standards. They were less likely than ever to say something like this: Basic research is the most expensive research, research that industry can't or won't pay for. The university had long served as a means for socializing the cost of very expensive research that was beyond the reach of even the largest corporations. Another way of saying "expensive" is "risky"—the university's most distinctive role is to perform the most exciting, incredible, uncertain research whose financial payoff is unknown. The university is the unique site of the ultra-basic, the most fundamental, the deepest background, the highest of the blue sky. And why not? We see the university as a magnet for the least financially oriented people, the least inhibited imaginers, the big-time intellectual gamblers, the strangest dreamers, the people who love working in the dark. We offer a perfect match: ultra-basic research and super-visionary inventors. We tolerate high risk, we embrace uncertainty, we offer a context for trying anything. And by the way, we therefore shield our people from market incentives. We still keep the books. We just don't let them influence research decisions.

In order to enable this path, the university would have had to embark on a full-scale publicity campaign for deep research. This would have promoted the history of publicly funded, bureaucratically protected breakthroughs that ignored practical goals, the legends of creativity, the lore of the value of *non*market research. University leaders would have described research that could not be driven by market incentives, that was *not* compatible with market returns. They would have had to move from a limited notion of public service to one of serving the entire spectrum of public needs. They would have announced the desirability of the so-cialized work environments that in fact the university had already built, where overhead costs were shared, wealthier fields subsidized worthy but poorer ones, salary differentials were modest, and the good if unexciting salary took a back seat to professional recognition and the experience of the work. Such a path would have reflected the outlook of many if not most researchers already working in the university. It would have sup-ported partnership with industry, but on the basis of principles quite different from those of industry itself. They would be principles we have seen before: professional craft labor, self-organized, in an organization that recognizes strong individual and collaborative agency.

The university neither rejected nor chose this path. University leaders continued to describe the university's role in classical postwar terms — basic research, public service, and intellectual freedom (especially, open publication). They also qualified the difference between each of these terms and its opposite. The university meant research that was basic, public, and open, and yet also applied, commercial and proprietary. The tension within these sets of terms would, over time, begin to blur the uniqueness of the university's intellectual activities and social function. These terms certainly did overlap and needed to be linked in a practical way. But how would the relationship be decided? After Bayh-Dole, mar-ket incentives increasingly stood in for the complicated, social discovery process that the university actually housed. This meant the eclipsing of the role of human development by its economic twin. The university was less likely to be the distinctive defender of the former as it sought scope for the latter. Most of its personnel continued to see the university as unique and to value the university's independence from financial incen-tives. And yet by 1980 the theory of nonmarket research and educational activity was increasingly difficult to generate in the technological domains that led the university.

# CHAPTER 9

. . . . . . . . . . . . . . . . . . . . . . . .

## *Corporate Pleasure and Business Humanism*

If the changes of the 1970s inspired the university to softpedal its non-commercial labors, were there other parties inspired by the same changes to push them? Much of the economy depended on nonprofit work, of course. But among the university's immediate partners, it was for-profit business itself that most visibly embraced partially unmanaged aspects of workplace behavior. Some management theorists worked tirelessly to persuade executives that the crisis in business of the 1970s was in large part a crisis of human development.

### · · · *Business as Fulfillment* · · ·

As the economy continued to change, talk of corporate freedom went mainstream. James K. Sims, the CEO of Cambridge Technology Partners, said that "free access to information eliminates the need for hierarchical management systems that existed before."[1] Michael Hammer, coauthor of *Reengineering the Corporation,* claimed that "organizations need fewer and fewer of better and better people. . . . [Future] jobs are going to be better jobs."[2] Joseph Stiffarm, a track foreman at Burlington Northern, announced the end of autocratic rule. "Now," he remarked, "you have to listen to your men. They have empowered us so much that we don't have to do a job if we think it's unsafe."[3] Fortune 500 companies were claiming to liberate human potential.

   Employee freedom was a core claim of what came to be known in the 1990s as the "new economy," a claim with deep roots in the 1960s and 1970s. The new economy was a mixture of conflicting trends. It emerged from, and did not end, years of wage stagnation, job insecurity, dissatisfaction with life in cubicles, wealth booms for the top 1 percent and 10 percent, and widespread overwork. But if life got tougher, corporate work supposedly got better. As jobs outside the corporate world seemed more difficult, scarce, and despotic, jobs on the inside were said to be more liberating and democratic.

New economy discourse evolved both carrots and sticks. The first carrot involved remodeling the corporation as a global village. In this vision of borderless capitalism, the winning business would offer its citizens wealth and happiness, and national and local governments would be little more than obliging brokers. The second carrot required transforming work into pleasure. The two were assembled into one wholesome but exciting corporate self: the power of communitarian governance was synthesized with the pleasure of individual autonomy.

This synthesis tried to respond to new conditions while building on a combination long at the heart of American liberalism. One major version emerged from the economic crisis of the 1970s. Robert Reich, the first secretary of labor in the Clinton administration, had first become prominent in the late 1970s by advocating Japanese strategies of managing markets. He defined "the next American frontier" as the implementation of stronger forms of flexibility in manufacturing and its management.[4] In *The Resurgent Liberal,* he rejected the idea of freedom as individual autonomy in favor of freedom as interdependence. He reaffirmed corporate individualism as the preeminent national model for the successful self.[5] He instructed us to see "the team as hero": "To the extent that we continue to celebrate the traditional myth of the entrepreneurial hero, we will slow the progress of change and adaptation that is essential to our economic success. If we are to compete effectively in today's world, we must begin to celebrate collective entrepreneurship."[6]

In his most renowned book, *The Work of Nations,* Reich described this corporate individual's ideal suitors: global companies made of "webs of enterprise." These webs consist of delayered or horizontal networks of individuals who come together to generate high-value products. Organizations do not give orders but convene "problem-identifiers," "problem-solvers," and "strategic brokers."[7] Made of self-managed teams and integrated computer systems, these organizations are civil societies that gradually replace the diminishing nation-state. Compared to the new corporation, which offers decentered flexibility, global communications, and world-class systems of knowledge, civil society is in a Hobbesian state of nature. Corporations could act, in this view, as though individuals had come together voluntarily to form enterprise webs for their mutual benefit.

But on the general scale of corporate individualism, Reich was a prudish moralist. Even his title gave him away: nations are not about wealth but work. Unlike many other business writers, Reich conceded the existence of the nonbusiness sector, and even regretted its decline. The last six chapters of *The Work of Nations* are much closer to *Blade Runner* than to *Business Week*. Reich criticized the collapse of public investment and told a tale of two nations, one consisting of workers tied to a shrinking local economy, the other of "symbolic analysts" who, in tandem with their kindred élites around the world, secede from their home society by withdrawing their financial resources into garrison enclaves.[8] Reich's cure for this was the business version of "common culture," which he called "positive economic nationalism," but it was born already rent into pieces by intensified inequality.

Management discourse has always tried to avoid these unhappy endings. It has been less overwhelmed by Darwinist rage than are many national Republican politicians. And its liberal wing has always insisted on the corporate nurturance of individual potential. Getting under way during the business disarray of the 1970s, it reached its culmination during the downturn of the early 1990s. Anyone flipping through an issue of the *Harvard Business Review* for March–April 1994 could find, sandwiched between articles entitled "Putting the Service-Profit Chain to Work" and "What Asbestos Taught Me about Managing Risk," one called "Does New Age Business Have a Message for Managers?" The answer, according to the author, is a resounding yes. "Today's company," she noted, "is a place with the emotional tone of a family or a friendly village, where managers encourage employees to do community work on office time and where everyone creates products that they themselves love. . . . Professionals now fear . . . isolation and loss of self, purpose, and stability. [Thus,] . . . creating meaning for employees may be the true managerial task of the future."[9] The two halves of corporate self-making went together: first, a regenerated community of mutual care, and second, personal meaning and fulfillment.

The business dream was that the two halves are one. The dream gathered much of its power from its liberalism. Conventional wisdom has been quite wrong in assuming that the corporate middle class historically favors laissez-faire liberalisms and fully deregulated markets and individuals, for American liberalism has always been obsessed with collective management. The dream of corporate individualism built on a long tradition in the United States of seeking individualist fulfillment through community harmony. But by the 1980s, this looked possible to business liberals only within the borders of the business firm.

· · · Liberation from Management? · · ·

Writing off society is depressing, but write-offs were a hallmark of the transitional economy after 1970. They were justified by the single most important slogan of the last thirty years of economic change: "creative destruction." As we have seen, the term was coined by Joseph Schumpeter, who used it to define the "fundamental impulse" of capitalism as the perpetual creation of the new — "new consumer's goods, the new methods of production or transportation, the new markets, the new forms of industrial organization."[10] Write-offs were intrinsic to renewal, Schumpeter argued. Capitalist progress was an "organic process," and this meant that its pain and suffering had to be judged "over time" and in the context of the overall system, which was essentially creative. Destruction could be explained by Schumpeter and his followers as a central element of the creative process, which was in turn none other than life itself. One of Schumpeter's most influential ideas was that a firm's real competition is not with existing products but with new or unborn ones. Schumpeter thus enshrined innovation as the indispensable center of strategic and financial planning, explaining both paranoia and destruction through the capitalist life-process.[11]

It's not surprising that Schumpeter should have been embraced by economists and executives, for he took the Depression-era capitalist, widely seen as a ruthless exploiter and authoritarian enemy of social change, and transformed him into a creator of economic life. In the period after 1970, his ideas were reworked by writers such as George Gilder, whose influential tome Wealth and Poverty (1981) ignited the trend toward admiring entrepreneurs because their lives were consecrated to innovation.[12] The successes of the era's most prominent CEOs were increasingly traced to their courageous, farsighted faith in creative destruction — destroying the better to create. Summing up the career of Jack Welch, whose triumphant tenure as CEO of General Electric (1980–2001) coincided with the post-Fordist period, one analyst observed: "What Mr. Welch recognized is that destroying one's own businesses — or knowing when to let go of them and move in a different direction — is a far surer way to generate value and outperform the market than to buckle down and try to protect what you've built, regardless of how grand."[13] Most observers agreed that by the 1970s American business had become rigid and over-weight. Only the destroyers could revive it.

But this bioeconomics of continuous change was far from becoming a popular ideology with the large numbers of people who felt the pain and none of the gain. Some major works of economic synthesis described the destruction and argued that it was not the natural byproduct of innovation. *The Deindustrialization of America* (1982), by Barry Bluestone and Bennett Harrison, argued that enormous blue-collar job losses were the product of unnecessary and wasteful management strategies rather than of economic laws. Ten years later, David M. Gordon traced continuing problems with job insecurity and wage stagnation to American business's preference for con-flictual over cooperative labor relations. Far from shedding layers of man-agement fat, business had increased its proportion of supervisory labor and increased bureaucratic control.[14] Regardless of the specific influence of these books and others like them, they described a lived reality for millions of workers in the United States: the post-Fordist economy put a new stress on lower wage costs and increased labor discipline. A broad section of the workforce experienced more destruction and less creativity.

The economy's antidepressants were not those who celebrated ab-stract, systemic creativity but those who planted creativity in the liberated worker. These were the preachers of the new business self, the ones who unmade *homo hierarchicus* with the corporate version of Huey Long's phrase, "every man a king."[15] Arguably the most important of these was Tom Peters, a management consultant at McKinsey and Co. when he published *In Search of Excellence* (1982). This book synthesized trends that had been gathering momentum for years and brought them into the performance-oriented mainstream of management debate. Peters fol-lowed this book with others such as *Thriving on Chaos* (1987), and at-tempted a full-scale synthesis with *Liberation Management* (1992). Other books in the 1990s went one step further toward becoming helter-skelter picture scrapbooks of business pleasure.[16]

All the books described corporate America as a state of purgatory that could be redeemed by individual passion. Peters would begin by an-nouncing the market death of tyrannical bureaucracy. He would declare the future to be "horizontal" and all successful power to lack hierarchy. He would combine a "just do it" individualism with a "relationship revo-lution" on behalf of flexible collaboration. He would ratify the "shift to softness" while reassuring us that "soft is hard."[17] But most importantly, he would repeatedly extol the new economic order for offering unending personal liberation and total business fun. Peters would never be caught writing an essay for the *Harvard Business Review* with a title like "Staple Yourself to an Order." His motto, to borrow from the comic Kate Clinton, describing her ideal workout, was "no pain . . . no pain." He would celebrate intensive and endless effort, but only of the exhilarating, creative kind, as evidenced by his effusions on "Building 'Wow Factories.'"[18] He would proclaim a French Revolution for the businessperson: liberty ("just do it" in a "world gone bonkers"), equality ("going 'horizontal'"), and fraternity ("toward projects for all").[19]

Peters's revolution rested on the idea that there is no pleasure like corporate pleasure. Liberty is fulfilled in maximum "businessing." He and his associates, Peters says, "are indeed trying 'to business' everyone: to turn all employees into mom-and-pop enterprises."[20] Once fully businessed, the new individualist builds and rebuilds the product in a spirit of endless transformation:

> I beg you to start a list like mine, to go berserk over floors labeled two that should be labeled one, shampoo containers that a pointy-toothed genius couldn't crack, and watch straps that snag sweaters. Don't be like that company secretary and assume it's your fault. . . . I urge you to become aware. Allow design and usability of everyday objects to worm their way into your consciousness. Allow yourself to become irritated, even furious, at the designer instead of feeling frustrated at yourself. It should convince you of how much can be done better, how big a little difference can be, and how important the whole idea is.
>
> The battle for competitive advantage is increasingly over nonobvious sources of value-added.[21]

Peters offered huge helpings of this kind of individualism. Almost all of it claims an emancipation in business much greater than that which his audience could expect to find in its public or private spheres. Tired of politicians, your colleagues, and your friends? The crazy organization is better than all of them. Drop your futile civic labors and follow us.

Peters took for granted that creativity can and should be harnessed to capitalist production. This and other features of his work, like his admiration for the free-market apostle F. A. Hayek's *Fatal Conceit: The Errors of Socialism,* may encourage some of us to dismiss him as Horatio Alger's Ragged Dick reincarnated in a perpetually adolescent Silicon Valley tycoon, now described as though Nietzsche had been in marketing.[22] I will return to these limitations, but they do not invalidate Peters's permanent theme that absolutely anyone can be creative. Peters has been part of a movement in management theory that developed the corporate version of something I would call, in a term that the movement would never use, *mass creativity*. For all its compromises with standard business practice, it has stuck to its defenses of the freedom of individual activity. Reading Peters, I couldn't help notice that any ten pages of his later work offer more passionate denunciations of creativity's bureaucratic death than anything I was hearing on university campuses. Writing like his has raised an odd possibility: what if the most visible defense of craft freedoms against Taylorized control, though focused on the business middle class, had moved out of the university into the business world itself, as idealized by management theory?

## ··· *Humanistic Management* ···

Peters is best understood as a corporate humanist. His ideas build on a long tradition of "humanistic" management theory, one which began to develop out of hostility to the reigning Taylorist paradigm of scientific management.[23] The humanistic branch has generally rested on three fundamental claims. First, people naturally prefer to do good rather than sloppy or minimal work. Second, managers should seek positive work experience as much as they seek production efficiency. Third, positive work experience *and* production efficiency are increased by significant self-management by employees.

Management humanism overlaps with traditional aesthetic humanism, though these domains have had little contact. Both emphasize the free development of individual faculties through independent and collective activities. The management version ties development explicitly to labor, which aesthetic humanism has both encouraged and disparaged. Humanistic management theory has intellectual ties to the business-friendly humanism we observed in the thinking of university leaders like William Rainey Harper, who insisted that personal development was different from and yet served economic growth. Management humanism raised a crucial question, one too often ignored by academic humanists: what kind of free labor would be possible *inside* organizations? Company employees could not withdraw into their own work as many academics could, so coordinated work was taken for granted. How would the employee acquire meaningful autonomy within a managed work process?

Some version of this question received consistent attention in the humanistic management tradition from the time of major early figures like Mary Parker Follett and Elton Mayo down to the present day. It received a boost in the World War II era from European refugees such as Kurt Lewin and the longstanding dean of management theory, Peter Drucker. Under rubrics such as "human relations" management, it housed itself in a range of institutes and consulting groups that included the National Training Laboratories (NTL) in the United States and the Tavistock Institute in Britain. Many influential contemporary management theorists —Rosabeth Moss Kanter, Chris Argyris, Judy Rosener, and R. Roosevelt Thomas, among others—owe their core insights to this tradition. Human relations has been institutionalized as a default position for several generations of personnel professionals. It has also underwritten the work of race, gender, and sexuality consultants who created the field of "diversity management"; many of them, like Elsie Cross, were veterans of the civil rights movement or dissident alumni of institutes like NTL.[24]

In spite of its presence, human relations theory offered many weak and misguided solutions to routinely authoritarian management structures. It was regarded by many managers as naive and soft, and by many critics of business as collaborationist.[25] For all its problems, it was nonetheless focused on workplace autonomy for the main subjects of this book, the college-educated middle classes whose livelihoods were hitched to the corporate world but who did not want their dependence on it to mean the loss of meaning or autonomy on the job.

If we had to identify a major modern source of Peters's tradition, a leading candidate would be a book called *The Human Side of Enterprise* (1960).[26] Its author, the MIT industrial psychologist Douglas McGregor, reduced existing American corporate management to a contrast between a coercive, hierarchical view of human nature that he labeled "Theory X" and its near-opposite, "Theory Y." In 1982 Peters and his co-author, Robert Waterman, invoked McGregor as a founding father of "what was to become the 'human relations' school of management." McGregor, they noted, "termed Theory X 'the assumption of the mediocrity of the masses.'" The masses "need to be coerced, controlled, directed, and threatened with punishment to get them to put forward adequate effort," McGregor wrote. Theory Y, by contrast, assumes "(1) that the expenditure of physical and mental effort in work is as natural as in play or rest—the typical human doesn't inherently dislike work; (2) external control and threat of punishment are not the only means for bringing about effort toward a company's ends; (3) commitment to objec-

tives is a function of the rewards associated with their achievement . . .
(4) the average human being learns, under the right conditions, not only to
accept but to seek responsibility; and (5) *the capacity to exercise a relatively high
degree of imagination, ingenuity, and creativity in the solution of organizational
problems is widely, not narrowly, distributed in the population.*[27] McGregor used
X and Y to avoid reductive labeling, but it's fairly clear that X and Y mark the
spots of a reigning scientific and an insurgent humanistic, even democratic
theory of so-called economic man. Theory Y asserted that self-managed and
relatively egalitarian groups will be as productive as coerced and hierarchical
ones. Command-and-control management could not justify itself by invoking the wisdom of the behavioral sciences. To the contrary, McGregor
justified much flatter and more open organizations on the fundamental level
of human nature itself.[28]

Management humanism was widely popularized by Alvin Toffler's
blockbuster *Future Shock* (1970). Toffler blended the "knowledge industry" theories of Daniel Bell, Fritz Matchlup, Clark Kerr, and others with
cybernetics, communication theory, and a sense of pervasive social transformation indebted to the 1960s. The result was a very early description of
the "new economy" that seemed so new to observers in the mid-1990s.
One of Toffler's central claims was that hierarchical bureaucracies were
gradually being extinguished not by left-wing social movements but by
internal changes in capitalist economies. Technology in general and information technology in particular were revolutionizing social systems and
individual lives; the result was not only revolutionary change, but the
revolutionizing of the pace of change beyond anything in previous human experience:

> As machines take over routine tasks and the accelerative thrust in-
> creases the amount of novelty in the environment, more and more
> of the energy of society (and its organizations) must turn toward
> the solution of non-routine problems. This requires a degree of
> imagination and creativity that bureaucracy, with its man-in-a-slot
> organization, its permanent structures, and its hierarchies, is not
> well equipped to provide. Thus it is not surprising to find that
> wherever organizations today are caught up in the stream of tech-
> nological or social change, wherever research and development is
> important, wherever men must cope with first-time problems, the
> decline of bureaucratic forms is most pronounced. In these frontier
> organizations a new system of human relations is springing up.[29]

The slot-filler would have to molt into creative maturity, would "assume decision-making responsibility," would become empowered and creative. The decline of bureaucracy would mean the massive "humanization" of rational planning.[30] If McGregor supplied the empowerable human raw material, Toffler provided the tidal wave of global change that was sweeping bureaucracy away.

A decade after Toffler, several books consolidated the human relations approach. William G. Ouchi advocated "Theory Z," by which he meant the proposition "that involved workers are the key to increased productivity." How do you involve workers in the right way? Well you start by not assuming, in business's Theory X way, that they are lazy or incompetent. "Productivity, I believe, is a problem of social organization or, in business terms, managerial organization. Productivity is a problem that can be worked out through coordinating individual efforts . . . [and through] taking a cooperative, long-range view."[31] The two general lessons of Theory Z, Ouchi declared, were the need for "trust" in colleagues and "subtlety" in information, especially the inexplicit or informal information that often made the difference between success and failure. Trust and subtlety required clear, continually revised understandings of the complex relationships that characterized the firm. They required *intimacy*.[32] Productivity hinged on better—more intimate, more complex, more supported—group psychology. It hinged on upping mutual involvement. It did not hinge on upping the control or punishment of individuals.

Peters and Waterman claimed that excellent management is part of an indigenous American tradition and need not be an exotic import. Its fundamentals were apparently straightforward: "There is good news from America. Good management practice today is not resident only in Japan. But, more important, the good news comes from treating people decently and asking them to shine, and from producing things that work. Scale efficiencies give way to small units with turned-on people. Precisely planned R&D efforts aimed at big bang products are replaced by armies of dedicated champions. A numbing focus on cost gives way to an enhancing focus on quality. Hierarchy and three-piece suits give way to first names, shirtsleeves, hoopla, and project-based flexibility. Working according to fat rule books is replaced by everyone's contributing."[33] By liberating employee passions from the dimwitted yoke of hierarchical authority, corporations could transcend their floundering Fordist systems.

Ouchi, Peters, Waterman, Rosabeth Moss Kanter, and others boosted human relations' basic participatory insights by intensifying two major features of the tradition. First, they all stressed their financial evidence of the superiority of involved workers. *In Search of Excellence* and *Change-Masters* rested on significant samples in which companies known for progressive human relations policies had their numbers compared to those of a relatively traditional group. Kanter studied forty-seven pairs of companies.[34] Peters and Waterman had a data base of sixty-two American companies which they evaluated according to six measures of long-term financial performance. Having selected "excellent" companies on financial grounds, they then tried to itemize the common features of the group's excellent corporate culture.[35] Ouchi backed up his argument by pointing to the superior financial performance in the 1970s of all of Japanese industry. These writers added to a growing body of research that claimed that involving and empowering employees would help people and profits at the same time.[36]

Second, these writers offered a point-blank targeting of "rational actor" theory that dominated management thinking, economics, and most of the social sciences. Rational actor theory supported the "paraphernalia of modern information and accounting systems, formal planning, management by objectives, and all of the other formal, explicit mechanisms of control characterizing" the conventional firm.[37] It assumed that the best decisions are made on the basis of quantitative measurement, objective detachment, impersonal distance, routinized procedures, and other familiar practices of large bureaucracies. "Western management," Ouchi wrote, thinks that "rational is better than non-rational, objective is more nearly rational than subjective, quantitative is more objective than non-quantitative, and thus quantitative analysis is preferred over judgements based on wisdom, experience, and subtlety." By contrast, Z companies retain financial measures and use them "for their information, but [they] rarely dominate in major decisions. . . . The explicit and the implicit seem to exist in a state of balance."

Though the human relations authors acknowledged that quantitative knowledge has an important role to play, they hated its power to demote and dismiss the "human side" — the relationships, intimacy, and subtlety, the informal and qualitative face-to-face interactive contact on which real knowledge depends. As Peters put it to me, "relative to the dominant B-school paradigm, what Waterman and I were researching and writing about [in 1980] was an attack on structural solutions as the *only* type; we were trying to bring humanity into enterprise."[38] The important insight here involved the treatment of financial factors. Management humanists acknowledged their power and importance while rendering them logically subordinate to human factors. Profit was an index of successful, creative work rather than its driver or standard. Reversing the dominant trend at least in theory, management humanists made economic development dependent on human development.

Peters and Waterman assumed that both kinds of development occurred in groups. They thus tried to replace the rational actor with the social actor. Everyone used to assume, they wrote, that "clear purposes and objectives for organizations exist, and that these can be determined straightforwardly," usually through financial objectives. Everyone used to assume that firms were "closed systems" in which little outside the organization need be considered. Those ideas, they said, should be hauled to the boneyard. They announced a new phase in management thinking as of 1970, one based on *open* systems and *social* actors: "The social view supposes that decisions about objectives are value choices, not mechanical ones. Such choices are made not so much by clear-headed thinking as by social coalition, past habit patterns, and other dynamics that affect people working in groups."[39] Toffler used *The Third Wave* (1980) to weigh in with a similar emphasis on social and interpersonal factors. The new corporation, he wrote, will "combine economic and trans-economic objectives. It will have multiple bottom lines."[40]

By the early 1980s, management humanism had spent decades rejecting Taylorist supervision for the white-collar workplace.[41] It had tried to reform management so as to allow autonomy and satisfaction at work without compromising management's powers of coordination and decision. This work overlapped with John Dewey's efforts to socialize individualism while preserving older forms of autonomy within a complex, organizational society. Their work was drastically limited, though, because the "society" in question was the corporate firm, which led, in figures like Reich and Dewey, to a reluctance to confront the ease with which individual agency is lost in complex systems, even without a Taylorist boss. Peters, however, is less reticent. His version of management humanism comes as close as it ever has to an open attack on the concept of management. At various moments in his work, managerial processes are intrinsically opposed to the craft labor ethos to which he appeals. At these times, revolution against management is the only recourse. At these times, revolution against management flows from the long history of necessary revolts against tyranny. Business means overthrowing the regime, "unabashedly championing revolution, and getting the company anarchists to the barricades." Business is "perpetual revolution": "Whatever you've built, the best thing you can do . . . is to burn it down every few years. . . . Don't change it, but b-u-r-n i-t d-o-w-n."[42] Management is cast as a quasi-royalist despotism that damages individual and commonwealth alike, and must be reduced to ruins.

Peters stayed within the corporate world while repudiating many features of its disciplinary agenda. For him, people are not screwed up; the systems are. People aren't lazy; they are suffocated or even oppressed. It's not your fault; it's the fault of management. You were born creative, so be spontaneous. "Try anything," just do it, grope along like Einstein did since there's an Einstein in you. "The average employee can deliver far more than his or her current job demands — and far more than the terms 'employee empowerment,' 'participative management,' and 'multiple job skills' imply." You too can find one of those bosses who are turning America around by being "oblivious to the hurdles, who assume . . . that people can do damn near anything they have the will to do so long as they don't wait for one more analysis before starting." In short, "Do what turns you on, not what the statistics say is best."[43] Even in his sober youth, Peters insisted on "productivity through people": "There was hardly a more pervasive theme in the excellent companies than *respect for the individual*."[44] In his wilder middle age, Peters insisted on an irrepressible anarchism that challenged centrist syntheses of managed autonomy, whether they occur in industry or in academia.

### · · · *Mired in Middle Management* · · ·

It may seem naive to think that defending autonomous work against financial measures could change the course of business management. It is also true that humanistic management theory was frequently used as a Trojan horse that introduced new pressures in the name of empowerment.[45] While defenses of employee rights do not insure changes in the business system, the failure to defend them can insure that the system stays in place.

Literary labor offers circumstantial evidence for this claim. The job market in literary studies boomed through most of the 1960s and then crashed around 1970. With the exception of the last few years of the 1980s, the market for literature faculty has never come close to the hiring levels of the boom.[46] Undergraduate enrollments have flattened or declined: the critic Louis Menand has reported that the English majors fell from 7.6 percent of all bachelors degrees in 1970 to 4.3 percent in 1997.[47] There has been correspondingly little need for growth in overall faculty numbers. To make matters worse, after 1970 many full-time tenured positions in universities were gradually converted to part-time and untenurable positions, and literary study has been even more subject than other humanities fields to a reduction in its permanent ranks.[48]

Literary studies has of course been caught in the crossfire of various large-scale social forces. I don't want to blame the victims of major market pressures for their troubles. But the university's traditional business model, in conjunction with literature's acceptance of middle-management practices, contributed to the problem.

Even the wealthiest private universities had never achieved financial independence; the large majority of public universities lived at the mercy of economic ups and downs from year to year. Change in the university was dependent on growth: not only was growth the general currency of American business success, but the university had a hard time undoing existing departmental and disciplinary structures and needed to change by adding to them. Universities had direct financial control over few financial variables other than labor costs, which they had sought to minimize as much as any private firm. Low-cost, highly skilled labor was one of the services the university provided to industry, and university-industry ties would be preserved partly for that reason. And as time went on, research universities became less immediately influenced by their liberal arts traditions — which were at many schools the realm of a small minority — and by their example of nonmarket production. When funds and enrollments dropped, administrations used market forces to justify significant cuts.[49]

The time-honored mode of market adaptation is austerity: the least obtrusive way to restore an equilibrium between supply and demand is to cut supply to match a supposedly unalterable demand. This strategy was implicit in literary academia's familiar good-year, bad-year strategies. In good years departments grew and gave some support to emerging or innovative fields. But these additions were treated as electives or options that in bad years could be trimmed. Richard Ohmann summarized this tendency on the basis of a departmental survey from the early 1970s. English departments, he wrote, "have allowed a proliferation of new studies and approaches, new 'relevant' contents and styles — yet without yielding any ground near the professional heart of the curriculum. In all but a few of the 71 institutions he surveyed, [John] Kinnaird found the standard requirements for the English *major* more or less intact. . . . Yet the departments had added dozens of new courses: black literature, ethnic literature, film . . . In short, the opportunity for English departments to reconceive their task has been bypassed in favor of a set of conveniences that preserve *both* the professional habits of a lifetime and the popularity of the department's offerings."[50] This kind of semi-diversification preserves the traditional core, and in any case it takes place only in flush years. In tight years, English departments readily cut supply. Here's Ohmann again: "In 1977 . . . leaders in [English and foreign languages] recommended addressing the crisis either by making the best of a rotten situation (be glad that Ph.D.s unable to find careers will humanize the places where they find jobs), or by changing the services we offer the public (more practical training in literacy and communications, less Culture); or by amending the internal procedures we use to regulate the size of the profession and, thus, its market leverage (reduce graduate admissions, slow down the tenure clock, facilitate early retirement)."[51] English departments cut supply to match market demand, and failed to develop counter-cyclical strategies that might have pulled them out later on. Moreover, English departments tended to cut in the peripheral growth areas while saving the traditional core.

These responses were probably not driven by enrollments. There is no evidence that the demand for Shakespeare or Milton studies grew in proportion to the growth in student population. On the other hand, the growth of related interdisciplinary programs suggested potential growth in demand for the newer fields — film, black studies, Chicano and Latino studies, and women's studies, among others. In addition, students seeking careers in law and business often majored in standard departments of history, economics, sociology, and political science, in part because these provided skills in analyzing the systems of contemporary society; English might have skimmed some of these enrollments with a stronger emphasis on contemporary studies, or on creative skill development, whether in technical writing or composition or literature or journalism. Some diversifications came to pass, but they remained marginal in numbers and influence. The periphery stayed underdeveloped in proportion to likely student interest, which helped to preserve a static core.

The core-periphery model also affected the work of untenured teachers, including grad students, lecturers, or "freeway flyers" being paid by the course. "Nontraditional faculty" grew at a much faster rate than tenured and tenure-track faculty did.[52] Again, this seems like the effect of national and international economic forces, and it to some extent is. But English departments readied sections of their curricula for outsourcing by identifying levels and topics that could allegedly be taught as easily with temporary as with permanent faculty. This occurred in composition, which was relegated to a low-end service function provided by nonresearch faculty, mostly grad students and lecturers.[53] To a lesser extent the same thing occurred in ethnic studies, which were often located in nondepartmental programs that relied on soft money for much of their instructional staff.[54] This was a period in economic history when the professional middle class was beginning to segment according to income level, with knowledge specialists like doctors and lawyers making many times the average incomes of also well-educated service providers like professors and counselors.[55] This divergence was occurring in the university, as salaries in the humanities failed to keep up with those in engineering, sciences, and professional schools.[56] But the same thing was happening within literary studies itself, as a two-tier teaching hierarchy developed. English departments, often without wishing to, endorsed the idea that core disciplines required tenured research faculty while the periphery could make do with temporary staff. The consequence of this, in turn, was that craft labor became the privilege of a distinct faculty minority rather than the precondition of the field as a whole.

Many factors influenced these trends. One was certainly the self-interest that practitioners have in protecting the fields in which they already work. But the one that may have been decisive was the absence from mainstream literary studies of a vision of *organizational* life. The management issues of large research universities were seen as irrelevant to literary study as such. I've argued that indifference to management did not spare literary studies from a managerial unconscious.[57] Quite the contrary: indifference most likely weakened the power of the discipline to confront management in its damaging aspects. A nonmanagerial vision might have insisted on the institutional relevance of unmanaged subjectivity, at least as much as Tom Peters did. It might also have fought financial measures by explicating the practical public value of labor that lacked a product. It further might have confronted organizational forces by seeing them as entities that could be remade by culture and literature and professional artisanal activity, properly self-organized. It might have embraced and let newer fields like ethnic and feminist studies take the lead for the sake of justice, or the social good, or human development. It might have asserted the need for craft-labor conditions, including permanent employment, for all its teachers. It might have, in short, done battle with its own managerial condition.[58]

Many literary academics did do battle: some, for example, advocated passionately for the protection and growth of initially peripheral fields. But they were generally cast as dissidents, were not particularly trusted, and were often seen as a menace to the field's scholarly bedrock. Such disputes are of course normal—change always takes struggle and time. But institutions that require too much struggle and take too long and lose too many innovative thinkers will recover too late. By the early 1980s, most English faculty members had resigned themselves to a job market that was bad enough to threaten their power to reproduce themselves. They assumed that financial measures could not be redesigned and like the hierarchy of fields and administrators was an established fact. They accepted their secondary status in a university that their forerunners had invented.

### · · · *The Absorption of Self-Development* · · ·

Though it's not much comfort, business humanism was also making less of a difference than it had initially planned. As with academic humanism, much of this was beyond its control. The crisis of profitability of the 1970s ultimately intensified attention on financial results rather than working conditions. One crucial tactic that ensued was the "wage squeeze." The wages that had risen steadily by several percentage points each year for the three decades after World War II stopped rising.[59] Another major tactic was the squeeze placed on executives by some powerful shareholders. Usually called the "shareholders' revolt," it forced managers to return more of their cash flow to stockholders.[60] The range of predominant strategies could be summarized as what the sociologist Neil Fligstein called "the financial conception of control." Fligstein concludes that "the financial controls that supported the multidivisional form [became] the chief source of power in the large corporation" after 1960, replacing the "sales and marketing conception of the firm."[61] Financial control was of course exactly what humanistic management was resisting. Given the background of economic uncertainty, financial issues gained rather than lost influence. Theorists of the human factors who had head-on collisions with finance generally suffered the fate of a bicycle meeting a snowplow.

But like the academic humanists, Peters also weakened his own position. The problem can be seen in one of his typical crescendos, this one delivered to a live audience of managers:

> I told you I think words are important. I came across this the other day and I just love this and oh it would make me so happy if you could put this into your language. It's from Guy Kawasaki, who was one of the top software developers for the Macintosh at Apple. And Kawasaki says the objective is simple: turn everyone on your payroll into, quote, a raging inexorable thunderlizard evangelist. I love that. I'm saying look, your boss asked you for MBO's this year. MBO number 1 for 1993: turn the 11 people in my purchasing organization into raging inexorable thunderlizard evangelists.
>
> There are a lot of messages I hope you take out of this discussion, but none of them is much more important in my mind than what I call learning how to use hot words instead of cold words. Learning to take seriously as a business proposition words like weird, crazy, zany, thrill, delight, wow, renegade, traitor, anarchist, raging inexorable thunderlizard evangelist. . . .
>
> I'm now 50 instead of 40 and thinking some different thoughts. I think excellence is as good an idea as I thought it was 10 years ago, except I've redefined it. And let me suggest that maybe this is the way that we should be thinking for a marketplace that has come unglued, that does call for curiosity and imagination. And my definition of excellence today is very simple, nonfinancial, and a one-sentence definition. And that is, would you want your son or daughter to work here? And that to me is the acid test, because the place that could tap the spirit and the courage and the curiosity and the imagination of a young man or a young woman, then the odds are reasonably high that it's a place that can continue to be imaginative in a world that continues to call for more imagination.
>
> Now is a fantastic time. The marketplace is loaded with exciting Japanese products and German products and Swiss products and Swedish products and the Mexicans are coming on strong and the Indians are coming on strong and some people are predicting that China will be the biggest economy in the world by the year 2010 and the nature of products is changing, and it's just fantastic to be in charge of anything.
>
> The beautiful thing about what's going on is that nobody in Japan, nobody in Germany, nobody in the United States, nobody

in Chicago, nobody in San Jose, nobody in Pittsburgh, nobody in Dallas, has a sweet clue as to what the hell they're doing. And since you don't know what the hell you're doing, that means that the only way to screw up is by not trying something. Really. And it's just a wonderful time to try to test to experiment to fail to get fired to be curious to ask questions to be dumb, and that to me is the ultimate joy. That's why we ended up choosing *liberation* as the first word.

It's going to be a hell of a long and tough and bumpy ride. We're going to have to reinvent our country, reinvent our companies, and reinvent ourselves and our careers. But that's a challenge that sounds to me like fun, frankly.

And so my final advice is a) be weird and figure out how to tap the raging inexorable thunderlizard evangelist which I think resides in the hearts and minds and souls of the people in this room.[62]

Note that there is no "B"; there is only "A" — there is only being weird and unleashing the monster that sleeps within. At the same time, in the passage overall, there is nothing but service to the organization. Peters was trying to invent a popular humanism for the middle-class cadres of the corporate world, and to do it with his call to radical personal agency in a revolutionary time. But this agency appears here as the maximum capacity of response to market forces. Craft freedoms are expressed through engagement with the sales process. Liberation takes place through management — through its transmission of financial conditions.

Management humanists like Peters sacrificed even minimal leverage on the economy. They claimed that economic development depended on self-development *and* that self-development was expressed through the economic. They celebrated human development while binding it to business processes. They solved the conflict between the two by making them the same, fusing personal agency with commercial agency, which came to mean the power to respond quickly and flexibly to new economic conditions. Their humanism, with deep roots in American liberalism, all but abandoned political agency, meaning the mode in which individuals rewrite the basic rules of collective order in collaborations *not* ruled by the product. Taking Peters as its paradigm, corporate humanism all but abandoned the combination of individual and collaborative agency that underlies both cultural and political expression.

In this tale of two humanisms, the academic and the business types ignored each other while experiencing parallel fates. At crucial junctures,

both types covered up the conflict between developing persons and developing economies, damaging their ability to offer alternatives. Though
working under fewer constraints, academic humanists through the early
1980s made a crucial case only on their margins — that self-development
occurred outside of markets, was in basic ways noncapitalist. Management humanists didn't help by submitting their newly minted craft workers to the commodity markets as though doing so made no difference.
Much would depend on whether academic humanists could devise *institutions* that supported self-development regardless of market outcome.
But the weakness of both academic and management humanists continued through the era of post-1960s reform.

# CHAPTER 10

. . . . . . . . . . . . . . . . . . . . . .

*Epilogue: The Second Story*

I have been comparing the development of the business, scientific, and humanistic features of the university. The results have suggested that twentieth-century humanist "man" is not first and foremost aesthetic man or historical man or anti-political man but organization man. The reverse is also true: organization man has always had humanist roots, and figures like Tom Peters are only the most visible recent incarnations. I have argued that humanism and management are tied together in conflict: humanist tendencies contain both managerial and anti-managerial elements. Academics, and the middle classes that they produce, exist with a divided consciousness about their organizational lives and the administered world they have made. Academics are neither artists nor bureaucrats but both at the same time. They have *not* transcended their managerial function to become a straightforwardly "creative class."[1] Nor have they remained merely managerial. The drama of the university's development and of the changing economy is shaped by the conflict between these contradictory and yet interconnected impulses, even when, as in chapter 9, the managerial impulse prevails.

This division or doubleness of mind is an effect of university training. For generations, the university fed and fostered the highly managed workplace that followed the first corporate revolution in the nineteenth century. The university adopted, where it did not invent, many features of corporate working conditions. Protected white-collar workers relied directly on often poorly paid employees who did the routine work: for example, both scientific and cultural research throve in proportion to the amount of undergraduate teaching and grading performed by untenured lecturers and teaching assistants.[2] At the same time, university faculty experienced a workplace at least as good as any in American society. In the office, the classroom, the laboratory, the curriculum or admissions meeting, the ostensibly lost ideals of self-managed craft labor continued to exist.

Thus on the one hand, the postwar professional middle class had come to accept managerial hierarchy, restraint, even exploitation as the price of success. On the other hand, most tenured faculty experienced their careers as offering interesting, rewarding work with unusually high levels of freedom, challenge, and security on the job. The university was part of a Taylorizing industrial system that preserved anti-Taylorist conditions on campus. Its faculty could be described as "semi-autonomous wage-earners" who were their own bosses on the job though they had little influence on the overall institution or educational system.[3] This distinctively hybridized university culture, to repeat, shaped and sustained the divisions within middle-class consciousness. The collegiality model is only one example of workplace features that would incline faculty to encourage their imagination about good work rather than suppress it as unreal. In focusing on the university version of middle-class work culture, I have wanted to make visible what we too easily dismiss as a naive or self-dealing petty-bourgeois idealism, even when it belongs to us. The story of the American middle class changes dramatically depending on whether we ignore this divided consciousness or factor in its idealist half.

· · · *First Draft* · · ·

American culture has sponsored a long, distinguished tradition of commentary that elaborates the managerial heart of the modern middle class. William Whyte's *The Organization Man* (1956) and C. Wright Mills's *White Collar* (1956) were pivotal works that confirmed the middle class's image of its productive yet circumscribed social role. Subsequent descriptions of industrial *and* post-industrial society shared a sense that the middle class's mission has been to serve as the expert managers though not the main decision makers of that society. Writers like Daniel Bell, Clark Kerr, and John Kenneth Galbraith continued in the 1960s to remind the middle class about its managerial vocation, confirming the postwar sense that modern managerial society was set in stone. This society, everyone seemed to agree, was enormously intricate and complex, and had to be run by experts in the innumerable subsystems on which prosperity and efficiency hinged. Defense planning, television production, criminal justice, health care, mutual fund management, environmental science, retail sales, auto design, electricity generation, casino operations, book editing, special effects development, urban planning, marriage and divorce, birth and death — every corner of society or private life depended on professional experts and managers to operate and develop them. By 1980 few university graduates could identify features of society or experience that could *not* be improved by expert management.

In 1979 two books added a crucial twist to the managerial story. One of these, Barbara and John Ehrenreich's "The Professional-Managerial Class," collapsed the distinction between professional and managerial functions.[4] The newly anointed PMC consisted not so much of the politically neutral servants of society's technical systems but of a "new class" that like other social classes used its work to advance its class interests.[5] The Ehrenreichs defined this new class as "salaried mental workers who do not own the means of production and whose major function in the social division of labor may be described broadly as the reproduction of capitalist culture and capitalist class relations."[6] Though these interests were sharply distinct from those of the upper classes as well as the lower, the Ehrenreichs saw PMC labor as generally serving the top. They noted that their analysis was inspired by their own repeated experiences of antagonism between the middle-class and working-class members in activist organizations.[7] The consistent, operational feature of the PMC, they claimed, was an "objectively antagonistic relation" to ordinary wage earners that made practical alliances nearly impossible. The PMC's primary service was to manage labor on behalf of capital even when it felt alienated from or opposed to business owners and leaders. Its historical mission was to manage labor without the violence and repression by which capital tried to control labor in earlier times.

As a class, the PMC is not a unified group but, like all social classes, a changing "position within class relations."[8] As a sign of how complicated the PMC's social position was, the essays in *Between Labor and Capital* argued that the PMC sided with capital, and that it was independent of capital, and that at important points it sided with the working class. While some commentators held that these contradictions discredited the idea of a PMC, others saw them as typical of increasingly common "contradictory" class relations.[9] In the context of this book, I would add that the new middle class had been developing for decades in tandem with the rising research university. The university endowed this new class with concrete experiences of craft-labor conditions while helping it place its professional training in managerial service.

I have sought to recenter the story of management on the research university. I have insisted that the university is a major producer of American culture in its own right, and of its middle-class sectors in particular. It has functioned alongside the music and publishing industries, mosques, churches, and temples, Hollywood, Silicon Valley, and the Pentagon, all of which steadily generate ideas, techniques, practices, selves, and ways of life. For the professional middle class, however, the university is arguably more formative and fundamental than any of these, not so much because it operates on younger, more impressionable people as because it is where professional techniques and practices are acquired. It is the university, more than any other institution, that systematically links a student's success with her adaptation to the sensibility and behavior of professional and managerial life.

I have not only argued that the central historical function of the university has been to make these future managers, but have been at some pains to detail what that means — what it means *culturally* to be a university-trained manager, especially in the humanities. In a broad sense this has historically meant a deep comfort with nondemocratic group life, if not an active belief in it. It has meant a willingness to preserve craft labor ideals while directing them toward market production.

I will return to the self-division of the PMC below, but will first note how *parts* of my analysis support and extend the prevailing story about the rise of a managerial class for a managed society. As we know, the research university was created to serve a newly corporate form of capitalism's educational and technological needs, and this service involved adapting to the economic values of that society and creating a large number of cooperative employees to make it work. Cooperation entailed agreement with the emphasis business placed on productivity and efficiency and on economic development as the major purpose of American society. But the university's business sponsors were generally willing for the university to consent only passively, meaning that business influenced the university less through the direct manipulation of financial contributions and governing boards, though these were constant possibilities, than through business culture.[10] Universities were of course multidivisional accountancy-based organizations by the end of World War I, and their financial administration had become complex and burdensome by the end of World War II. The university was not oppositional to corporate capitalism, but developed divided and hybrid approaches to it. The middle classes were not formed in quasi-monastic isolation from economic forces, but were learning at school how to manage them.

Contemporary analyses of business in higher education tend to see business coming onto campus through disciplines that work with business directly. They note the trend of undergraduate enrollments away from the traditional liberal arts and toward vocational and preprofessional programs like business economics.[11] With more historical depth, we can see that business has always been on campus — having helped build it in the first place — and that fields with no connection to business participate in business culture. This has been the case with the liberal arts themselves, where humanism provided some of the crucial elements that allowed managerialism to work as a consent-based, ostensibly liberating middle-class ideology. Freedom, concrete personal experience, and the right to self-development were all essential to the humanization of management in a sense that mixed manipulation with genuine progress toward better work for managers. I have given a number of examples of dueling humanisms in which the version more closely adapted to the ethos of large organizations prevailed: Irving Babbitt and T. S. Eliot over Cardinal Newman and William James, Ransom and Tate over Burke and Dewey. The point of such comparisons is not to polarize figures who have generally retained much influence, but to suggest that institutional norms can be traced to the more strongly managerial side of the humanist tradition.

The research university helped form the American middle class through a distinctive culture that I have called *managerial humanism*. Within this culture, generations of university staff and students learned to stress self-development and to see the economic system as functionally prior to their individual activity and uninfluenced by it. The economy was a given, even in relation to the collaborative labor of the PMC in large organizations. The PMC accepted the independence of the organizational system from human agents and saw its hierarchical form as inevitable. Hierarchy expressed not an unnecessarily instrumental, ultimately political device built by people much like themselves, but necessary differences in human activity. Were we to look for a formula to express managerial humanism, it might be *work without agency*. As craft ideals lost their autonomy from market signals, the market increasingly served as the director of production. Management served the market rather than the craft and its practitioners.

By 1980 members of the university-educated middle class were being asked to see themselves not as the victims of organizational forms but as its beneficiaries. They were not only white-collar dependents but a managerial class with a historic mission. The old middle class had lacked monopoly powers and economies of scale, and was limited economically. Members of the new PMC had a direct pipeline to corporate revenues, and as a result, their economic fortunes were transformed. Their financial self-interest came into full alignment with their managerial function, and this only increased their distance from a vast popular majority that allegedly lacked true culture and the power to govern itself. PMC experts handled everything from foster care placement and criminal prosecution to weapons development and corporate mergers. Their scientific and legal branches were accompanied by a cultural or media branch, which managed public opinion about popular culture.[12] Commentators noted that the American postwar political left had mostly been a middle-class left, and yet this middle class's long-term loyalties opposed the left's mass constituency. It observed the conflicts within the PMC but generally saw the conflicts as resolved in favor of employer and capital interests. There were few explicit alliances with labor. Nor were there alliances that reflected, in this book's terms, a shared advocacy of craft-labor ideals that brought white- and blue- and pink-collar workers together. Most of those that had participated in attempts at such alliances came to see them as doomed.

We could say that by 1980, to be self-conscious as a member of the PMC was to be conscious of one's de facto rejection of craft-labor practices and alliances in favor of expert management. When business prophets like Tom Peters appeared on the scene, their audience consisted of a PMC which had been taught that its conformity was the condition of its security and influence. After 1980 commentators described a professional middle class that redoubled its efforts to leave ordinary Americans behind.[13] The PMC continued to leave racially and economically mixed neighborhoods and schools for exclusive suburbs. The PMC largely supported the tax revolts of the late 1970s and 1980s that reduced their own investment in the larger society. When it was not supporting Republican opponents of an inclusive system of social services — and a majority of white college graduates were now Republicans — it was supporting "new Democrat" versions of the same policies. New Democrats were also noteworthy for attempts to reach out to "ordinary" white voters by offering neither economic justice nor blue-collar uplift but appeals to a resentment of black and other alleged government dependents. These appeals made no attempt to overcome the distance between the working-class targets and the PMC authors of these political strategies but instead reinforced the distance through their patronizing, cynical "realism" and their denial of how much the PMC depended on governmental largesse.[14] The PMC's own intellectuals intensified these mixed feelings and desires, praising the PMC's work ethic while belittling its dissenting impulses.[15]

In fact, these mixed feelings were contained in a class-conscious way. PMC commentators endlessly reiterated the alienation of the middle class not from its bosses but from its subordinates, the working masses, otherwise known as "ordinary Americans." They showed how stray idealism undermined middle-class finances, a realization which would bring the middle class back in line. They described the wishful, unoriginal, and self-defeating nature of PMC revolt. In the midst of this pervasive tale, who could imagine the American middle class giving anything up for basic reform or the general good? They were the intellectuals and opinion makers, so they would simply define reform and the general good as what they were already doing: deregulating markets, shipping jobs overseas, building gated communities, shifting education toward commercial technology. The most decisive strategy for fixing and settling the PMC was to show that it had already split into two more homogeneous classes, an upper PMC that devoted itself to high incomes and other rewards of the market, and a lower PMC that stuck with the "social trusteeship" model and suffered financially.[16]

Of the Ehrenreichs' two main claims about the PMC in 1979 — that it was dissociated from working people, and that it sought independence from capital — only the first survived. Professional and managerial practices no longer seemed to seek meaningful independence from markets and finance. The PMC had virtually ceased to exist as a separate interest in society. Its upper strata formed a classic bourgeoisie, while those downstairs remained managed employees.

Portions of every chapter of this book confirm this story about the rise and fall of the university's middle-class graduates. It is a partial, first-draft narrative, and it goes like this: The university's middle class rose as reformers and socioeconomic managers in the late 1800s, but compromised in ways that led to their cultural and intellectual insignificance a century later. The research university was as important as business and government in engineering these compromises. The business structure of the university meant that it depended on outside funding, and it normalized this dependence for its middle classes (chapter 2). The humanities disciplines, supposedly turning students into free, democratic citizens, lacked the confidence and vision to shape them for an organizational society and tied them to vanished worlds (chapter 3). As management became more central to university life, universities divided administration from education in a way that deprived the faculty of managerial authority over the system. Self-development was a private and not a public principle, associated with solitude rather than organizational life (chapter 4). As educators adopted meritocractic systems, hierarchy and standardized evaluation came to seem the natural expression of middle-class work. Merit was no longer a process of personal unfolding but a measurable performance (chapter 5). After World War II, when mass higher education became a (largely segregated) reality, knowledge production became increasingly distant from teaching; socially important knowledge was esoteric and beyond the powers of the popular mind (chapter 6). Though scholars had developed a version of modern, even radical humanism that imagined democratic agency within organizational life, this was set aside as literary critics wrongly equated aesthetic response with a withdrawal from a manifestly multiracial and multicultural society (chapter 7). Universities had long insisted on the difference between curiosity-driven and commercial research, but by 1980 they had eroded the philosophical and institutional status of nonmarket research (chapter 8). When the university's adult middle classes finally demanded their liberation, that cry arose from management consultants under contract with large, fading corporations and on the market's terms (chapter 9).

If we recall the origins of this story in the years following the Civil War, we can see that it ends up where we thought it would. It is a tale of historical determinism, in which the irresistible rise of corporate capitalism sweeps everything in its wake — the old college, the liberal arts curriculum, the craft-labor system, the independent worker, immigrants and freedpersons, the old rich now forced to build industrial empires, the old middle class now sent to glorified boarding schools where they learned the rules of their new service. Through this history, autonomy and liberty come to seem like echoes of pre-capitalist nostalgia, tokens of personal worth now used to justify special privileges. The compensation for sacrificing autonomy is unprecedented affluence and technological power, improved material lives for the popular majority. Compared to this increased freedom from want, the fate of the liberal arts or the liberal arts university seems a minor issue. Why don't humanities people just adapt like everyone else, everyone else meaning not just finance executives but museum curators and ballet dancers and classical musicians and social novelists and feature journalists and all our other contemporaries whose creative work keeps going just fine? The humanities fields look backward, declining guardians of a grown-up culture, unable to challenge their own second-class status, preferring isolated élitism to disciplinary change, unable to support society's freedom movements though they rested in part on liberal arts values. The university made the professional middle class a complacent and sheltered though hardworking and efficient group, one that has usually seen university training as the basis of its demonstrated superiority, client service as measurable through market returns, and "shock therapy" as a valid treatment for others' ways of life. Craft freedoms were associated with a pleasure principle long since obliterated by corporate capitalism. The framework sought to fit graduates to the business system starting with the half-formed impulses of the research university's Civil War founders. Such are the manifest effects of managerial humanism.

### · · · Second Draft · · ·

But this narrative is only half right. I have not just been showing that the university has played a central role in containing the middle class. I have been showing that the university constantly pushed the middle class out of its subordinate role. A second draft recovers the rest of the story by incorporating other elements of the preceding chapters. The research university has always had enormous experience with business. It has had nearly a century and a half of practice pursuing truth and personal development in the context of economic development. Even in instrumentalist terms, the university was the place where knowledge would determine the shape of economics, and not the other way around (chapter 2). The humanities had a central place in the early university, and rested on a narrative of human emancipation. Though this narrative was ethnocentric and élitist, it recognized itself as realizable through free labor, including artistic craft (chapter 3). The rise of academic management led, among other things, to relative autonomy for academic disciplines and faculty. Organization was the new condition of modern life, but it was compatible with freedom and agency (chapter 4). Freedom and agency were also actively suppressed, as the New Humanism served to do. But cultural criticism generated a wide array of alternatives to the centralized management of cultural tradition: racial pluralism was one, merit defined as craft process was another (chapter 5). After World War II, big science discovered that bureaucratic life could sponsor freedom of invention by sheltering the investigation from the market (chapter 6). Democratic and radical humanism were marginalized by, but survived, a critical mainstream in conceptual and practical retreat from its constitutive social world (chapter 7). Even after the Bayh-Dole Act gave universities financial reasons to commercialize research, universities continued to define themselves as sites of unfettered, curiosity-driven research. The university's autonomy remained a fundamental academic value (chapter 8). By 1980 the PMC had for some time been enduring a crisis of coercion. Even management literature — one branch of it — claimed to endorse a pervasive drive to free up pleasure and autonomy in large organizations. Employees hadn't so much accepted top-down management as they had unhappily endured it. Liberation narratives would have to engage with managerial forms, which would forever reincite these narratives (chapter 9).

This second half of the story reflects middle-class experience if not its standard history. This second half is rarely recognized as such: even the relatively sympathetic Ehrenreichs failed to develop their account of subjective PMC goals. Praise of middle-class virtues has appeared most frequently on the political right and among those who seek the right's approval. Many of these virtues are in fact not virtues to the center and left, who have correctly questioned the frequent insularity of the university, its slowness in embracing racial integration, its rigid disciplines, its suspicion of social movements and non-academics, and its dependence on America's boardrooms. All these criticisms are rightly lain at the door of the PMC who runs the university for its particular benefit. And yet the criticisms wrongly sever the PMC from its own progressive tradition and from its partial forms of freedom, ones which it has been taught to suspect, and which it thus neglects.

Part of the problem is the first, incomplete draft of this story, which by now has become a self-fulfilling prophecy: the PMC gates its academic and other communities because it learns to forget its interest in everything but self-interest, such as its interest in freedom and justice and serving society. I have focused on managerial humanism in this book because it is the foundation of the first draft that does this damage. I noted above that the effect of this outlook might be summarized as work without agency. Another way of saying this is that managerial humanism has suppressed what we might call a craft-labor approach to management. This approach does not mean the denial of managerial forms or disengagement from them, which have been strategic and intellectual disasters. It means the opposite: seeing management as constituted by, and changeable through, work as an active and constitutive process. Craft-labor management means not replacing management with self-management, but overcoming this opposition by building large-scale managerial systems on craft-labor practices.

The university has simultaneously preserved the craft impulse and cast it as backward in relation to advanced economic life. It has maintained a false opposition between craft labor and modern organization, helping organizations to isolate an artisanal independence that they cannot do without. The university's crucial move has been to cast craft desires as important but preliminary to one's actual work, as private and bourgeois, as preoccupied with self-development and happiness as opposed to progress, efficiency, and justice. Literary criticism has played its part, describing the great artist as a (rare) agent and the critic as a watcher, reader, and scribe, to say nothing of the general public whose concern for practical affairs casts doubt on its cultivation. The university became the instrument of a great dissociation in which the middle class came to see itself as an entitled servant class by learning to distrust its craft impulses even as it preserved them as a special privilege and private indulgence. Modernity, through the university, became the condition in which the middle classes were convinced that non-instrumental thought and work have been exhausted. Economic determinism and other symptoms of modernity arose from the PMC's loss of belief in the historical agency of all members of a culture, themselves included, which in turn flowed from the dissociation of craft and management, of art and the social processes of organizations.

Management is neither good nor bad: it depends on whether it reflects the agency of its members. Measuring agency is a complex matter of case-by-case interpretation, one that must be referred in part to the experiences, interests, and pleasures of the members of the system. Agency requires that these members in fact be authors: good management is that which starts from the cadres' insistence on their right to — the fact of — their agency in the making of the managerial condition.

A renewed PMC would need to act in relation to the other working classes of society, to see itself as a working class in the craft senses I have discussed. Its special sociocultural function is managerial, and its renewal would require taking management back as its own invention. Such a readoption of management would require the university's faculty and staff to recognize their own labor as the craft that has made and remakes managerial systems day by day. Such a readoption would require that they recover a sense of their own agency in the operation of these systems, and in the making of their social effects. Such a readoption would require them to see their inner and their organizational lives as mutually created, as different but indissociable, as private and public at the same time. Such a readoption would require the PMC to see its managerial work as craft, as a generative activity that makes the managerial world through a continuing process in which the individual is made as well.

Similarly, humanism is neither good nor bad: it depends on whether the strain in question confronts or evades the challenges of managerial systems. Liberal humanism does not confront managerial life, though I've praised it for its insistence on autonomy and some related qualities. My preferred academic kind took its early form through William James and John Dewey, among others: I've called it democratic humanism and radical humanism. The radical humanist saw that freedom is a feature not only of individual lives but of societies: the freedom that finally matters is mass freedom in which freedom requires its own extension to the entirety of the society in which it operates. The concept of mass higher education following World War II was a down payment on this kind of freedom, though many of the later payments were never made. The radical humanist held that freedom expresses itself as free labor, a fundamentally social activity that constructs selves and organizations alike. The radical humanist regarded managerial systems as the product of collaborative labor rather than as predetermined social system, one that could be remade if necessary. The radical humanist insisted that the PMC recognize and use its own agency within expert systems as it emerges from its everyday work.[17]

Radical humanism has attempted to reassemble pieces of PMC experience that the university, like the business world, had separated. Academics were attracted to ideas of self-managed craft and nonmarket investigation; they pursued them individually *and* regarded them as impractical or marginal to public life, best suited to exceptional people at the top of their fields. The strong forms of intellectual independence were less a core value than a privilege, the result of merit rather than its logical cause. Knowledge came to be seen as dependent on complex managerial structures far more than on subjective states of independence. Academic freedom remained an important value, but it was constituted by procedural safeguards rather than by the actual work process of individuals or groups. As an academic subject, literary study was increasingly defining itself as a provider of skills and evaluations more than states of liberty and collaborative self-governance that might lead to genius. In contrast, the radical humanist held that the managerial condition, though pervasive, was unnecessary, the result of a first-draft narrative, the result of dissociation and forgetting. Elements of this radicalism circulated at the highest levels of the university, which continued to stand for an intellectual autonomy forever on the verge of collegiality.

By the 1980s leaders in both academia and business were faced with a difficult challenge. How would free inquiry be subject to market tests and product pressures and yet remain independent? How would the university's two missions — economic and personal development — stay distinct if they were intertwined? How could academic labor be reconciled with knowledge management? How could the university change as its student and faculty became racially and culturally more diverse, as its class composition gradually widened, as some of its disciplines reflected new social movements?

Good answers would depend on the much-postponed confrontation between the university's middle classes and their own organizational life. That confrontation would be propelled by humanism's radicals, those holding out for relatively unmanaged individual agency within the social processes in which knowledge was always produced. By 1980 this radicalism was beginning to find a place at the table. Feminist and ethnic studies reminded the university of the ties between the progress of knowledge and the emancipation of humanity. Poststructuralist thought reconnected individual and systemic phenomena. Various advances in critical theory allowed work activity to be understood as process-based, nonessentialist, operating without linear determinants. Technology transfer raised new questions about the world-making power of academic knowledge. I will consider the rest of my second story in a sequel to this book, but we can already see the enormous potential for the research university to take a central role in a range of positive developments, with its humanities disciplines reassembling the basis of a democratic society — expertise reconnected to craft, human development at the center of an organizational world.

# NOTES

. . . . . . . . . . . . . . . . . . . . . . . .

## Chapter 1

1 The authors continue: "The managers of higher education's mini-cities must oversee a rapidly expanding infrastructure that includes security and police; real-estate acquisition, management, and development; budgeting and finance; legal services; human resources; technology and information systems; public affairs, development, and alumni relations; community relations; sometimes hospitals and medical centers; and a host of other business services." Marvin Lazerson, Ursula Wagener, and Larry Moneta, "Like the Cities They Increasingly Resemble, Colleges Must Train and Retain Competent Managers," *Chronicle of Higher Education*, 28 July 2000, A64.

2 Blair Sheppard, Duke Corporate Education, conversation with the author, Duke University, 24 July 2000.

3 Manuel Castells, *The Rise of the Network Society*, vol. 1 of *The Information Age: Economy, Society and Culture* (Malden, Mass.: Blackwell, 1996), 22. The Touraine citation is Castells's translation from *Qu'est-ce que la démocratie?* (Paris: Fayard, 1994), 168 (emphasis omitted). Castells continues: "I understand by identity the process by which a social actor recognizes itself and constructs meaning primarily on the basis of a given cultural attribute or set of attributes, to the exclusion of a broader reference to other social structures. Affirmation of identity does not necessarily mean incapacity to relate to other identities (for example, women still relate to men), or to embrace the whole society under such identity . . . But social relationships are defined *vis-à-vis* the others on the basis of those cultural attributes that specify identity" (22).

4 For an especially useful discussion of these trends, see Steven Brint, *In an Age of Experts: The Changing Role of Professionals in Politics and Public Life* (Princeton, N.J.: Princeton University Press, 1994). Brint analyzes "the triumph of the idea of professionals as agents of formal knowledge over the older idea of professionals as 'trustees' of socially important knowledge" (5). Agents of formal knowledge are also more likely to focus on finding the highest market value for

their skills instead of on social results. Brint argues, following Eliot Freidson, that professions had rested on "an *occupational principle* of authority, based on ties to universities and organizations of practitioners. This occupational principle serves as an alternative to the more common *administrative principle* of organization, based on hierarchical authority" (6). The university is increasingly divided between these two, in part because it remains rooted in the former.

## Chapter 2

1 See Immanuel Kant, *The Conflict of the Faculties*, trans. Mary J. Gregor (1794; Lincoln: University of Nebraska Press, 1992). For influential modern accounts of the German ideal, see François Lyotard, *The Postmodern Condition: A Report on Knowledge* (1979; Minneapolis: University of Minnesota Press, 1984), and Bill Readings, *The University in Ruins* (Cambridge: Harvard University Press, 1997), chapters 3–4.

2 John Jay Chapman, "The Harvard Classics and Harvard," *Science* 30 (1909): 440; cited in Laurence Veysey, *The Emergence of the American University* (Chicago: University of Chicago Press, 1970), 346.

3 Alfred D. Chandler Jr., *The Visible Hand: The Managerial Revolution in American Business* (Cambridge: Harvard University Press, 1976), 1, 3.

4 Albert H. Teich, "The Outlook for Federal Support of University Research," in Roger G. Noll, ed., *Challenges to Research Universities* (Washington: Brookings Institution Press, 1998), 89. For the higher figure, see Stuart W. Leslie, *The Cold War and American Science: The Military-Industrial-Academic Complex at MIT and Stanford* (New York: Columbia University Press, 1993), 1; Greenberg, *Science, Money, and Politics: Political Triumph and Ethical Erosion* (Chicago: University of Chicago Press, 2001), table 4: Federal Obligations for Academic R&D, by Agency, 1970–1999, pp. 484–85.

5 Roger G. Noll, "The American Research University: An Introduction," in Noll, ed., *Challenges*, 25.

6 Sheila Slaughter and Larry L. Leslie, *Academic Capitalism: Politics, Policies, and the Entrepreneurial University* (Baltimore: Johns Hopkins University Press, 1997), is probably the best single large-scale synthesis now available of overall economic trends in higher education. Slaughter and Leslie use qualitative and quantitative data on the subject, in this case compared across four English-speaking countries.

7 Slaughter and Leslie, *Academic Capitalism*, 7–8.

8 David F. Noble, "The New University," speech to the California Faculty Association, 1999.

9 For a relatively early modern lament about business opportunities compromising a faculty's commitment to their universities, see A. Bartlett Giamatti, "Free Market and Free Inquiry" (1982), reprinted in *A Free and Ordered Space: The Real World of the University* (New York: W. W. Norton, 1988), esp. 264–65. At the time of writing, Giamatti was president of Yale University.

10  Albert H. Teich, "The Outlook for Federal Support of University Research," in Noll, ed., *Challenges*, 89.

11  See for example Jurgen Herbst, *From Crisis to Crisis: American College Government, 1636–1819* (Cambridge: Harvard University Press, 1982): the "prevailing view of American colonial colleges and private and primarily religious institutions has obscured their status as civil corporations. It has made it difficult to see the importance of the Great Awakening and the growing religious heterogeneity of the colonies in strengthening public supervision of the colleges during the eighteenth century. . . . It has prevented an appreciation of just how radical an innovation the American private college was when it first emerged at the end of the eighteenth century in reaction to the early moves for state universities during the Revolution" (x). The history of the colonial college is at the very least a three-sided struggle among religious, civic, and commercial interests.

12  Frederick Rudolph, *The American College and University: A History* (New York: Alfred A. Knopf, 1962; Athens: University of Georgia Press, 1990), 208–9.

13  *Trustees of Dartmouth College v. Woodward*, 17 U.S. 518 (1819) at 563.

14  *Dartmouth* at 696. Justice Story continued to discuss grants: "The truth is, that the government has no power to revoke a grant, even of its own funds, when given to a private person, or a corporation for special uses. It cannot recall its own endowments granted to any hospital, or college, or city, or town, for the use of such corporations. The only authority remaining to the government is judicial, to ascertain the validity of the grant, to enforce its proper uses, to suppress frauds, and, if the uses are charitable, to secure their regular administration through the means of equitable tribunals, in cases where there would otherwise be a failure of justice" *Dartmouth* at 698.

15  William G. Roy, *Socializing Capital: The Rise of the Large Industrial Corporation in America* (Princeton, N.J.: Princeton University Press, 1997), 282. For a substantial reading of the *Dartmouth* case in the context of college governance, see Herbst, *From Crisis to Crisis,* chapter 17. Brook Thomas also concludes that after *Dartmouth*, "new corporations of all kinds could appeal to their original charters as sacred contracts under the law, not to be altered by legislative attempts to control them," *Cross-Examinations of Law and Literature: Cooper, Hawthorne, Stowe, and Melville* (Cambridge: Cambridge University Press, 1987), 49.

16  William Warren Ferrier, *Origin and Development of the University of California* (Berkeley: Sather Gate Book Shop, 1930), 205.

17  Verne A. Stadtman, *The University of California, 1868–1968* (New York: McGraw Hill, 1968), 64.

18  Ferrier, *Origin and Development*, 355, 361, 357. For a more comprehensive account, see Stadtman, *The University of California,* chapter 6.

19  Herbst, *From Crisis to Crisis,* 241. Everything I've read confirms Herbst's astute summary of the early connection between industry and university: "the Dartmouth case [had] recognized the rights of nonpublic college corporations to legal protection equal to that accorded to private business corporations. It recognized that colleges, as a means for development, were as important as

business corporations. . . . As a result, the distinctions of status between education and business began to grow dim . . . A passion for economic expansion and development motivated both business and education and placed private venture capitalism next to government as the custodian of the public weal. Higher education found its place in both the private and the public spheres."

20 For the example of the University of California, see John A. Douglass, *The California Idea and American Higher Education: 1850 to the 1960 Master Plan* (Stanford: Stanford University Press, 2000), especially chapters 2–3.

21 Rudolph, *The American College and University,* 219.

22 Ibid., 184.

23 Ibid., 185.

24 Ibid., 186–87.

25 On early UC financing, see Stadtman, *The University of California,* chapter 8.

26 Although Cornell originated with Ezra Cornell's private endowment, "his gift of $500,000 toward the founding of the university secured for it the proceeds of New York's federal land grant, thus providing the new institution with an unusually solid financial base for this period." Roger L. Geiger, *To Advance Knowledge: The Growth of American Universities, 1900–1940* (New York: Oxford University Press, 1986), 6.

27 Veysey, *The Emergence of the American University,* 84.

28 Ferrier, *Origin and Development,* 336.

29 Act of 2 July 1862, ch. 130, 12 Stat. 503, 7 U.S.C. 301, Sec. 4. A web text is available at http://www.reeusda.gov/1700/legis/morrill1.htm.

30 Ferrier, *Origin and Development,* 43.

31 Laurence Veysey offers the fullest modern description of the decentralized university, and has influenced my thinking at a number of points.

32 Geiger, *To Advance Knowledge,* 40 and appendix C.

33 Veysey, *The Emergence of the American University,* 356. The Eliot quotations appear on this page.

34 Geiger, *To Advance Knowledge,* 40. "In their annual reports the presidents consistently underscored each year's progress, gave statistics on the geographical extent of the institution's drawing power, made impressive comparisons with the recent past, and infrequently rationalized a temporary reversal" (13).

35 "The proportion of funds spent on faculty salaries as compared with those spent on administration at Harvard remained about constant between 1868 and 1903." Veysey, *The Emergence of the American University,* 307. I have been unable to find reliable figures on the growth of administration relative to enrollments and endowments. A partial exception is Marx, "Some Trends in Higher Education," *Science* 29 (1909): 784 and table IV.

36 Veysey, *The Emergence of the American University,* 305–6.

37 Ibid., 306; Geiger, 16.

38 William Rainey Harper, *The Trend in Higher Education* (Chicago: University of Chicago Press, 1905), 163, 161, 177.

39 Geiger, *To Advance Knowledge,* appendix C; Chandler, *The Visible Hand,*

168; William G. Roy, *Socializing Capital: The Rise of the Large Industrial Corporation in America* (Princeton, N.J.: Princeton University Press, 1997), 233.

40  Geiger, *To Advance Knowledge,* 13. Half was the recommended proportion of income from tuition during this period (47).

41  Geiger, *To Advance Knowledge,* 273. Thirty years later these figures were still 75 percent for Wisconsin and 80 percent for California.

42  Geiger, *To Advance Knowledge,* 42, 47.

43  Rudolph, *The American College and University,* 194.

44  Between 1981 and 1999, faculty numbers grew 46 percent nationwide, while part-time faculty totals grew 76 percent. Eugene L. Anderson, *The New Professoriate: Characteristics, Composition, and Compensation* (Washington: American Council on Education, 2002), 1.

45  Taylor and scientific management are covered by an enormous literature. An especially useful overview can be found in Daniel Nelson, *Managers and Workers: Origins of the Twentieth-Century Factory System in the United States, 1880–1920,* 2d ed. (Madison: University of Wisconsin Press, 1995), chapter 4. Taylor describes his interest in efficiency through "close, intimate, personal cooperation between the management and the men" in *The Principles of Scientific Management* (1911; New York: W. W. Norton, 1967), chapter 1.

46  "After the war, the large general-purpose foundations led the way in providing voluntary philanthropic support explicitly for university research. Most important, over the long run the extramural support for university research tended to flow to those institutions that had most successfully developed their research capabilities." Geiger, *To Advance Knowledge,* vii.

47  Clyde W. Barrow, *Universities and the Capitalist State: Corporate Liberalism and the Reconstruction of American Higher Education, 1894–1928* (Madison: University of Wisconsin Press, 1990), 61–71.

48  White and Gilman are cited in Burton J. Bledstein, *The Culture of Professionalism: The Middle Class and the Development of Higher Education in America* (New York: W. W. Norton, 1976), 321, 292.

49  Ibid., 293.

50  Ibid., 289.

51  David F. Noble, *America by Design: Science, Technology, and the Rise of Corporate Capitalism* (New York: Alfred A. Knopf, 1977), 130.

52  Geiger, *To Advance Knowledge,* 176. Geiger observes that "there are no reliable figures for corporate support before the IRS began tracking these deductions in 1936."

53  Ibid., 191.

54  Noble, *America by Design,* 122–23.

55  Ibid., 123: "The purpose of the system . . . was to enable the universities to keep abreast of the changes in the industries and to enable the manufacturer to obtain needed expertise."

56  Henry Etzkowitz, "Bridging the Gap: The Evolution of Industry-University Links

in the United States," in *Industrializing Knowledge*, ed. Lewis M. Branscomb, Fumio Kodama, and Richard Florida (Cambridge: MIT Press, 1999), 203.

57 Noble, *America by Design*, 136.

58 Ibid., 138.

59 Ibid., 143.

60 See Rebecca S. Lowen, *Creating the Cold War University: The Transformation of Stanford* (Berkeley: University of California Press, 1997).

61 In *To Advance Knowledge*, Geiger writes that by the turn of the century, universities "increasingly employed organization and foresight in order to stimulate, solicit and channel existing eleemosynary possibilities"; they no longer treated individual philanthropic gestures as acts of providence. "The field in which these energies were unloosed can be broken into three components . . . they were the great foundations created by Andrew Carnegie and John D. Rockefeller, major individual givers who commanded the vast personal fortunes of the day, and the increasingly numerous and prosperous graduates of these universities" (43). The Carnegie Corporation appeared in 1911, offering $125 million "to promote the advancement and diffusion of knowledge and understanding among the people of the United States"; Rockefeller's $182 million was designated in 1913 "to promote the well-being of mankind throughout the world". Universities benefited enormously from these funds but never controlled them. "When the interwar period is viewed as a whole, the foundations appear as the most dynamic element in the research system. They warmed to the cause of university research in the mid twenties, and the volume of such grants then rose to a peak by the end of the decade" before declining in the 1930s (171). "These arrangements placed enormous resources in the hands of the trustees and staff and gave them great latitude to determine how these broad purposes might be served" (143).

62 Carol Gruber, *Mars and Minerva: World War I and the Uses of Higher Learning* (Baton Rouge: Louisiana State University Press, 1975), 28.

## Chapter 3

1 U.S. Commission on Education, *Report* (1889–90) II:1143, cited in Laurence Veysey, *The Emergence of the American University* (Chicago: University of Chicago Press, 1970), 13–14.

2 The position is a composite, one ventriloquized by advocates of a new university in "Boys of California," *The Pacific*, cited in William Warren Ferrier, *Origin and Development of the University of California* (Berkeley: Sather Gate Book Shop, 1930), 231.

3 Philip Lindsley, Henry Tappan, and Gilman are cited in Frederick Rudolph, *The American College and University: A History* (New York: Alfred A. Knopf, 1962; Athens: University of Georgia Press, 1990), 214, 219–20, 273–74.

4 Veysey, *The Emergence of the American University*, 257.

5 See Veysey, *The Emergence of the American University*, and note 13, below. As another more recent example of the general story, see Christopher J. Lucas.

Specialization, he writes, was allied with "yet another social movement that originated in the latter half of the nineteenth century and has continued virtually undiminished ever since: a drive towards the 'professionalization' of occupations and vocations. . . . The Morrill Acts of 1862 and 1890 supplied the opening wedge. If agricultural pursuits required formal preparatory training in the university, and 'mechanics,' or engineering, was also to become an academic discipline, the same logic could be applied to practically any other vocation with equal force. Business administration, journalism, nursing, teacher education, library science, home economics, and the domestic arts — all began clamoring for a place within the university. If the university as a seat of learning was to be the place where the specialized knowledge required by emergent professions would be acquired, no occupation aspiring to recognition as a true profession wanted to be left out. . . . What few anticipated was the extent to which professional training would begin to expand and encroach upon general undergraduate education." *Crisis in the Academy: Rethinking Higher Education in America* (New York: St. Martin's, 1996), 67, 69.

6  For a useful overview of the concept of liberal culture in the nineteenth century, see Veysey, *The Emergence of the American University,* chapter 4.

7  This view is nicely encapsulated by Gerald Graff: "The story of academic literary studies in America is a tale not of triumphant humanism, or any single professional model, but of a series of conflicts that have tended to be masked by their very failure to find visible institutional expression. This emphasis on conflicts is seen in the successive oppositions that organize my narrative: classicists versus modern language scholars; research investigators versus generalists; historical scholars versus critics; New Humanists versus New Critics; academic critics versus literary journalists and culture critics; critics and scholars versus theorists." *Professing Literature: An Institutional History* (Chicago: University of Chicago Press, 1987), 14.

8  For a recent detailing of this argument, see Julie A. Reuben, *The Making of the Modern University: Intellectual Transformation and the Marginalization of Morality* (Chicago: University of Chicago Press, 1996), chapter 7. Similarly, John Guillory claims that "the New Criticism's doxical failure and institutional success oriented its representation of literature toward *orthodoxy,* toward an increased investment in the university as an institution taking over some of the cultural functions of the church." *Cultural Capital: The Problem of Literary Canon Formation* (Chicago: University of Chicago Press, 1993), 140.

9  Gerald Graff and Michael Warner, Introduction, *The Origins of Literary Studies in America: A Documentary Anthology,* ed. Graff and Warner (New York: Routledge, 1989), 11.

10  For some quotations of characteristic conservative views, see Richard Ohmann, *English in America: A Radical View of the Profession* (New York: Oxford University Press, 1976; Hanover, N.H.: University Press of New England, 1996), 248–49.

11  A sampling of these views: Bruce Kuklick writes, "'Our' humanities, as they

came into existence from 1890 to 1920, composed the least worldly leavings in the university, after the hiving off of the social sciences. The old moral philosophy spawned all those disciplinary studies of the human world that most easily fit the stress of the new universities on applied science. What was left could not be easily applied and was justified as being the home of eternal truths; what was left had no obvious extrinsic value and was often, therefore, legitimated because of its absolute value." "The Emergence of the Humanities," in *The Politics of Liberal Education*, ed. Darryl J. Gless and Barbara Herrnstein Smith (Durham: Duke University Press, 1990), 209. Laurence Veysey states that "liberal culture thrived most splendidly in the classroom. The men who sought to combine its values with those of administration seemed doomed, before 1910, either to complacent mediocrity or else, in the case of Woodrow Wilson, to the frustrations of failure." *The Emergence of the American University*, 233. John Higham concludes, "Instead of bringing a larger dimension into specialized thought, the champions of liberal education for the most part concentrated on holding their own within the setting in which they felt at home: the undergraduate college." In doing so, they conceded to specialists the control of graduate and professional studies. "The Matrix of Specialization," in *The Organization of Knowledge in Modern America, 1860–1920*, ed. Alexandra Oleson and John Voss (Baltimore: Johns Hopkins University Press, 1979), 6. Generally speaking, college leaders argued that true liberal culture could be found only in the college, while university leaders claimed that liberal culture could also be found in the university, in successful coexistence with research specialization.

12  Caroline Winterer, "Victorian Antigone: Classicism and Women's Education in America, 1840–1900," *American Quarterly* 53 (March 2001): 71.

13  Benjamin Ide Wheeler, "The Liberal Education," *The Abundant Life*, ed. Monroe E. Deutsch (Berkeley: University of California Press, 1926), 179–81. Wheeler offers a sweeping, developmentalist history: "The ideals of the German university laid hold upon us first in the [eighteen-]sixties, then with increasing strength in the seventies and eighties. . . . The college was tending fast toward absorption in the specialized subjects, and the old ideals of the liberal culture shrank back into the freshman and sophomore years, disputing the ground as they retreated, but slowly and surely yielding in a failing cause. . . . The process of jack-screwing up the college into the university was held in check by the inertia of the many, and especially by the vested interests of the 'small colleges.' . . . The upshot of the whole movement has been that just at the time when the old liberal culture and its adaptability to American uses has been called into question, the type of educational institution which stood to represent it has seemed to be preparing to exit from the scene."

14  Tony Davies, *Humanism* (London: Routledge, 1997), 130–31.

15  For a critique of the anti-political agenda of 1950s humanism, see Ohmann, *English in America*. Later critiques will be considered in later chapters.

16  Davies, *Humanism*, 131.

17  My preferred definition is that of Barbara and John Ehrenreich: the PMC, they

wrote, has an "objectively antagonistic relation to another class of wage earn-ers." It is distinctive to monopoly capitalism, which was forming itself as the research university was taking root after the Civil War. I will, however, contest the second part of this definition, in which the PMC consists of "salaried mental workers who do not own the means of production and whose major function in the social division of labor may be described broadly as the reproduction of capitalist culture and capitalist class relations." Barbara and John Ehrenreich, "The Professional-Managerial Class," in *Between Labor and Capital,* ed. Pat Walker (Boston: South End Press, 1979), 9–10, 12.

18  One of the best explications of dialectical criticism remains the final chapter of Fredric Jameson, *Marxism and Form: Twentieth-Century Dialectical Theories of Literature* (Princeton, N.J.: Princeton University Press, 1971), 306–416. Mar-shall Berman provides some useful distillations. Writing of Marx, he notes, "We encounter a problem we have met before: the tension between Marx's critical insights and his radical hopes. . . . Some readers may be inclined to take only the criticism and self-criticism to heart, and throw out the hopes as utopian and naive. To do this, however, would be to miss what Marx saw as the essential point of critical thinking. Criticism, as he understood it, was part of an ongoing dialectical process. It was meant to be dynamic, to drive and inspire the person criticized to overcome both his critics and himself, to propel both parties to-ward a new synthesis. Thus, to unmask phony claims of transcendence is to demand and fight for real transcendence. To give up the quest for transcendence is to put a halo on one's own stagnation and resignation, and to betray not only Marx but ourselves." *Adventures in Marxism* (New York: Verso, 1999), 137.

19  One of the few weaknesses of Veysey's book is his tendency to embed the views of humanists in the context of their character flaws or institutional defeats, thus strewing his history with annoying malcontents fighting a lost cause. See the discussion of Woodrow Wilson in chapter 4 and the discussions of William James, George Santayana, Thorstein Veblen, and other "misfits" in chapter 7. Recent revisionist histories have offered a clearer picture of humanism's un-broken impact on literary studies. Gerald Graff argued in *Professing Literature* (1987) that the history of literary studies consisted of the continuous interaction among generalist and specialist models, among others, such that the generalist-humanist position remained a continuous presence. The historian Julie A. Reu-ben challenged the "revolution" model in which the research university replaced the old college; she showed that the university hung on to much of the old college mission of making individuals. Reuben writes, "My research indicates that university reformers continued to view piety and moral discipline as one of the aims of higher education, but wanted to replace older, authoritarian methods with new ones." *The Making of the Modern University,* 12.

20  *Oxford English Dictionary.*

21  Even sympathetic modern scholars stress the dullness of actual liberal arts cur-ricula. See for example Graff, *Professing Literature,* 36: "The college teaching of English literature in the preprofessional era suffered from the same limitation

marking the teaching of the classics: the routine of study obscured the theory supposedly justifying it. This was not surprising, since the earliest methods of teaching English literature were copied from those used to teach the classics. Literature was subordinated to grammar, etymology, rhetoric, logic, elocution, theme writing, and textbook literary history and biography — everything, a later generation would complain, except a truly literary study. And whatever the emphasis, the recitation method remained in force" (36). See also Robert Scholes, *The Rise and Fall of English: Reconstructing English as a Discipline* (New Haven: Yale University Press, 1998).

22 "In later use, of condition, pursuits, occupations: Pertaining to or suitable to persons of superior social station; 'becoming a gentleman'" (*O.E.D.*). This is partly the responsibility of the enormously influential nineteenth-century humanist John Henry Newman, who tended to use "liberal knowledge, or a gentleman's knowledge," interchangeably. *The Idea of a University* (Oxford: Clarendon, 1976), discourse V, p 103.

23 My thanks to Wolf Kittler, professor of German at the University of California, Santa Barbara, for informing me about this etymology.

24 In 1713 Addison wrote that these studies existed "to cultivate the wild licentious savage with wisdom, discipline, and liberal arts." *Cato* I, cited in *O.E.D.*

25 For this view of the university's German origins, see Bill Readings, *The University in Ruins* (Cambridge: Harvard University Press, 1997), especially chapters 3–5. The national agenda was also a racial one. On the American dimension see Philip A. Klinkner and Rogers M. Smith, *The Unsteady March: The Rise and Decline of Racial Equality in America* (Chicago: University of Chicago Press, 1999), 95. I take up this issue in chapter 5.

26 This view had classical antecedents. Martha Nussbaum identifies this shift in "liberal" — from "fitted for freedom" to characterizing the "free citizen" — with the thought of Seneca in *Cultivating Humanity: A Classical Defense of Reform in Liberal Education* (Cambridge: Harvard University Press, 1997), 293.

27 See for example Immanuel Kant, *Critique of Practical Reason* and *The Critique of Judgment;* J. G. Fichte, *The Science of Knowledge;* and Friedrich Schiller, *On the Aesthetic Education of Man.*

28 Wilhelm von Humboldt, "On the Imagination," trans. Ralph R. Read, in *German Romantic Criticism,* ed. A. Leslie Willson (New York: Continuum, 1982), 137.

29 Humboldt continued the passage cited above by writing, "The poet does not need to lift us from earth to heaven, as it is often expressed; rather, he should diffuse the sublimity and immovable constancy of these high spheres upon the earth itself." This process involves the poet in transforming our own faculties by releasing us "from the limitations of present existence and transport[ing] us to that realm of deep and sublime ideas in which alone the better part of our essence finds itself." "On the Imagination," 138. I interpret this "essence" as the experience of oneself as free.

30 This general conception of self-formation through the aesthetic imagination was complicated, criticized, and in some cases jettisoned by literary thought

after the New Criticism. For important examples, see Thomas Weiskel, *The Romantic Sublime: Studies in the Structure and Psychology of Transcendence* (Baltimore: Johns Hopkins University Press, 1976); Neil Hertz, *The End of the Line: Essays on Psychoanalysis and the Sublime* (New York: Columbia University Press, 1985), especially chapter 3 and the afterword; and Paul de Man, "Intentional Structure of the Romantic Image" (1960), in Harold Bloom, ed., *Romanticism and Consciousness: Essays in Criticism* (New York: W. W. Norton, 1970), 65–76, as well as, for the fully developed version of de Man's career-long concern with false plenitudes and unities in language and consciousness, *The Aesthetic Ideology* (Minneapolis: University of Minnesota Press, 1996). These critiques have helped to make permanent changes in what freedom can mean, and yet they are not adequate theorizations of subjective freedom.

31  Samuel Taylor Coleridge, *Biographia Literaria,* ed. James Engell and W. Jackson Bate (Princeton, N.J.: Princeton University Press, 1983), 1:304. Coleridge is distinguishing here between the "primary" and "secondary" imagination. Though this distinction has attracted much complicated debate, I think Coleridge is making a fairly simple distinction between what we would now call unconscious and conscious forms of creative agency. He is most concerned with contrasting imagination with "fancy," a mode in which the mind is comparatively passive, since "it must receive all its materials ready made from the law of association" (1:305). In keeping with this definition of the imagination, Coleridge later notes that "original genius" appears in a poet's representations "only as far as they are modified by a predominant passion; or . . . when a human and intellectual life is transferred to them from the poet's own spirit, 'Which shoots its being through earth, sea, and air'" (2:23).

32  Ralph Waldo Emerson, "The Poet," *Essays: Second Series,* in *Essays and Lectures* (New York: Library of America, 1983), 462–63. For a discussion of Emerson's larger refusal to liberate language from transcendental essences, see my *The Emerson Effect: Individualism and Submission in America* (Chicago: University of Chicago Press, 1996), chapter 2.

33  Frank Lentricchia, *After the New Criticism* (Chicago: University of Chicago Press, 1980), 21, 20. For the most thoroughgoing critique of Schiller's aestheticism, see de Man, *Aesthetic Ideology.* Lyotard claims that with the German understanding of speculative knowledge, "the humanist principle that humanity rise up in dignity and freedom through knowledge is left by the wayside." But he also notes that the other principle of the legitimation of knowledge, which he associates with the French revolution, did not in fact disappear: "the problem of legitimacy can be solved using the other procedure as well. . . . According to this version, knowledge finds its validity not within itself, not in a subject that develops by actualizing its learning possibilities, but in a practical subject — humanity. The principle of the movement animating the people is not the self-legitimation of knowledge, but the self-grounding of freedom or, if preferred, its self-management." François Lyotard, *The Postmodern Condition: A Report on Knowledge* (1979; Minneapolis: University of Minnesota Press, 1984), 35.

34 The classic modern account remains that contained in the early chapters of Raymond Williams, *Culture and Society, 1780–1950* (New York: Columbia University Press, 1952).

35 Hannah Arendt, "The Crisis in Culture: Its Social and Political Significance," in *Between Past and Future: Six Exercises in Political Thought* (New York: Viking, 1961; New York, Penguin, 1993), 225. I should note that I am not giving full due the Christian tradition of spiritual development and its significant role in college and university humanism, one which imputed some ministerial functions to literary faculty and lent a pastoral air to college teaching. The Christian connection is central to standard accounts of the development of the humanities, but has unfortunately eclipsed the elements I am retrieving here.

36 The concept of free inquiry certainly did not exclude science. To the contrary, as we will see, reformers cited it as a central virtue of scientific investigation. Reuben writes, "Within higher education, supporters of university reforms came to view science as a particularly successful form of inquiry because it rejected common-sense beliefs. . . . The superiority of science depended on openness: scientists had to be free to question received knowledge." *The Making of the Modern University,* 5.

37 Charles W. Eliot, *University Administration* (Boston: Houghton Mifflin, 1908), 153, 173.

38 Herbert Spencer, *Social Statics* (London: John Chapman, 1851), 59.

39 William Rainey Harper, *The Trend in Higher Education* (Chicago: University of Chicago Press, 1905), 321–25.

40 Ibid., 268.

41 C. S. Schiller, cited in "humanism" entry, *Oxford English Dictionary*.

42 Lionel Trilling, *The Liberal Imagination: Essays on Literature and Society* (New York: Viking, 1950), xi–xiii.

43 William James, *Pragmatism* (1907; New York: Meridian, 1955), 165–66.

44 William James, *Essays in Radical Empiricism,* vol. 1 (New York: Longman, 1947), 193.

45 William James, *The Principles of Psychology* (London: Macmillan, 1910), 2:110.

46 William James, "Humanism and Truth Once More," *Mind,* new ser. 14, no. 54 (April 1905): 191.

47 For an accessible condensation of Tomkins's definition of affect and of the various affects he considered fundamental, see Eve Kosofsky Sedgwick and Adam Frank, eds., *Shame and Its Sisters: A Silvan Tomkins Reader* (Durham: Duke University Press, 1995).

48 James, *Essays in Radical Empiricism,* 99.

49 John Dewey, *Democracy and Education: An Introduction to the Philosophy of Education* (New York: Free Press, 1916), 120.

50 Cited in George E. Peterson, *The New England College in the Age of the University* (Amherst: Amherst College Press, 1964), 31.

51 Peterson, *The New England College,* 33.

52 Harper, *The Trend,* 324.

53  Ibid., 23.

54  Harper puts a pious twist on this in his next sentence: "Communion with self, study of self, is, where rightly understood, communion with God and study of God." I read this last phrase as a partial covering of Harper's more radical moment, based both on my knowledge of the big-business politics in which he operated and the secularity of nearly all his discussions of the self.

55  Sedgwick and Frank, *Shame and Its Sisters,* 35, 36. Tomkins writes that "the freedom of any feedback system is, consequently, a conjoint function of its complexity and the complexity of its surround."

56  Andrew S. Draper, "The University Presidency," *Atlantic Monthly,* Jan 1906, 34.

57  Cited in William Warren Ferrier, *Origin and Development of the University of California* (Berkeley: Sather Gate Book Shop, 1930), 376.

58  Eliot, *University Administration,* 176.

59  See for example William James, "The Dilemma of Determinism," in *The Will to Believe* (New York: Longmans Green, 1915). For useful modern overviews of James's epistemology, pragmatism, and related matters, see John Patrick Diggins, *The Promise of Pragmatism* (Chicago: University of Chicago Press, 1994), chapter 3; Giles Gunn, *Thinking across the American Grain: Ideology, Intellect, and the New Pragmatism* (Chicago: University of Chicago Press, 1992), chapter 2; Cornel West, *The American Evasion of Philosophy: A Genealogy of Pragmatism* (Madison: University of Wisconsin, 1989), chapter 2; and Louis Menand, *The Metaphysical Club: A Story of Ideas in America* (New York: Farrar, Straus & Giroux, 2001).

60  Newman, *The Idea of a University,* ed. I. T. Ker (Oxford: Clarendon, 1976), 102 (emphasis in original).

61  Richard G. Moulton, *Shakespeare as a Dramatic Artist: A Study of Inductive Literary Criticism,* in Graff and Warner, eds., *The Origins of Literary Studies,* 62.

62  Moulton, *Shakespeare,* 71.

63  "Laws of literature, in the sense of external obligations limiting an author, there are none: if he were voluntarily to bind himself by such external laws, he would be so far curtailing art." Moulton, *Shakespeare,* 71.

64  Ibid., 65.

65  Ibid., 66.

66  Ibid., 73 (emphasis in original).

67  James Morgan Hart, *German Universities: A Narrative of Personal Experience* (1874), in Graff and Warner, eds., *The Origins of Literary Studies,* 21.

68  Martin Wright Sampson, contribution to *English in American Universities* (1895), in Graff and Warner, eds., *The Origins of Literary Studies,* 54.

69  Charles Mills Gayley, contribution to *English in American Universities* (1895), in Graff and Warner, *The Origins of Literary Studies,* 59–60.

70  Bliss Perry, *The Amateur Spirit* (1904), in Graff and Warner, eds., *The Origins of Literary Studies,* 107.

71  Charles Hall Grandgent, "The Dark Ages" (1913), reprinted in Graff and Warner, eds., *The Origins of Literary Studies,* 127.

72 David Montgomery, *The Fall of the House of Labor: The Workplace, the State, and American Labor Activism, 1865–1925* (Cambridge: Cambridge University Press, 1987), 13. For the American version of the craft-labor movement, see Eileen Boris, *Art and Labor: Ruskin, Morris, and the Craftsman Ideal in America* (Philadelphia: Temple University Press, 1985).

73 Cited in Christopher Lasch, *The Revolt of the Elites and the Betrayal of Democracy* (New York: W. W. Norton, 1995), 66. For major interpretations of free labor theory, see Eric Foner, *Free Soil, Free Labor, Free Men: The Ideology of the Republican Party before the Civil War* (New York: Oxford University Press, 1970), chapter 1; Eric Foner, *Reconstruction: America's Unfinished Revolution, 1863–1877* (New York: Harper and Row, 1988), chapters 4, 10, 11; Christine Stansell, *City of Women: Sex and Class in New York, 1789–1860* (New York: Alfred A. Knopf, 1986), chapter 7; Sean Wilentz, *Chants Democratic: New York City and the Rise of the American Working Class, 1788–1850* (New York: Oxford University Press, 1984), chapter 4; Nelson Lichtenstein, *State of the Union: A Century of American Labor* (Princeton, N.J.: Princeton University Press, 2002), chapters 1–2; Evelyn Nakano Glenn, *Unequal Freedom: How Race and Gender Shaped American Citizenship and Labor* (Cambridge: Harvard University Press, 2002).

74 Herbert G. Gutman, *Work, Culture and Society in Industrializing America: Essays in American Working-Class and Social History* (New York: Vintage, 1977), 69.

75 Burton J. Bledstein, *The Culture of Professionalism: The Middle Class and the Development of Higher Education in America* (New York: W. W. Norton, 1976), 90.

76 Bledstein, *The Culture of Professionalism*, 87–88.

77 Ibid.

78 For a brief, relatively positive overview, see Gary G. Hamilton and John R. Sutton, "The Problem of Control in the Weak State: Domination in the United States, 1880–1920," *Theory and Society* 18 (1989): 1. This movement has received widespread criticism from the left. For one classic, largely critical appraisal, see R. Jeffrey Lustig, *Corporate Liberalism: The Origins of Modern American Political Theory, 1890–1920* (Berkeley: University of California Press, 1982). For the continuing shift toward a copyright and patenting system that linked labor to the creation of individual property, see Corynne McSherry, *Who Owns Academic Work? Battling for Control of Intellectual Property* (Cambridge: Harvard University Press, 2001), chapter 1.

79 Lasch, *The Revolt of the Elites*, 64. The best analysis of literary study as a "different order of work" is Evan Watkins, *Work Time: English Departments and the Circulation of Cultural Value* (Stanford: Stanford University Press, 1989).

80 See especially Linda Gordon, *Pitied but Not Entitled: Single Mothers and the History of Welfare* (New York: Free Press, 1994); and Alice Kessler-Harris, *In Pursuit of Equity: Women, Men, and the Quest for Economic Citizenship in Twentieth-Century America* (New York: Oxford University Press, 2001).

81 W. E. B. Du Bois, *The Souls of Black Folk* (1903; New York: Bantam, 1989), chapter 7, pp. 75–76.

## Chapter 4

1 The clearest evidence of the constant business effort to control markets is the sheer, brute existence of the corporation itself. Corporations came into existence in part to suspend and circumvent market relations, to control market relations with managerial relations. Ronald H. Coase, a Nobel laureate in economics, showed in a famous paper in 1937 that "the distinguishing mark of the firm is the supersession of the price mechanism." Ronald H. Coase, "The Nature of the Firm," *Economica* 4 (1937): 386–405, cited in Doug Henwood, *Wall Street: How It Works and for Whom* (London: Verso, 1997), 249. Corporations reduce "transaction costs" by replacing bidding and contracting procedures with stable bureaucratic relations. For confirmation of Coase with specific reference to the "market for corporate control" of the 1980s, see William Lazonick, "Controlling the Market for Corporate Control: The Historical Significance of Managerial Capitalism," *Industrial and Corporate Change* (Oxford: Oxford University Press, 1992), 445–88. After World War I other influential writers described a fully formed "managerial revolution" against "free market" capitalism. Influential examples include A. A. Berle and Gardiner C. Means, *The Modern Corporation and Private Property* (New York: Macmillan, 1932); and James Burnham, *The Managerial Revolution: What Is Happening in the World* (New York: John Day, 1941). After World War II the most prominent inheritor of the managerial vision of the modern economy became John Kenneth Galbraith, notably in *The New Industrial State* (New York: Houghton Mifflin, 1967). Alfred Chandler's classic study *The Visible Hand* argued that corporations developed because they were more efficient than markets at coordination, distribution, and other economic tasks. Alfred D. Chandler Jr., *The Visible Hand: The Managerial Revolution in American Business* (New York: Harvard University Press, 1977). Though politics, ideology, and other factors were also involved, corporate management expressed businesspeople's profound need to increase their control over the market environment. For a strong recent critique of Chandler's "efficiency" paradigm, see William G. Roy, *Socializing Capital: The Rise of the Large Industrial Corporation in America* (Princeton, N.J.: Princeton University Press, 1997).

2 Karl Marx, *Capital*, vol. 1 (New York: Vintage, 1976), 453.

3 Saint-Simon, Charles Fourier, and other "utopian socialists" had detailed precorporate cooperative schemes. Marx thought the socialization of labor historically necessary, and he did not seek to reverse this process so much as to give labor self-management and full returns. As the corporation and the university were developing, Edward Bellamy envisioned a future in which "the principle of fraternal co-operation" would be managed by self-regulating, benevolent government. *Looking Backward, 2000–1887* (Boston: Ticknor, 1888; New York: Penguin, 1982).

4 Chandler, *The Visible Hand,* 1.

5 I am not making any claims here about causes, or engaging in important,

complex, longstanding debates about the purposes and political or ethical effects of bureaucracy. Functionalists argue that bureaucratic forms arose from technical and economic necessity: see for example Chandler, *The Visible Hand;* and Louis Galambos, "The Emerging Organizational Synthesis in Modern American History," *Business History Review* 44 (autumn 1970): 279–90. Critics of bureaucracy argue that it is simply an instrument by means of which the ruling class dominates labor or a subtler form of control sometimes known as "corporate liberalism": for the latter perspective see for example Richard Edwards, *Contested Terrain: The Transformation of the Workplace in the Twentieth Century* (New York: Basic Books, 1979), R. Jeffrey Lustig, *Corporate Liberalism: The Origins of Modern American Political Theory, 1890–1920* (Berkeley: University of California Press, 1982), and Stephen P. Waring, *Taylorism Transformed: Scientific Management Theory since 1945* (Chapel Hill: University of North Carolina Press, 1991). For a "third way" perspective, see Sanford M. Jacoby, *Employing Bureaucracy: Managers, Unions, and the Transformation of Work in American Industry, 1900–1945* (New York: Columbia University Press, 1985).

6 Robert H. Wiebe, *The Search for Order, 1877–1920* (New York: Hill and Wang, 1967), 145–46.

7 Karl Marx, cited in David F. Noble, *America by Design: Science, Technology, and the Rise of Corporate Capitalism* (New York: Alfred A. Knopf, 1977), xxiv. I rely in this section on Noble's comprehensive research.

8 Noble, *America by Design,* 111.

9 Ibid., 128.

10 Ibid., 118.

11 Ibid., 82–83.

12 Ibid., 119, 170.

13 Cited in ibid., 175.

14 Anonymous, "The Perplexities of a College President," *Atlantic Monthly* 85 (1900): 485, 493. The article is extreme enough to have made Veysey wonder if it was meant as parody.

15 William Rainey Harper, *The Trend in Higher Education* (Chicago: University of Chicago Press, 1905), 268–69, 272.

16 Charles W. Eliot, *University Administration* (Boston: Houghton Mifflin, 1908), 37–39.

17 Andrew S. Draper, "The University Presidency," *Atlantic Monthly,* Jan 1906, 36.

18 Clark Kerr, *The Uses of the University* (Cambridge: Harvard University Press, 1963), 48.

19 Ibid., 58.

20 Ibid., 59–60.

21 Henry, C. Metcalf and L. Urwick, *Dynamic Administration: The Collected Papers of Mary Parker Follett* (New York: Harper and Brothers, 1940), 32. Taylor himself was more liberal than Taylorism, but his strict labor engineering overwhelmed other elements of his thought.

22 Eliot, *University Administration,* 238.

23  Laurence Veysey, *The Emergence of the American University* (Chicago: University of Chicago Press, 1970), 311.

24  Daniel Nelson, *Managers and Workers: Origins of the Twentieth-Century Factory System in the United States, 1880–1920,* 2d ed. (Madison: University of Wisconsin Press, 1995), 49–50.

25  For example, engineers in the late nineteenth century recommended three main kinds of policies: "cost accounting systems to promote vertical integration; production and inventory plans to facilitate horizontal integration; and wage payment plans to stimulate production and reduce unit costs. In each case the objective was to enhance the manager's control over production, including the foremen and the production workers." Nelson, *Managers and Workers,* 51.

26  Veysey, *The Emergence of the American University,* 311, 315. I have omitted Veysey's claim that administrators applied bureaucratic norms uniformly. Uniformity was more an ideal than a practice, and the claim is less accurate than Veysey's later claim that academic bureaucracy works through compartmentalization.

27  Ibid., 338.

28  Michel Foucault, "Governmentality," in *The Foucault Effect: Studies in Governmentality,* ed. Graham Burchell, Colin Gordon, and Peter Miller (Chicago: University of Chicago Press, 1991), 93.

29  Ibid., 95.

30  Ibid., 101.

31  Veysey, *The Emergence of the American University,* 302–3.

32  Ibid., 305.

33  Author's interview with Clark Kerr, Cerritos, California, 13 Aug 1997; also mentioned in Clark Kerr, *The Gold and the Blue: A Personal Memoir of the University of California, 1949–1967,* vol. 1, *Academic Triumph* (Berkeley: University of California Press, 2001), 146.

34  Frederick Rudolph writes, "The professionalization of the professors had not brought them any new authority in college or university affairs; actually it had only helped to widen the gap between them and the governing board, a gap which had existed even in the era of the colleges, when the professors were already on the road from being fellows charged with ultimate responsibility to being hirelings of those men of the world who increasingly dominated collegiate governing boards." Frederick Rudolph, *The American College and University: A History* (New York: Alfred A. Knopf, 1962; Athens: University of Georgia Press, 1990), 427. For my discussion of the professional middle class as divided between capital and labor, see chapter 10, and the important work of Erik Olin Wright on intellectuals and other PMC workers occupying contradictory class locations in "Intellectuals and the Class Structure of Capitalist Society," *Between Labor and Capital,* ed. Pat Walker (Boston: South End, 1979), 191–212, and *Class Counts: Comparative Studies in Class Analysis* (Cambridge: Cambridge University Press, 1997).

35  Veysey, *The Emergence of the American University,* 304.

36  Ibid., 305.

37 Faculty power is limited even in academic matters and is quite personalistic, as I will discuss in a later chapter.

38 See chapter 5, note 6.

39 Rebecca S. Lowen, *Creating the Cold War University: The Transformation of Stanford* (Berkeley: University of California Press, 1997).

40 See the AAUP documents "Statement of Principles on Academic Freedom and Tenure" (1940), "Statement on Government of Colleges and Universities" (1966), and "On the Relationship of Faculty Governance to Academic Freedom" (1994).

41 Burton R. Clark, *The Academic Life: Small Worlds, Different Worlds,* Carnegie Foundation Special Report (Princeton, N.J.: Carnegie Foundation for the Advancement of Teaching, 1987), 157.

42 See in particular Charles Heckscher, *White-Collar Blues: Management Loyalties in an Age of Corporate Restructuring* (New York: Basic Books, 1995).

43 Veysey, *The Emergence of the American University,* 317, 337–38.

44 Clark Kerr, *The Uses of the University* (Cambridge: Harvard University Press, 1964), 99–102.

45 Clark, *The Academic Life,* 186.

46 Veysey, *The Emergence of the American University,* 393.

47 Hannah Arendt, "What Is Freedom?" *Between Past and Future: Six Exercises in Political Thought* (New York: Viking, 1961; New York, Penguin, 1993), 147.

48 Heckscher, *White-Collar Blues,* 49, 53, 52, 83.

49 These faculty are implicitly defined as technological researchers, though humanities faculty have tagged along on the deal, partly because they represent the great tradition that forms selves and souls, and partly because the university required some equity across divisions for the sake of internal peace.

*Chapter 5*

1 Philip Lindsley, University of Nashville (1825), cited in Frederick Rudolph, *The American College and University: A History* (New York: Alfred A. Knopf, 1962; Athens: University of Georgia Press, 1990), 214.

2 On the evolution of professional management, see, among many strong accounts, Alfred D. Chandler Jr., *The Visible Hand: The Managerial Revolution in American Business* (Cambridge: Harvard University Press, 1977), especially part V; Sanford M. Jacoby, *Employing Bureaucracy: Managers, Unions, and the Transformation of Work in American Industry, 1900–1945* (New York: Columbia University Press, 1985); and David Montgomery, *The Fall of the House of Labor: The Workplace, the State, and American Labor Activism, 1865–1925* (New York: Cambridge University Press, 1988), especially chapter 5.

3 John Aubrey Douglass, *The California Idea and American Higher Education: 1850 to the 1960 Master Plan* (Stanford: Stanford University Press, 2000), 104.

4 "In 1901 Wheeler declared that 'life has no . . . easy-going elective system, and colleges ought not to have [one]. Life wants men who do things . . . Because it

is their duty to do them, not because they elect to do them.'" Laurence Veysey, *The Emergence of the American University* (Chicago: University of Chicago Press, 1970), 363. In "The Liberal Education" (discussed below), Wheeler wrote, "The unlimited 'elective system' concerning which there has been so much ill-judged flourishing of trumpets, is merely a state of revolution and anarchy historically intruded between two systems of order." Benjamin Ide Wheeler, *The Abundant Life*, ed. Monroe E. Deutsch (Berkeley: University of California Press, 1926), 183.

5  Veysey, *The Emergence of the American University*, 363–64.

6  Wheeler's autocratic hand is generally held responsible for the "great revolt" of 1919–20, in which some administrative powers were handed over to the faculty senate. Douglass, *The California Idea*, 379n45; Veysey, *The Emergence of the American University*, 363; Verne Stadtman, *The University of California, 1868–1968* (New York: McGraw-Hill, 1968), 290. Stadtman writes, "The principal grievances of the revolutionaries were that they had little voice in appointments, promotions, budget decisions, educational policy, the choice of department chairmen, or the selection of the presiding officer of the senate. . . . The revolt achieved its purposes: a Committee on Budget was provided for in the standing orders of the Regents; a Committee on Committees, elected by the senate, made committee appointments; and the senate chose its own presiding officer. Further, the chairman of a department was no longer its senior member, who had achieved his position by remaining alive longer than his colleagues, but was appointed by the President in consultation with members of the department." Stadtman claims that as a result of the successful revolt, "the faculty regained control of its destinies," producing a system that had changed little to the time of Stadtman's writing.

7  Benjamin Ide Wheeler, "What the University Aims to Give the Student," in *The Abundant Life*, ed. Deutsch, 187–88.

8  Benjamin Ide Wheeler, "The Liberal Education," in *The Abundant Life*, ed. Deutsch, 181.

9  Ibid., 182.

10  Ibid., 184.

11  Ibid., 185.

12  Ibid., 186.

13  Mary Kupiec Cayton, *Emerson's Emergence: Self and Society in the Transformation of New England, 1800–1845* (Chapel Hill: University of North Carolina Press, 1989), 8.

14  In addition to the large current literature on republicanism in political thought in the United States, see Daniel Walker Howe, *The Political Culture of the American Whigs* (Chicago: University of Chicago Press, 1979), especially the introduction and chapters 1, 2, 5.

15  Jefferson to Adams, cited in Nicholas Lemann, *The Big Test: The Secret History of American Meritocracy* (New York: Farrar, Straus and Giroux, 1999), 43. Lemann also cites Adams's rejection of Jefferson's idea.

16  Charles W. Eliot, "Inaugural Address of Dr. Eliot," delivered 19 Oct 1869, in *Charles W. Eliot: The Man and His Beliefs,* vol. 1, ed. William Allan Neilson (New York: Harper and Brothers, 1926), 21.

17  Eliot claimed that Harvard was "intensely democratic in temper" because it "has always attracted and still attracts students in all conditions of life." Ibid., 18.

18  On radical Reconstruction, see W. E. B. Du Bois, *Black Reconstruction in America* (New York: Harcourt, Brace, 1935), especially chapters 7, 9, 14; and Eric Foner, *Reconstruction: America's Unfinished Revolution, 1863–1877* (New York: Harper and Row, 1988), especially chapters 6, 8, 10. On the interaction of Emerson's social outlook and his later racial views, see my book *The Emerson Effect: Individualism and Submission in America* (Chicago: University of Chicago Press, 1996), chapter 7.

19  Emerson, "Aristocracy," in *The Complete Works of Ralph Waldo Emerson, 1803–1882,* introduction and notes by Edward Waldo Emerson (Boston: Houghton Mifflin, 1903–4), 10:48–49.

20  Ibid., 10:52. Only a certain "class" should be leaders, and Emerson goes on to say that the test of a leader should be whether he is "a man of talent" (53) and whether he has a "will," both of which are "gift[s] of nature."

21  Ibid., 51–52.

22  This pricing of persons was actually put in place by the English biologist and founder of mental testing Sir Francis Galton. In the Thomas Huxley lecture of 1901, Galton reported the results of his program in calculating "the Worth of Children." He found the child of the wife of an Essex laborer, for example, to be worth five pounds. Sir Francis Galton, "The possible Improvement of the Human Breed Under the Existing Conditions of Law and Sentiment," *Nature,* 31 Oct 1901, 659–65, cited in a Ralph Nader report, Allan Nairn, *The Reign of* ETS: *The Corporation That Makes Up Minds* (1980), 164.

23  *The Nation,* 12 Nov 1868, 387. There is reason to think that the moderate liberalism of E. L. Godkin, founding and longstanding editor of *The Nation,* was not remote from Emerson's views. Writing to Godkin on 31 January 1868, Charles Eliot Norton somewhat flatteringly observes that "Emerson, who had been cold toward [*The Nation*], who thought a mistake had been made in putting you at the head of it, spoke to me last week in warmest terms of its excellence, its superiority to any other journal we have or have had." *Letters of Charles Eliot Norton,* vol. 1 (Boston: Houghton Mifflin, 1913), 297. I have taken parts of the foregoing discussion from my *The Emerson Effect,* chapter 7.

24  William Rainey Harper, *The Trend in Higher Education* (Chicago: University of Chicago Press, 1905), 322–23. For similar ambiguities in the thinking of a major university leader, see the discussion of David Starr Jordan, president of Cornell and Stanford, in Douglass, *The California Idea,* 98–100.

25  Nicolas Murray Butler, "True and False Democracy," *Educational Review* 33 (April 1907): 330–31, cited in Harold S. Wechsler, *The Qualified Student: A History of Selective College Admission in America* (New York: John Wiley and Sons, 1977), 73.

26  Some observers have found little evidence that meritocracy was explicitly designed to exclude African Americans (and later, immigrants from Asia, Southern and Eastern Europe, and Latin America). Nicholas Lemann asserts, for example, that "The new system hadn't been set up with the intention of excluding Negroes . . . During all the time that ETS and other testing companies had been promoting the use of tests as a hiring instrument by American business, it never occurred to them that the results would be used to exclude Negroes or, for that matter, that there could be any bad side to the miracle of testing." *The Big Test,* 156–57. This is to take the idea of intention in the narrowest sense. Meritocracy took for granted a social order based on class stratification and racial and ethnic exclusion, and used racial differences as the prime example of natural stratification.

27  *South Dakota v. Yankton Sioux Tribe,* 522 U.S. 329 (1998). Unanimous opinion by Justice O'Connor, referencing hearings on H.R. 7902 before the House Committee on Indian Affairs, 73d Cong., 2d sess., 428 (1934) (statement of D. S. Otis on the history of the allotment policy).

28  W. E. B. Du Bois, *The Souls of Black Folk* (New York: Bantam, 1988), 8.

29  Cited in Arthur Schlesinger Jr., *The Disuniting of America* (Knoxville: Whittle Direct, 1991), 13. This section is based on the discussion of Kallen to be found in my "Multiculturalism's Unfinished Business," in *Mapping Multiculturalism* (Minneapolis: University of Minnesota Press, 1996), written with Avery F. Gordon.

30  Horace M. Kallen, *Cultural Pluralism and the American Idea: An Essay in Social Philosophy,* with comments by Stanley H. Chapman et al. (Philadelphia: University of Pennsylvania Press, 1956), 85.

31  Ibid., 97.

32  Ibid., 82.

33  Ibid., 23. I have omitted Kallen's biologistic continuation, which mixes complicatedly with his culturalism.

34  Ibid.

35  Ibid.

36  Ibid., 98.

37  Ibid.

38  Gerald Graff, *Professing Literature: An Institutional History* (Chicago: University of Chicago Press, 1987), 85, 83.

39  Irving Babbitt, *Literature and the American College: Essays in Defense of the Humanities* (Boston: Houghton Mifflin, 1908), 8, 18, 14, 13.

40  Ibid., 7, 8, 12.

41  Ibid., 8, 9.

42  "Interest" is the psychologist Silvan Tomkins's term, but the same principle is at work in much psychological theory, including Freud's sense of the extreme danger posed by melancholic cathexes on lost or missing objects.

43  Babbitt, *Literature,* 22–23.

44  Ibid., 26–27.

45  Ibid., 26–27, 22–23, 23.

46 Sinclair Lewis, *Babbitt* (1922), chapter 3.

47 Ibid.

48 Ibid, chapter 34.

49 The term "grey flannel rebel" comes from Barbara Ehrenreich's description of the suburban breadwinners of the 1950s in *The Hearts of Men* (New York: Anchor, 1983).

50 Irving Babbitt had many objections to specialization and philology. Nonetheless, his new humanist would accept the subjectivity and organizational structure of professionalism.

51 This status in turn affected the kind of cultural and social studies that the university conducted and the parameters of "scientific knowledge." This issue is beyond my scope here, but for an important discussion of the limits of the social science generated at the University of Chicago after 1920, see Alice O'Connor, *Poverty Knowledge: Social Science, Social Policy, and the Poor in Twentieth-Century U.S. History* (Princeton, N.J.: Princeton University Press, 2001). Chicago-school sociology, for example, removed professional research from the precincts of "feminized" and "amateur" community research (18). Academic and experiential knowledge were becoming increasingly incompatible.

## Chapter 6

1 For the drama and conflict of campus development during the interwar period, see David O. Levine, *The American College and the Culture of Aspiration, 1915–1940* (Ithaca, N.Y.: Cornell University Press, 1986).

2 Clark Kerr wrote that "higher education in 1960 received about $1.5 billion from the federal government — a hundredfold increase in twenty years. About one third of this $1.5 billion was for university-affiliated research centers; about one third for project research within universities; and about one third for other things, such as residence hall loans, scholarships, and teaching programs. This last third was expended at colleges as well as universities, but the first two thirds almost exclusively at universities, and at relatively few of them." *The Uses of the University* (Cambridge: Harvard University Press, 1963), 52–53.

3 Ibid., 53.

4 Ibid., 55.

5 John Aubrey Douglass, *The California Idea and American Higher Education: 1850 to the 1960 Master Plan* (Stanford: Stanford University Press, 2000), 194, 256.

6 Christopher J. Lucas, *Crisis in the Academy: Rethinking Higher Education in America* (Boston: St. Martins, 1996), 12.

7 Ibid., 17–18; William G. Bowen and Derek Bok note that "in 1965, only 4.8 percent of all U.S. college students were African American." *The Shape of the River: Long-Term Consequences of Considering Race in College and University Admissions* (Princeton, N.J.: Princeton University Press, 1998). Lucas's numbers are not exactly equivalent to those of Bowen and Bok, but they are comparable before 1965. The situation was even more restrictive at the élite schools in the

Mellon study "College and Beyond" on which Bowen and Bok base their conclusions. "In the fall of 1951, black students averaged 0.8 percent of the entering
class at the nineteen College and Beyond schools for which adequate records are
available." By the mid-1960s, "the numbers actually enrolled remained small,
with blacks making up only 1 percent of the enrollments of selective New
England colleges in 1965." Similarly, "in 1965, barely 1 percent of all law students in America were black, and over one-third of them were enrolled in all-
black schools. Barely 2 percent of all medical students were African American,
and more than three-fourths of them attended two all-black institutions,
Howard University and Meharry Medical College" (5). Measurable change
followed intensified political protest and civil rights legislation. "The percentage of blacks enrolled in Ivy League colleges rose from 2.3 percent in 1967 to 6.3
in 1976, while the percentages in other 'prestigious' colleges grew from 1.7 to
4.8. Meanwhile, the proportion of black medical students had climbed to 6.3
percent by 1975, and black law students had increased their share to 4.5 percent." (7).

8  Sheila Slaughter and Larry L. Leslie, *Academic Capitalism: Politics, Policies, and
   the Entrepreneurial University* (Baltimore: Johns Hopkins University Press,
   1997), 100.

9  See Martin Duberman, *Black Mountain: An Exploration in Community* (1972;
   New York: W. W. Norton, 1993); and Constance Cappel, *Utopian Colleges*
   (New York: Peter Lang, 1999). For contemporary commentary, see Arthur E.
   Morgan, "The Antioch Program," *Journal of Higher Education,* Dec 1930, 497–
   502; Dorothy Hall, "Democracy Begins at Home," *Journal of Higher Education,*
   Oct 1940, 360–62; Clarence Leuba, "New Ways of Organization," *Journal of
   Higher Education,* March 1934, 136–40; and Charles W. Coulter, "The Present
   Challenge," *Journal of Higher Education,* Oct 1934, 355–64.

10 See for example Cary Nelson, *Repression and Recovery: Modern American Poetry
   and the Politics of Cultural Memory* (Madison: University of Wisconsin Press,
   1989), and Michael Denning, *The Cultural Front: The Laboring of American
   Culture in the Twentieth Century* (New York: Verso, 1996).

11 For the difficulty and complexity of Kerr's (and UC's) costly battles for the
   Master Plan, see Douglass, *The California Idea,* chapters 9–11.

12 Clark Kerr, *The Uses of the University,* 122.

13 Ibid., 123.

14 For an important discussion of the relationship between granting agencies and
   university scientists, see Jessica Wang, *American Science in the Age of Anxiety:
   Scientists, Anticommunism, and the Cold War* (Chapel Hill: University of North
   Carolina Press, 1999).

15 Clark Kerr, *The Uses of the University,* v–vi. Kerr relies on the pioneering research
   of the Princeton economist Fritz Machlup in *The Production and Distribution of
   Knowledge in the United States* (Princeton, N.J.: Princeton University Press,
   1962). Machlup estimated that "the production, distribution, and consumption of 'knowledge' in all its forms" accounted for "29 percent of gross national

product . . .; and 'knowledge production' is growing at about twice the rate of the rest of the economy." *The Uses of the University*, 88.

16  Kerr, *The Uses of the University*, 89.

17  Ibid., 89–90.

18  Ibid., 90.

19  Ibid., 59. See also the discussion in chapter 3. On the shift from teaching to research as a primary faculty activity see Christopher Jencks and David Reisman, *The Academic Revolution* (Garden City, N.Y.: Anchor, 1969).

20  R. C. Lewontin, "The Cold War and the Transformation of the Academy," in *The Cold War and the University: Towards an Intellectual History of the Postwar Years* (New York: New Press, 1997), 8–9. Lewontin itemizes the reasons why competitive capitalism can block innovation: "First, capital in excess of what is available even to the largest individual enterprises is needed both for the education of scientists and engineers and for many research projects. Although the American Telephone and Telegraph Company could fund the most successful corporate research enterprise in existence, Bell Laboratories, it could not also create the universities, their faculties, laboratories, and libraries in which Bell Laboratory scientists were formed. Second, investment in research is not only risky, but even if successful will not usually produce a return for ten or more years, while the typical corporate investment horizon is two to three years. . . . Third, successful innovation usually depends on a wide sharing of preliminary results in an international community of scientific workers with similar interests. But the proprietary interests of corporations prevent that sharing."

21  Lewontin also notes that American culture's strong bias against state management means that state coordination of research needs special incentives. The greatest of these was war—first the world wars and then the permanent cold war with the communist world. It's also clear that state subsidy goes down better if it uses proxy agents. The research university was an ideal proxy: it served national security and economic growth at the same time. The explosion of postwar research funding was accompanied by an explosion in undergraduate enrollments. A public that might have balked at taxpayer underwriting of basic research with uncertain payouts could hardly say no to the university's promise of both national security and upward mobility.

22  Kerr, *The Uses of the University*, 95.

23  For a characteristic recent view that the cold war forged university-government relations that have been increasingly replaced by university-business relations, see Robert W. Conn, "University-Industry Partnering: A New Era Requires New Thinking," in *The University of California's Relationships with Industry in Research and Technology Transfer* (Proceedings of the President's Retreat, UCLA, 30–31 Jan 1997), 65–79. Conn was dean of engineering at UC San Diego. But Rebecca S. Lowen, in her study of the rise of Stanford University to national prominence, notes that throughout the cold war golden age of federal funding, Stanford attracted substantial industry sponsorship and modified its academic programs to attract more. Industry remained the preferred partner among the

research university's conservative leadership; between 1944 and 1947 seventy university departments developed arrangements with industry. A partnership with General Electric was fully in place by the mid-1950s, before the National Science Foundation boom was under way. By 1957 university "spin-off" companies were springing up in Stanford's dedicated industrial park; industry models of management were increasingly influential on campus; and an Industrial Affiliates Program, set up by David Packard and a Stanford professor, was offering industry access to prepublication campus research. *Making the Cold War University: The Transformation of Stanford* (Berkeley: University of California Press, 1997), 99, 121, 130–31. Lowen concludes that "the genius of the postwar generation of university administrators, such as Frederick Terman, was to recognize that the university's relationship to the federal government need not be seen as an alternative to a relationship to private industry; in fact, the university's relationship to one had to be intricately bound up in the university's relationship with the other if either were to prove lucrative. Terman understood that industry would see participation in this triangular relationship as a 'win'; it stood to profit from both research and the training of potential employees that was being paid for with taxpayer's money. The university 'won' its long-standing aims — industrial patronage, consulting opportunities for its scientists and employment for its students" (236).

24 For a critical account of Vannevar Bush's policy impact, diminished political influence, and enduring legend, see Daniel S. Greenberg, *Science, Money, and Politics: Political Triumph and Ethical Erosion* (Chicago: University of Chicago Press, 2001), chapter 3.

25 Vannevar Bush, *Science: The Endless Frontier: A Report to the President on a Program for Postwar Scientific Research* (1945; Washington: National Science Foundation, 1960), 6.

26 Ibid., 6–7.

27 Bush credits industry with this wisdom: "Industry learned many years ago that basic research cannot often be fruitfully conducted as an adjunct to or a subdivision of an operating agency or department. Operating agencies have immediate operating goals and are under constant pressure to produce in a tangible way, for that is the test of their value. None of these conditions is favorable to basic research." Ibid., 32.

28 A later director of the NSF noted how its funding was influenced by "the public reaction to the international and national political situation." The NSF's budget for its first operating year, 1951, was $3.5 million. "By the fifth year the National Science Foundation was operating at about thirteen per cent of the level suggested by Dr. Bush for that year. By 1960, however, the Foundation's appropriation for all activities was $159,200,000, almost ten times the 1956 level" and over forty-five times its budget of less than ten years before. What made the difference? "In the summer of 1955, the Foundation published a National Research Council study, *Soviet Professional Manpower*, which drew sobering comparisons between the rates at which the U.S. and the U.S.S.R. are training scientific and

technical manpower. One result of these findings was that the Congress sharply increased Foundation funds for education in the sciences. The Foundation appropriation for fiscal year 1957, $40 million, more than doubled that of the preceding year. The next large increment came in 1959 when $130 million was appropriated in the wake of intense national concern over the Russian sputnik and all that it implied." Alan T. Waterman, Introduction to Bush, *Science: The Endless Frontier,* xxiv–xv.

29  Joseph A. Schumpeter, *Capitalism, Socialism, and Democracy* (1942; 3d ed. New York: Harper and Row, 1950), 80.

30  Ibid., 82.

31  For a more critical reading of Bush see Steve Fuller, *Thomas Kuhn: A Philosophical History for Our Times* (Chicago: University of Chicago Press, 2000), 150–57.

32  Freeman Dyson, *The Sun, the Genome, and the Internet* (New York: Oxford University Press, 1999), 9–10.

33  Richard P. Feynman, *"Surely You're Joking, Mr. Feynman!" Adventures of a Curious Character* (New York: Bantam, 1985), 157–58.

34  For more systematic confirmation about creativity in a range of fields, see Mihaly Csikszentmihalyi, *Creativity: Flow and the Psychology of Discovery and Invention* (New York: Harper Collins, 1996), especially chapters 4 and 5.

35  I owe the concept of "not trying" to the Santa Barbara psychotherapist Dierdre Morse and to her unpublished manuscript on the psychological preconditions of innovation.

36  Norman Mailer, *The Armies of the Night* (New York: Random House, 1968), 24–25.

37  Rebecca S. Lowen, *Creating the Cold War University: The Transformation of Stanford* (Berkeley: University of California Press, 1997), e.g. 71–73, 121.

38  See for example Ellen W. Schrecker, *No Ivory Tower: McCarthyism and the Universities* (New York: Oxford University Press, 1986), Lewontin in *The Cold War and the University,* and Christopher Simpson, *Universities and Empire: Money and Politics in the Social Sciences During the Cold War* (New York: New Press, 1998).

39  Kenneth Burke, *Permanence and Change,* cited in Michael Denning, *Cultural Front: The Laboring of American Culture in the Twentieth Century* (New York: Verso, 1996), 436.

40  Sidney Hook, "Marxism, Metaphysics, and Modern Science," *Modern Quarterly* 4 (May–Aug 1928): 388–94, cited in Denning, *Cultural Front,* 429–30. Denning describes the American branch of "Western Marxism" linking Marxism to pragmatism, and uses Hook as a primary example. This linkage involved Dewey and his theories of progressive education.

41  C. L. R. James, *American Civilization* (1950; Cambridge, Mass.: Blackwell, 1993), 167.

42  Ibid., 171.

43  Ibid., 187, citing Drucker, *The Future of Industrial Man* (New York: John Day, 1942).

44 Market calculations often damage technological development, although this is not sufficiently recognized in the United States. Although it is beyond this book's chronological range, the "internet economy" offers a compelling recent example. The policy analyst and software company founder Charles H. Ferguson writes, "It has become fashionable to argue that industrial policy isn't possible in America and is anyway inherently a bad idea. But the record of government-supported Internet development versus the commercial online services industry clearly demonstrates exactly the opposite. The established technology companies, the Silicon Valley geniuses, the online services industry, and the venture capitalists all missed it for twenty years or more. Every brilliant, important, technically farsighted Internet development came either from government agencies or universities. In the meantime, decision making in the competitive marketplace was narrow, shortsighted, self-protective, and technically far inferior to its Internet equivalents." *High Stakes, No Prisoners: A Winner's Tale of Greed and Glory in the Internet Wars* (New York: Times Business, 1999), 49. Ferguson explains the difference in part through the damage done to innovative thinking by financial interests.

## Chapter 7

1 John Dewey, "Self-Realization as the Moral Ideal" (1893), in *The Early Works of John Dewey, 1882–1898*, vol 4, *1893–1894* (Carbondale: Southern Illinois University Press, 1971), 43.

2 Ibid.

3 John Dewey, *Democracy and Education: An Introduction to the Philosophy of Education* (New York: Free Press, 1916), 121.

4 Ibid., 51.

5 This enormously complex system of arguments was developed by figures as different as Ferdinand de Saussure, Edmund Husserl, Martin Heidegger, Ludwig Wittgenstein, W. V. O. Quine, Maurice Merleau-Ponty, Jacques Derrida, Michel Foucault, and Richard Rorty, among many others.

6 Dewey, *Democracy and Education*, 4. Commentators have sometimes stressed Dewey's interest in regularity and commonality, but difference and disparity were at least as fundamental to usable knowledge. Dewey did, however, encourage a focus on shared interests: see, e.g., *Democracy and Education*, 99.

7 Ibid., 238.

8 Ibid., 120–21.

9 John Patrick Diggins alleges Dewey's rejection of individualism in *The Promise of Pragmatism: Modernism and the Crisis of Knowledge and Authority* (Chicago: University of Chicago Press, 1994), 299–305. Other critics who grant Dewey's individualism tend to downplay the *combination* of the anomalous, "incommensurable" and the social, participatory self. Giles Gunn writes that Dewey "extrapolated two criteria for assessing the value of any form of social life" and cites Dewey himself: "the extent [to] which interests of a group are shared by all its

members, and the fullness and freedom with which it interacts with other groups." *Thinking across the American Grain: Ideology, Intellect, and the New Pragmatism* (Chicago: University of Chicago Press, 1992), 77. Cornel West underplays the incommensurable self in arguing that a vulnerability of Dewey's position is his belief "that social conflict can be resolved and societal problems overcome by a widely held consensus more characteristic of artisanal towns or farming communities than of industrial cities or urban capitalist societies." *The American Evasion of Philosophy: A Genealogy of Pragmatism* (Madison: University of Wisconsin Press, 1989), 102. Gunn and West are right that Dewey was drawn toward communitarian solutions, but his more promising notion of irreducible individuality survived nonetheless.

10 Dewey, *Democracy and Education*, 122.

11 Many of Dewey's followers admire his antidualism on epistemological issues like truth versus opinion, and show how Dewey demonstrates that truth is a version of context-dependent thought, how he rejects the correspondence theory of truth, and so on; yet they continue to read his politics through a dualism of private and public. See for example Richard Rorty's abundant uses of Dewey, which regularly lead to contrasts such as "Education as Socialization and Individualization" (the title of an essay in *Philosophy and Social Hope* [New York: Penguin, 1999], 114–26). For a compact, antidualist reading of Dewey's analysis of truth as social practice, see West, *The American Evasion of Philosophy,* chapter 3.

12 Dewey, *Democracy and Education*, 98.

13 Here's another example of how Dewey sounded on the subject: "There is no inherent opposition between working with others and working as an individual. On the contrary, certain capacities of an individual are not brought out except under the stimulus of associating with others. That a child must work alone and not engage in group activities in order to be free and let his individuality develop, is a notion which measures individuality by spatial distance and makes a physical thing of it." *Democracy and Education,* 302.

14 Ibid., 230.

15 Ibid., 286.

16 Ibid.

17 Ibid.

18 Ibid., 257.

19 Ibid., 314.

20 Ibid., 260.

21 Ibid., 314.

22 This periodization appears in Paul Jay, "Kenneth Burke and the Motives of Rhetoric," *American Literary History* 1 (fall 1989): 535–53. For the altered endings, as well as other insights into Burke's place in the history of criticism, see Michael Denning, *The Cultural Front: The Laboring of American Culture in the Twentieth Century* (New York: Verso, 1996), 434–55. Burke criticized the "Joyce-Stein-*transition*" school because an anti-authoritarianism that nonethe-

less "leaves the things of Caesar to take care of themselves" keeps the artist dependent "on some ruler who will accept the responsibility for doing the world's 'dirty work.'" *The Philosophy of Literary Form: Studies in Symbolic Action* (Baton Rouge: Louisiana State University Press, 1941; New York: Vintage, 1957), 200. The split between aesthetic and sociological approaches was "preparatory to political authoritarianism in its strictest forms." For commentary on the limits of Burke's uses of sociology and history, see Fredric Jameson, "The Symbolic Inference; or, The Poetics of Historiography" (1976), in *The Ideologies of Theory: Essays 1971–1986*, vol. 1, *Situations of Theory* (Minneapolis: University of Minnesota Press, 1988), 137–52.

23 Kenneth Burke, "Literature as Equipment for Living," in *The Philosophy of Literary Form*, 253; the second phrase is Jay's in "Kenneth Burke," 541.

24 Burke, *The Philosophy of Literary Form*, 260.

25 Ibid., 261.

26 Burke distinguished between "practical" and "symbolic" acts but held that they remain interconnected. "The symbolic act is the *dancing of an attitude,*" and "in this attitudinizing of the poem, the whole body may finally become involved, in ways suggested by the doctrines of behaviorism" (*The Philosophy of Literary Form*, 9). Burke sought an integrated approach to the relations among mind, body, and world.

27 Ibid., 51.

28 Ibid., 262.

29 Ibid., 263–65.

30 Ibid., 3.

31 Ibid., 259.

32 Ibid., 5.

33 Murray Krieger, *The New Apologists for Poetry* (Minneapolis: University of Minnesota Press, 1956), excluded Burke from his consideration of the New Critics — Burke "simply represents an extremely divergent approach," in part because he denied "any barrier between art and life" (216n18); cited in Vincent B. Leitch, *American Literary Criticism from the Thirties to the Eighties* (New York: Columbia University Press, 1988), 45.

34 Gerald Graff, *Professing Literature: An Institutional History* (Chicago: University of Chicago Press, 1987), 146.

35 Richard Ohmann, "English and the Cold War," in Noam Chomsky et al., *The Cold War and the University: Toward an Intellectual History of the Postwar Years* (New York: New Press, 1997), 73.

36 Morris Dickstein, *Double Agent: The Critic and Society* (New York: Oxford University Press, 1992), 145.

37 Guillory, *Cultural Capital: The Problem of Literary Canon Formation* (Chicago: University of Chicago Press, 1993), 168.

38 See for example Cleanth Brooks, *Modern Poetry and the Tradition* (Chapel Hill: University of North Carolina Press, 1939).

39 Guillory, *Cultural Capital*, 170.

40 See the example of Horace Kallen's concept of "cultural pluralism" in chapter 5.

41 Robert Maynard Hutchins, *The Higher Learning in America* (1936), cited in Graff, *Professing Literature*, 164. The humanities "core" remains a controversial issue; note for example the melodrama in Thomas Bartlett, "The Smearing of Chicago: A University Improves Its Teaching of Classic Texts, but Is Accused of Gutting 'Western Civilization,'" *Chronicle of Higher Education*, 28 June 2002, A10.

42 Cited in Gerald Graff, *Professing Literature*, 170.

43 Richard Ohmann, *English in America: A Radical View of the Profession* (New York: Oxford University Press, 1976; Hanover, N.H.: University Press of New England, 1996), 75.

44 Allen Tate, "Literature as Knowledge" (1941), in *Essays of Four Decades* (Chicago: Swallow, 1968).

45 Allen Tate, "Is Literary Criticism Possible?" *Partisan Review* 19 (1952): 551.

46 William J. Handy, *Kant and the Southern New Critics* (Austin: University of Texas Press, 1963), 76, 81. For an influential treatment of "neo-Kantianism" in the period's literary criticism, see Frank Lentricchia, *After the New Criticism* (Chicago: University of Chicago Press, 1980).

47 Tate, *On the Limits of Poetry: Selected Essays, 1928–1948* (New York: Swallow, 1948), 251; cited in Handy, *Kant*, 75.

48 Lionel Trilling, *The Liberal Imagination: Essays on Literature and Society* (New York: Viking, 1950), 36.

49 Trilling, *The Liberal Imagination*, xiii.

50 Ibid., 44.

51 Ibid., 45. Trilling notes that "the old myth of the mad scientist . . . no longer exists. The social position of science requires that it should cease, which leads us to remark that those partisans of art who insist on explaining artistic genius by means of psychic imbalance are in effect capitulating to the dominant mores which hold that the members of the respectable professions are, however dull they may be, free from neurosis" (170). Trilling rejects this distinction between artists and scientists.

52 Ibid., 178.

53 John Crowe Ransom, "Criticism as Pure Speculation," *The Intent of the Critic*, ed. D. A. Stauffer (Princeton, N.J.: Princeton University Press, 1941).

54 John Crowe Ransom, *The World's Body* (New York: Kennikat, 1938), cited in Leitch, *American Literary Criticism*, 39.

55 Irving Babbitt, "Romantic Melancholy," *Rousseau and Romanticism* (Boston: Houghton Mifflin, 1919), 328.

56 Northrop Frye, *Anatomy of Criticism: Four Essays* (New York: Atheneum, 1967), 5, 89; cited in Lentricchia, *After the New Criticism*, 11.

57 W. K. Wimsatt and Monroe C. Beardsley, "The Intentional Fallacy," in Wimsatt, *The Verbal Icon: Studies in the Meaning of Poetry* (Lexington: University of Kentucky Press, 1954), 5, 10, 3, 9, 4.

58 For example, they start their analysis by noting that "the separation of emotive

from referential meaning was urged persuasively about twenty years ago in the
earlier works of I. A. Richards. [He] created . . . a clean 'antithesis' between
'symbolic and emotive use of language.'" Wimsatt, *The Verbal Icon,* 22. Similarly, they affirm Matthew Arnold's belief that poetry "attaches the emotion to
the idea; the idea *is* the fact" (34).

59 "We venture to rehearse some generalities about objects, emotions, and words.
Emotion, it is true, has a well known capacity to fortify opinion, to inflame
cognition, and to grow upon itself in surprising proportion to grains of reason.
We have mob psychology, psychosis, and neurosis. We have 'free-floating anxiety' and all the vaguely understood and inchoate states of apprehension, depression, or elation, the prevailing complexions of melancholy or cheer. But it is
well to remember that these states are indeed inchoate or vague and by that fact
may even verge upon the unconscious. We have, again, the popular and self-
vindicatory forms of confessing emotion. 'He makes me boil.' 'It burns me up.'
Or in the novels of Evelyn Waugh a social event or a person is 'sick-making.'"
Wimsatt, *The Verbal Icon,* 26–27.

60 Ibid., 38.

61 J. F. Wolpert, "Notes on the American Intelligentsia," *Partisan Review* 14
(1947): 474.

62 Arthur Koestler, "The Intelligentsia," *Partisan Review* 11, no. 3 (1944): 276;
William Phillips and Philip Rahv, eds., "Our Country and Our Culture," special
issue of *Partisan Review* 19 (1952): 276, 573, 578, 557.

63 Trilling, *The Liberal Imagination,* 174–75.

64 Lionel Trilling, *Beyond Culture* (New York: Harcourt Brace Jovanovich, 1965),
184.

65 Ibid., 185–86.

66 Ibid., 195.

67 Ibid., 193.

68 Ibid., 196–97.

69 Ibid., 200.

70 Trilling ended the essay by demoting poetry too; the winner is "philosophy"
(citing Keats), which does not seem to originate with poet or critic or any
known agent (ibid., 202).

71 John Kenneth Galbraith, *The New Industrial State* (Boston: Houghton Mifflin,
1967).

72 For a collection of essays that includes some of the rebels, see Louis Kampf and
Paul Lauter, eds., *The Politics of Literature: Dissenting Essays on the Teaching of
English* (New York: Pantheon, 1972). On the MLA's convention in 1968, see pp.
34–40.

73 Stanley Fish, "Introduction, or How I Stopped Worrying and Learned to Love
Interpretation," in *Is There a Text in This Class? The Authority of Interpretive
Communities* (Cambridge: Harvard University Press, 1980), 9.

74 Ibid., 10.

75 Ibid., 11.

76 Ibid., 12.

77 Ibid., 14. Other fields were developing parallel ways of talking about the social basis of meaning. One of the most interesting involved the meaning of scientific discovery. In the course of analyzing Thomas Kuhn's views on the subjective aspects of an interpretive view, Paul Hoyningen-Huene notes, "Just as an individual can't *change* grammatical rules. . . . Neither can any individual change the structuring of the world inherent in a scientific or an everyday language. An individual might, of course, *lend impetus toward* linguistic change, but the success of such change in the appropriate community is an essentially social process." *Reconstructing Scientific Revolutions: Thomas S. Kuhn's Philosophy of Science* (Chicago: University of Chicago Press, 1993), 269. Kuhn's work on scientific revolutions was a major feature of the intellectual 1960s.

78 Harold Bloom, "The Internalization of Quest-Romance," in *Romanticism and Consciousness: Essays in Criticism,* ed. Bloom (New York: W. W. Norton, 1970), 13.

79 Ibid., 14.

80 Ibid., 21.

81 Harold Bloom, *Agon: Towards a Theory of Revisionism* (New York: Oxford University Press, 1982), 175.

82 Ibid.

83 Ibid., 231–32.

84 Ibid., 232.

## Chapter 8

1 For a fuller account of this transition, see my "Corporate Culture Wars," in *Corporate Futures: The Diffusion of the Culturally Sensitive Corporate Form,* ed. George Marcus (Chicago: University of Chicago Press, 1998), 23–62.

2 This chapter is based on material developed for a white paper on university-industry relations that I drafted for the Advisory Group on University-Industry Relations at UC Santa Barbara. The opinions expressed here are my own and not those of this group or its members.

3 University of California Office of the President, *Report of the University-Industry Relations Project* (Oakland: UCOP, 1982), 3.

4 The influence of this distinction owes much to Vannevar Bush's influence. In his criticism of Bush's position, Richard R. Nelson has noted that "Bush went out of his way to define basic research not only in terms of the search for fundamental knowledge that is involved in the activity, but also in terms of a lack of conscious targeting to specific areas of human need." "Why Bush's 'Science: The Endless Frontier' Has Been a Hindrance to the Development of an Effective Civilian Technology Policy," in *Science for the 21st Century: The Bush Report Revisited* (Washington: AEI Press, 1997), cited in Daniel S. Greenberg, *Science, Money, and Politics: Political Triumph and Ethical Erosion* (Chicago: University of Chicago Press, 2001), 46n5.

5 The grandfather of the University of California's Regulation no. 4 was University Regulation no. 3, instituted in 1935. It addressed "the problem of the relation between individual freedom and a 'planned economy,'" which it notes "is present in educational planning no less than in the domain of industry." Regulation no. 3 affirmed that "individual members of the faculty and the individual departments of the university are the instruments and servants of those ideal ends for the sake of which the university exists, such as the advancement of learning, the spread of knowledge, and the cultivation of capacities for intelligent and significant living." The regulation noted that these ends "can be furthered only through the free, willing and enthusiastic devotion to them of the individuals, comprising the university." But it also lays down the general principle that many of the university's ends require cooperation among many individuals and departments, and that academic planning does not in itself infringe academic freedom. The university, in other words, could make academic plans that would not, as long as they were "reasonable" and developed through "the democratic means of discussion and mutual give and take," illegitimately curtail the rights of individual faculty to conduct academic research. It stated that administrators were not infringing academic freedom by requiring budgetary accounting, among other things.

6 University of California Office of the President, *Report,* A-7. This same language recurs in later UCOP documents, as in the Policy on Outside Professional Activities of Faculty Members (1979). The "Principles" state that outside service is also to be monitored through the regular personnel review process, which is to consider whether the service is part of the evidence of "superior intellectual attainment." Academic Personnel Manual Section 51 (1977), cited in University of California Office of the President, *Report,* A-23.

7 University of California Office of the President (UCOP), Regulation no. 4, June 1958, at http://www.ucop.edu/ucophome/coordrev/policy/regulation4.html. The only stated exception is "when it is shown conclusively that satisfactory facilities for such services do not exist elsewhere."

8 Regulation no. 4, sec II, para. 5.

9 Cited in University of California Office of the President, *Report,* appendix A, p. A-9.

10 David Saxon, "Universities and the Common Good," MS 1979, cited in University of California Office of the President, *Report,* 15.

11 Ibid.

12 Ibid.

13 *Work in America: Report of a Special Task Force to the Secretary of Health, Education, and Welfare* (Washington: U.S. Government Printing Office, 1973), 4.

14 For an influential critique of techniques such as "management by numbers," see Robert H. Hayes and William J. Abernathy, "Managing Our Way to Economic Decline," *Harvard Business Review,* July–Aug 1980. For important portraits of the period's changing economic rules, see Ash Amin, ed., *Post-Fordism: A Reader* (Oxford: Blackwell, 1994), especially chapters 1, 4, 5, 7, 11; Giovanni

Arrighi, *The Long Twentieth Century: Money, Power, and the Origins of Our Times* (New York: Verso, 1994); Barry Bluestone and Bennett Harrison, *The Deindustrialization of America: Plant Closings, Community Abandonment, and the Dismantling of Basic Industry* (New York: Basic Books, 1982); David M. Gordon, *Fat and Mean: The Corporate Squeeze of Working Americans and the Myth of Managerial "Downsizing"* (New York: Free Press, 1996); Bennett Harrison, *Lean and Mean: The Changing Landscape of Corporate Power in the Age of Flexibility* (New York: Basic Books, 1994); David Harvey, *The Condition of Postmodernity: An Enquiry into the Origins of Cultural Change* (Oxford: Blackwell, 1989); Art Kleiner, *The Age of Heretics: Heroes, Outlaws, and the Forerunners of Corporate Change* (New York: Currency-Doubleday, 1996); Paul Krugman, *Peddling Prosperity: Economic Sense and Nonsense in the Age of Diminished Expectations* (New York: W. W. Norton, 1994); Robert Kuttner, *Everything for Sale: The Virtues and Limits of Markets* (New York: Alfred A. Knopf, 1996); and Anthony Sampson, *Company Man: the Rise and Fall of Corporate Life* (New York: Times Business–Random House, 1995).

15 See for example R. M. Burger, *An Analysis of the National Science Foundation's Innovation Centers Experiment (An Effort to Promote Technological Innovation and Entrepreneurship in an Academic Setting)* (Washington: U.S. Government Printing Office, 1977). Burger notes that the initial objective of the Innovation Centers program was to "increase . . . the probability of the . . . participants becoming successful entrepreneurs" (1). The interest in combining classroom and industry training stemmed from a decade-long sense that the American "tradition of innovation, invention, and entrepreneurship to which is ascribed a large measure of the Nation's success in achieving . . . a desirable 'quality of life' for its citizens" was "disappearing from the scene" (3). The result would be "an erosion of this country's leadership in the world." Burger cites the chairman of the President's Committee on Science and Technology, who noted that "use of science and technology for the Nation's benefit" had become "less bold, less innovative, more timid" (2). The report begins with charts that unfavorably compare the United States with Europe and Japan in terms of productivity growth, electronic patents, research and development as a percentage of gross national product, and so on.

16 In saying this I do not mean to slight the other major sources of the "new economy," such as wage reduction through union busting and increased unemployment; "deindustrialization" in the form of "sunbelt" and offshore manufacturing; increased "financialization" of economic activity, making manufacturing less important overall; and poorer working conditions, including longer hours and increased supervision. On the multidimensional "low road" to the new economy, see Gordon, *Fat and Mean*.

17 In addition to Robert Reich, *The Work of Nations* (New York: Random House, 1991), see Michael E. Porter, *The Competitive Advantage of Nations* (New York: Free Press, 1990).

18 Burger, *An Analysis*, 7. "Among the several responses to this distinct change in

the Foundation's charter were the establishment of RANN (Research Applied to National Needs) in 1971 and of the Experimental R&D Incentives (RDI) Program in 1972. The RDI objective was to identify and test incentives to stimulate technological innovation." The Innovation Centers program "combines education, clinical exposure for students, research, and outside business/inventor assistance" (9).

19 University of California Office of the President, *Report*, 7.

20 Ibid.

21 Ibid., 12.

22 University of California President's Budget Report, 2001.

23 Association of University Technology Managers, AUTM *Licensing Survey: FY 1998, 1999* (Washington: AUTM, 2000), 71.

24 National Science Foundation, "National Patterns of R&D Resources: 1996," Highlights, at http://www.nsf.gov/sbe/srs/nsf96333/general.htm#highlights. This figure measures expenditure by source. Measured by performer of work, the industry proportion is 73 percent; measured by full-time-equivalent R&D scientists and engineers, the industry proportion is 79 percent. See also Albert H. Teich, "The Outlook for Federal Support of University Research," reporting that corporate R&D overshadows university research: it "performs 70 percent of the nation's total R&D (supported both with firms' own funds and under federal contracts and grants), whereas academic institutions perform about 13 percent." Roger G. Noll, *Challenges to Research Universities* (Washington: Brookings Institution Press, 1998), 89.

25 In its report on university-industry relations, *Working Together, Creating Knowledge* (2001), the Business–Higher Education Forum claims that 40 percent of basic research is performed by industry.

26 David C. Mowery, Richard R. Nelson, Bhaven N. Sampat, and Arvids A. Ziedonis, "The Effects of the Bayh-Dole Act on U.S. University Research and Technology Transfer," in Lewis M. Branscomb, et al., eds., *Industrializing Knowledge: University-Industry Linkages in Japan and the United States* (Cambridge: MIT Press, 1999), 272–73.

27 Vannevar Bush had certainly meant to supplement industry's role in providing fundamental science, but he did not claim that industry's role should itself be negligible. Were business not responsible for basic research, it could devote more of its energy to profitable and perhaps socially useful applications. We are now in a position to see another dimension of Bush's support for basic research. Government support of universities would have the intended consequence of government laissez-faire with industry.

28 University of California Office of the President, *Report*, 10.

29 Ibid., 1, 16.

30 Ibid., 15.

31 As one study puts it, "Through much of the 1900–1940 period, U.S. universities, especially public universities, pursued extensive research collaboration with industry. Indeed, the academic discipline of chemical engineering was

largely developed through such collaboration between U.S. petroleum and chemicals firms and MIT and the University of Illinois." Mowery et al., "The Effects of the Bayh-Dole Act."

32 In the early 1960s, President Clark Kerr of the University of California had famously defined the university as the fountainhead of the information economy. He contrasted this with Cardinal Newman's strictly noncommercial university of the liberal arts, which seemed to Kerr an artifact of a bygone century. In the 1970s a future UC president, Richard C. Atkinson, the director of the National Science Foundation, assumed that technology transfer was a standard university practice requiring little defense.

33 The cold war context sometimes led to strong statements on behalf of free inquiry. Its competing imperatives appear in University Regulation no. 5, passed in June 1944, which declared, "The function of the University is to train students in processes whereby truth is to be made known. Its obligation is to see that conditions under which questions are examined are those which give play to intellect. To convert or make converts is alien and hostile to this dispassionate duty. When considering political, social, or sectarian movements, they are to be dissected and examined — not taught — and the conclusion left to the logic of the facts." Regulation summarized in "Compendium of Specialized University Policies, Guidelines, and Regulations Related to Conflict of Interest," in *Report of the University-Industry Relations Project* (1982), A-22.

34 The Standing Government Patent Policy through the 1970s read in part: "The Government shall normally acquire or reserve the right to acquire the principal or exclusive rights throughout the world in and to any inventions made in the course of or under a contract where: (1) A principal purpose of the contract is to create, develop, or improve products, processes, or methods which are intended for commercial use . . . by the general public at home or abroad, or which will be required for such use by government regulations; or (2) A principal purpose of the contract is for exploration into fields which directly concern the public health, public safety, or public welfare; or (3) The contract is in a field of science or technology in which there has been little significant experience outside of work funded by the Government, or where the Government has been the principal developer of the field, and the retention of exclusive rights at the time of contracting might confer on the contractor a preferred or dominant position." *Background Materials on Government Patent Policies,* vol 1, *Presidential Statements, Executive Orders, and Statutory Provisions,* Subcommittee on Domestic and Internal Scientific Planning and Analysis of the Committee on Science and Technology, U.S. House of Representatives, 94th Cong., Aug 1976, 27.

35 Richard C. Atkinson, "Visions and Values: The Research University in Transition," in *The University of California's Relationships with Industry in Research and Technology Transfer,* Proceedings of the President's Retreat, UCLA, 1997, 19.

36 "The Act's provisions represented a strong Congressional expression of support for the negotiation of exclusive licenses between universities and industrial

firms for the results of federally funded research." Mowery et al., "Effects of the Bayh-Dole Act," 274.

37  Mowery et al. mention two crucial developments on this point. The Supreme Court's decision in *Diamond v. Chakrabarty* (1980) upheld the validity of a broad patent in the new industry of biotechnology, opening the door to patenting the organisms, molecules, and research techniques emerging from biotechnology. And the new U.S. Court of Appeals for the Federal Circuit, established in 1982 as the court of appeal for patent cases throughout the federal judiciary, soon emerged as a strong champion of patentholder rights (274).

38  Leonard Minsky, "Dead Souls: The Aftermath of Bayh-Dole," *Campus, Inc.: Corporate Power in the Ivory Tower* (Amherst: Prometheus, 2000), 99.

39  Ralph Nader, Congressional testimony (1984), cited in Minsky, "Dead Souls," 97.

40  In 1982 Rickover testified as follows: "In 1980 the Congress reversed this long-standing government policy by giving universities and small business title to inventions developed at government expense. I testified against that because I recognized what would happen and it has happened. Now patent lobbyists are pressing Congress to extend that giveaway practice to large contractors. This would generate more business for patent lawyers, but, in the process, will promote even greater concentration of economic power in the hands of the large corporations which already get the lion's share of the governments research and developments budget." Cited in Minsky, "Dead Souls," 96.

41  Mowery et al., "Effects of the Bayh-Dole Act," 277, 290. Stanford's patenting data suggest that Bayh-Dole's effects may be exaggerated, as disclosures rose sharply in the late 1970s, before passage of the act, and plateaued in the mid-1980s. Ibid., figures 12–13, p. 291.

42  Ibid.

43  For example, California Labor Code section 2860 provides that "everything which an employee acquires by virtue of his employment, except compensation . . . belongs to the employer."

44  For example, University of California Office of the President, *Report,* notes that patent policy must seek to achieve "effective development of useful inventions by industry," achieve "reasonable revenues for the University from the licensing of patents," *and* maintain "good relations with industry" (21). Patent policy is also a proof of a state of mind that includes cooperativeness and interest in commercialization.

45  On the intensification of advertising in the 1960s, and its shift in tone toward a collaborative intimacy with its targets, see Thomas Frank, *The Conquest of Cool* (Chicago: University of Chicago Press, 1997).

46  Executive Summary, University of California Office of the President, *Report,* 1.

47  University of California Office of the President, *Report,* 3 (emphasis in original).

48  Minksy, "Dead Souls," 98.

49  Richard R. Nelson, "The Simple Economics of Basic Scientific Research," *Journal of Political Economy* 67 (1959): 300. See the similar argument in Kenneth. J.

Arrow, "Economic Welfare and the Allocation of Resources for Invention," in *The Rate and Direction of Inventive Activity: Economic and Social Factors: A Conference of the Universities-National Bureau Committee for Economic Research and the Committee on Economic Growth of The Social Science Research Council* (Princeton, N.J.: Princeton University Press, 1962), 609–24. Arrow concludes, "We expect a free enterprise economy to underinvest in invention and research (as compared with an ideal) because it is risky, because the product can be appropriated only to a limited extent, and because of increasing returns in use. This underinvestment will be greater for more basic research. Further, to the extent that a firm succeeds in engrossing the economic value of its inventive activity, there will be an underutilization of that information as compared with an ideal allocation" (619).

50  In Nelson's terms, "Applied research is relatively unlikely to result in significant breakthroughs in scientific knowledge save by accident, for, if significant breakthroughs are needed before a particular problem can be solved, the expected costs of achieving this breakthrough by a direct research effort are likely to be extremely high; hence applied research on the problem will not be undertaken, and invention will not be attempted. It is basic research, not applied research, from which significant advances have usually resulted." "The Simple Economics," 301.

51  As Nelson observed, "The incentives generated in a profit economy for firms to keep research findings secret produce results that are, in a static sense, economically inefficient." Ibid., 306.

52  Acknowledging this basic contradiction, Nelson advocated "the further growth of a 'basic-research industry,' a group of institutions that benefit from the results of almost any basic-research project they undertake. University laboratories should certainly continue to be a major part of this industry." In recent years, industries have established these kinds of research consortia, which I discuss elsewhere. Some versions of Nelson's dual system have been used to get around the contradiction between "static" and "dynamic" economic efficiency (his terms), or private and public efficiency, though most of these dual systems fail to acknowledge the contradiction as he does.

53  University of California Office of the President, *Report*, 2.

54  Ibid., 3.

55  Ibid., 21–22.

56  Ibid., 22.

57  Ibid.

58  Ibid.

59  Ibid., 21.

60  Ibid.

61  This includes situations where knowledge has market value but also has development costs that exceed that calculated value.

62  University of California Office of the President, *Report*, 2–3.

63  Ibid., 3 (emphasis omitted).

64  Ibid., 26. "Significant financial involvement, as defined by the policy, would

include a major equity interest, a position as a paid officer, or a consulting contract."

65  Ibid., 26.

66  Ibid., 27.

67  As paraphrased in ibid., 26.

68  Ibid.

69  The relevant policy at the time of the report was "Revised University Policy on Disclosure of Financial Interest in Private Sponsors of Research," issued by the Office of the President on 8 April 1982, almost simultaneously with the report itself.

70  University of California Office of the President, *Report*, 28.

71  Each campus should set up a "mechanism to review research proposals where it is disclosed that the principal investigator has a substantial financial interest in the sponsoring non-governmental entity." University of California Office of the President, *Report*, 4.

72  The report identified eight kinds of university-industry interactions (p. 9).

73  Cited in University of California Office of the President, *Report*, A-5. Standing Order of the Regents 103.1 reiterated that outside employment could not interfere with University duties and would not be compensated by the University.

74  Section I of Regulation no. 4 refers to "Special Services by Members of the Faculty." Section II refers to "Services involving the use of university facilities or conducted through university bureaus or other organizations, and under contracts between such organizations and the regents" (A-5). The contrast between basic and commercial research appears only in section II.

75  University of California Office of the President, *Report*, 25.

76  Ibid., 27–28.

## Chapter 9

1  Keith H. Hammonds, "The New World of Work," *Business Week*, 17 Oct 1994, 80.

2  Ibid., 81.

3  Ibid., 80.

4  Robert B. Reich, *The Next American Frontier* (New York: Times Books, 1983). Reich elaborated the argument in subsequent works such as (with John D. Donahue) *New Deals: The Chrysler Revival and the American System* (New York: Times Books, 1985) and *Tales of a New America: The Anxious Liberal's Guide to the Future* (New York: Times Books, 1987).

5  On the early genealogy of corporate individualism in the United States, see my "Emerson's Corporate Individualism," *American Literary History* 3 (1991): 657–84, and *The Emerson Effect: Individualism and Submission in America* (Chicago: University of Chicago Press, 1996).

6  Robert B. Reich, *The Resurgent Liberal (and Other Unfashionable Prophecies)* (New York: Times Books, 1989), 85.

7  Robert Reich, *The Work of Nations* (New York: Random House, 1991), 87.

8  For a description of an economic region already constructed around enclaves, see Mike Davis, *City of Quartz: Excavating the Future in Los Angeles* (New York: Verso, 1990), especially chapter 4.

9  Martha Nichols, "Does New Age Business Have a Message for Managers?" Executive Summary, *Harvard Business Review* 72, no. 2 (1994): 187.

10  Joseph A. Schumpeter, *Capitalism, Socialism, and Democracy* (1942; 3d ed. New York: Harper and Row, 1950), 83.

11  Ibid., 84. For my discussion of the limits of Schumpeter's endorsement of creative destruction, see chapter 6.

12  George Gilder, *Wealth and Poverty* (New York: Basic Books, 1981). Scott Cutler Shershow has noted that Gilder was part of a general shift among capitalism's defenders, who increasingly saw capitalism not as a production-oriented "restricted economy" but rather as a "general economy" based on a kind of gift exchange, and that Gilder explicitly drew on Marcel Mauss's theory of the gift. "Of Sinking: Marxism and the 'General' Economy," *Critical Inquiry* 27 (spring 2001): 471. Innovation is the entrepreneur's gift to the economy in the further sense that it cannot be traced to any contribution by labor.

13  Richard Foster, "The Welch Legacy: Creative Destruction." Foster, a director at McKinsey and Company, is the author of *Creative Destruction: Why Companies That Are Built to Last Underperform the Market—and How to Successfully Transform Them* (New York: Doubleday, 2001). Among many books on Welch, see Noel M. Tichy and Stratford Sherman, *Control Your Destiny or Someone Else Will: Lessons in Mastering Change—The Principles Jack Welch Is Using to Revolutionize General Electric* (New York: Harper Business, 1994). Praise of creative destruction has remained commonplace. For another example from high places, see Andy Grove, *Only the Paranoid Survive: How to Exploit the Crisis Points That Challenge Every Company* (New York: Currency-Doubleday, 1996); at the time, Grove was CEO of Intel.

14  David M. Gordon, *Fat and Mean: The Corporate Squeeze of Working Americans and the Myth of Managerial "Downsizing"* (New York: Free Press, 1996).

15  Mauro F. Guillén uses *homo hierarchicus* to describe the individual created by wage dependency and factory bureaucracy. See *Models of Management: Work, Authority, and Organization in a Comparative Perspective* (Chicago: University of Chicago Press, 1994), chapter 7.

16  The Peters canon: Thomas J. Peters and Robert H. Waterman Jr., *In Search of Excellence: Lessons from America's Best-Run Companies* (New York: Harper and Row, 1982); Tom Peters and Nancy Austin, *A Passion For Excellence: The Leadership Difference* (New York: Random House, 1985); Tom Peters, *Thriving on Chaos: Handbook for a Management Revolution* (New York: Alfred A. Knopf, 1987); Tom Peters, *Liberation Management: Necessary Disorganization for the Nanosecond Nineties* (New York: Alfred A. Knopf, 1992); Tom Peters, *The Tom Peters Seminar: Crazy Times Call for Crazy Organizations* (New York: Random House, 1994); Tom Peters, *The Pursuit of Wow! Every Person's Guide to Topsy-Turvy Times* (New York: Random House, 1994); Tom Peters, *The Circle of*

*Innovation: You Can't Shrink Your Way to Greatness* (New York: Alfred A. Knopf, 1997).

17  Peters, *Liberation Management,* 448, 66, 69, 5; Peters and Waterman, *In Search of Excellence,* 319.

18  Peters, *Liberation Management,* 701.

19  Ibid., 66, 33, 448, 222.

20  Ibid., 235.

21  Ibid., 737.

22  Peters, *The Pursuit of Wow!* 293.

23  The contrast between humanistic and scientific management is too easily simplified, as is the case in guides for the general reader. See for example John Micklethwait and Adrian Wooldridge, *The Witch Doctors: Making Sense of the Management Gurus* (New York: Times Books, 1996), e.g. 16, 65–67.

24  One of the group's bellwether publications was Warren Bennis and Philip Slater, "Democracy Is Inevitable," *Harvard Business Review* (1964). Other influential works connected one way or another with NTL include Robert Blake and Jane Srygley Mouton, *Corporate Excellence through Grid Organization Development: A Systems Approach* (1968), Leland P. Bradford, Jack R. Gibb, and Kenneth D. Benne, eds., *T-Group Theory and Laboratory Method* (1964), Kurt Lewin, *A Dynamic Theory of Personality: Selected Papers* (1935), Ronald Lippitt, *Training in Community Relations* (1949). These and other works constitute a democracy movement within management theory, one largely unknown in part because of the politics of most business leaders and the disciplinary divides in academia.

25  For a sympathetic overview of the human relations legacy, see Art Kleiner, *The Age of Heretics: Heroes, Outlaws, and the Forerunners of Corporate Change* (New York: Currency-Doubleday, 1996).

26  The next few pages of background on Peters's ideas are an adaptation of a portion of my essay "Corporate Culture Wars," in *Corporate Futures: The Diffusion of the Culturally Sensitive Corporate Form,* ed. George Marcus (Chicago: University of Chicago Press, 1998), 23–62.

27  Cited by Peters and Waterman, *In Search of Excellence,* 95 (emphasis in original).

28  Peters and Waterman displayed a common human relations embarrassment about applications in the 1960s of Theory Y "that went off the deep end on T-groups, bottom-up planning, democratic management, and other forms of a 'make everyone happy' work environment" (*In Search of Excellence,* 96). They claim that Theory X and Theory Y are not really opposed, that to contrast the authoritarian and the democratic is misleading since most managers — like good parents — are both. But they also display an uncommon honesty about Theory Y's importance to human relations thinking.

29  Alvin Toffler, *Future Shock* (New York: Random House, 1970), 134–35.

30  Ibid., 135, 408.

31  William G. Ouchi, *Theory Z: How American Business Can Meet the Japanese Challenge* (Reading, Mass.: Addison-Wesley, 1981), 4–5.

32 Ibid., 5–7.

33 Peters and Waterman, *In Search of Excellence,* xxiii.

34 Rosabeth Moss Kanter, *The Change-Masters: Innovation for Productivity in the American Corporation* (New York: Simon and Schuster, 1983).

35 One of Peters's recent cracks suggests that he's still irked, twelve years later, to have given this much credit to the numbers crowd. "In *In Search of Excellence*, Bob Waterman and I defined and measured excellence in terms of long-term financial health. Truth is, we could hardly have cared less. But we knew we needed to go through the drill to be taken seriously by the 5,000 conformists we hoped would buy the book." Having finished biting the hand, he continues, "Nothing wrong with financial measures, mind you. Can't live without them. But they're far from the whole picture." *The Tom Peters Seminar,* 219.

36 For other examples see Stephen P. Waring, *Taylorism Transformed: Scientific Management Theory since 1945* (Chapel Hill: University of North Carolina Press, 1991), 156–59.

37 Ouchi, *Theory Z,* 61.

38 Interview with the author, Feb 1996.

39 Peters and Waterman, *In Search of Excellence,* 92.

40 Alvin Toffler, *The Third Wave* (New York: William Morrow, 1980), 260.

41 The popularity of this effort can be crudely suggested by the fact that through the mid-1990s *In Search of Excellence* remained the number two best-selling management book in history. Number one was the how-to bible of self-development, Stephen R. Covey's *The Seven Habits of Highly Effective People* (New York: Simon and Schuster, 1989).

42 Peters, *The Pursuit of Wow!* 17, 81; Peters, *Crazy Organizations,* 167, 275, 285, 291.

43 Peters, *Crazy Organizations,* 71, 277; *The Pursuit of Wow!* 22.

44 Peters and Waterman, *In Search of Excellence,* 238 (emphasis in original).

45 There is a strong tradition of leftist critiques of liberal humanist management theory. For one that is particularly effective at criticizing this theory on its own terms, see Waring, *Taylorism Transformed,* especially chapter 5.

46 See the Final Report of the Committee on Professional Employment, Modern Languages Association, especially the section "The History of the Job Crisis in the Modern Languages," at http://www.mla.org.

47 Louis Menand, "College: The End of the Golden Age," *New York Review of Books,* 18 Oct 2001, 44.

48 See for example David Laurence, "The 1999 MLA Survey of Staffing in English and Foreign Language Departments," *Profession 2001* (New York: Modern Language Association, 2001). "Across responding departments, tenured and tenure-track faculty members made up only 35 percent of the total number of instructors teaching undergraduate courses in fall 1999 and less than half the faculty (i.e., after graduate TAs were excluded). Faculty members holding part-time appointments accounted for 32 percent of all instructors in the English departments and 29 percent of all instructors in the foreign language depart-

ments" (214). A significantly lower proportion of undergraduate courses are taught by full-time, tenure-track faculty in English than in other disciplines: about 42 percent, compared to 60 percent in history and 63 percent in philosophy. Modern Language Association, "Summary of Data from Surveys by the Coalition on the Academic Workforce," table 2, at http://www.mla.org/www _mla_org/home_middleframe.asp.

49 These features of the university business model summarize my discussion in chapters 2 and 8.

50 Richard Ohmann, *English in America: A Radical View of the Profession* (New York: Oxford University Press, 1976; Hanover, N.H.: University Press of New England, 1996), 226.

51 Ibid., xlv–xlvi.

52 The best recent study covers the period between 1981 and 1999, during which the number of faculty members grew by 46 percent nationwide, the number of part-time faculty by 76 percent; see note 44 to chapter 2.

53 See note 48.

54 I have been unable to find reliable figures on national trends in ethnic studies, and rely here on anecdotal evidence.

55 See note 4 to the introduction.

56 For a recent summary of academic salary patterns, see Sharon Walsh, "Lawyers Top Faculty-Salary List — Again," *Chronicle of Higher Education,* 9 Sept 2002. "At the low end of the scale were faculty members in library science ($44,206) and English composition ($44,616) at private colleges. At public institutions, English-composition professors ($48,503) and professors of foreign languages and literatures ($51,176) were at the bottom. Those salaries are not likely to leave the basement over the next decade . . . because a surplus of Ph.D.'s will persist in those fields." The survey's supervisor added, "There's not really much hope of catching up, because the English professors are starting at $40,000, while the financial people are starting at $70,000" (A21).

57 See chapters 5 and 7.

58 Corporate ethnography is relevant here. The sociologist Charles Heckscher, for example, found that "middle management *typically* does not understand business strategy. What they understand is product performance . . . Top managers build sophisticated pictures of how these factors come together in a coherent plan. But few of the middle managers could speak intelligently at this level. . . . Their refusal — the word is not too strong — to engage in real discussions about strategy indicates a *motivation not to understand the business.* . . . Middle managers frequently complained about the weakness of upper management, but these complaints were matched by *refusing to do anything about it.* When I say 'refusing,' I mean that the level of resistance to all options was so high as to amount nearly to panic." *White-Collar Blues: Management Loyalties in an Age of Corporate Restructuring* (New York: Basic Books, 1995), 91, 84 (emphases in original).

59 Although these numbers can be calculated in different ways with different sectors of the working population, the general trend remains the same. For exam-

ple, from 1973 to 1993, "family median incomes rose by $66," corrected for inflation, or "exactly 0.2 percent" David M. Gordon, *Fat and Mean: The Corporate Squeeze of Working Americans and the Myth of Managerial "Downsizing"* (New York: Free Press, 1996), 102. For a useful analysis of thirty-year trends using a range of federal data, see Doug Henwood, "Income and Poverty," *Left Business Observer* (1997), updated online at http://www.panix.com/~dhenwood/Stats_incpov.html.

60  For a summary by one of the movement's major theorists, see Michael C. Jensen, "Eclipse of the Public Corporation," *Harvard Business Review* 89 (Nov–Dec 1989): 13–33.

61  Neil Fligstein, *The Transformation of Corporate Control* (Cambridge: Harvard University Press, 1990), 15, 227. Finance's overall goal was simply to "increase assets and profits." To do this, it "emphasizes control through the use of financial tools which measure performance according to profit rates. Product lines are evaluated on their short-run profitability and important management decisions are based on the potential profitability of each line. Firms are viewed as collections of assets earning differing rates of return, not as producers of given goods. . . . The problem for management from this perspective is to maximize short-run rates of return by altering product mix, thereby increasing shareholder equity and keeping the stock price high."

62  Tom Peters, *Liberation Management: Necessary Disorganization for the Nanosecond Nineties* (PBS broadcast, 1993), transcription mine.

## Chapter 10

1  The notion that the white-collar functionary had become a "free agent" or self-starting "intrapreneur" was a staple of management writing in the 1990s. Peter Drucker argued that in the "knowledge society" the employee's intellectual capital is the only true form of capital. "Capital now serves the employee, where under Capitalism the employee served capital." Peter F. Drucker, *Post-Capitalist Society* (New York: Harper Business, 1993), 67. But Drucker was quite clear that management was a constitutive feature of the knowledge society as much as of the earlier industrial version, e.g., 52. Recently, extraordinary claims have been made for the rise of a new "creative class": see especially Richard Florida, *The Rise of the Creative Class, and How It's Transforming Work, Leisure, Community, and Everyday Life* (New York: Basic Books, 2002). Florida numbers this class at around 38 million in the United States; a higher estimate appears in Paul H. Ray et al., *The Cultural Creatives: How 50 Million People Are Changing the World* (Pittsburgh: Three Rivers, 2001). Florida is especially insightful when he traces cultural transformation to new social relations and work practices rather than technology, but he tends toward a dualistic view in which creativity transcends ongoing managerial functions: "Today's professionals see themselves as members of a broad creative force, not as corporate officers or organization

men" (11). A more convincing view of knowledge workers appears in Andrew Ross, *No Collar: The Humane Workplace and Its Hidden Costs* (New York: Basic Books, 2003).

2 Research universities have wider gaps than teaching colleges do between administrators and senior faculty, whose lives may resemble those of research executives, and large numbers of low-wage workers. Many of these are blue- and pink-collar employees: clerks, secretaries, cafeteria workers, gardeners. But many others are brainworkers — lower-division classrooms and laboratories are largely staffed by low-wage students and untenured technicians. The university has played a role in the widening wage stratification *within* the white-collar middle class since 1980; I will take up this topic in a sequel to this book.

3 Erik Olin Wright, "Intellectuals and the Class Structure of Capitalist Society," *Between Labor and Capital,* ed. Pat Walker (Boston: South End, 1979), 205–6.

4 The Ehrenreichs' essay appeared in *Between Labor and Capital,* 5–45. The other major work on this subject that year was Alvin Gouldner, *The Future of Intellectuals and the Rise of the New Class* (New York: Seabury, 1979).

5 The term "new class" is generally traced to Milovan Djilas, *The New Class: An Analysis of the Communist System* (New York: Praeger, 1957). His new class was the "political bureaucracy" produced by state-led Soviet-style industrialization, one whose power depended on its "administrative monopoly" (38–39). Djilas influenced analysis in the United States in part because his description of how expertise dominates was familiar to those acquainted with certain views of American society, later synthesized in John Kenneth Galbraith's *The New Industrial State* (1967). The new class was replacing rather than administering the political will: "The once live, compact party, full of initiative, is disappearing to become transformed into the traditional oligarchy of the new class, irresistibly drawing into its ranks those who aspire to join the new class and repressing those who have any ideals" (40).

6 Barbara and John Ehrenreich, "The Professional-Managerial Class," *Between Labor and Capital,* 5–45.

7 Barbara and John Ehrenreich, "Rejoinder," in *Between Labor and Capital,* 314–17. This essay puts Marx's class analysis in a particular historical context and notes ambiguities that limit its contemporary value (321–27).

8 Erik Olin Wright, *Class Counts: Comparative Studies in Class Analysis* (Cambridge: Cambridge University Press, 1997), chapter 2. In this complex work, Wright details the constitution and viewpoints of four to six positions within class relations in a number of industrial societies. Among the many features of his analysis that are relevant here, he confirms the importance of the positions of "experts" in the structuring of class relations; estimates the proportion of middle class "expert-managers" as no more than 10–15 percent of the workforce in industrial countries; shows that self-employment and self-management remain important in the United States (chapter 4); justifies the linkage of professional and managerial functions while noting variable relations between them (e.g.

57); shows that the working classes of the United States increasingly consist of women and people of color (69); and suggests that American society has been characterized by a steady "expansion, rather than a decline, of contradictory locations within class relations" (111).

9 Speaking of teachers, Wright made the useful comment that it is "only a first step in the analysis to demonstrate that teachers occupy contradictory class relations. It is equally important to specify the variability within those relations and to examine the processes of change in the class location of given categories of teachers." *Between Labor and Capital,* 210.

10 Here as elsewhere in this book, I accept Antonio Gramsci's claim that modern social governance rests on hegemony more than on explicit coercion and violence, though hegemony is often strengthened through the threat of these. See *Selections from the Prison Notebooks* (1971); for a particularly helpful and detailed discussion, see Perry Anderson, "The Antinomies of Antonio Gramsci," *New Left Review* 100 (1976–77): 5–78.

11 Louis Menand, "The End of the Golden Age," *New York Review of Books,* 18 October 2001, 44–47.

12 Andrew Ross, *No Respect: Intellectuals and Popular Culture* (New York: Routledge, 1989).

13 To name a few of the strongest entries: Barbara Ehrenreich, *Fear of Falling: The Inner Life of the Middle Class* (New York: Harper Collins, 1989); Robert Reich, *The Work of Nations: Preparing Ourselves for 21st Century Capitalism* (New York: Vintage, 1991), especially part II; Robert H. Frank and Philip J. Cook, *The Winner-Take-All Society: Why the Few at the Top Get So Much More Than the Rest of Us* (New York: Penguin, 1995); Thomas Frank, *The Conquest of Cool: Business Culture, Counterculture, and the Rise of Hip Consumerism* (Chicago: University of Chicago Press, 1997).

14 Major statements included E. J. Dionne Jr., *Why Americans Hate Politics* (New York: Simon and Schuster, 1991); Thomas Byrne Edsall and Mary D. Edsall, *Chain Reaction: The Impact of Race, Rights, and Taxes on American Politics* (New York: W. W. Norton, 1991); Mickey Kaus, *The End of Equality* (New York: Basic Books, 1992); and Stanley B. Greenberg, *Middle Class Dreams: The Politics and Power of the New American Majority* (New York: Times Books, 1995).

15 One example is David Brooks, *Bobos in Paradise: The New Upper Class and How it Got There* (New York: Touchstone, 2001).

16 Perhaps the best of these studies is Steven Brint, *In an Age of Experts: The Changing Role of Professionals in Politics and Public Life* (Princeton, N.J.: Princeton University Press, 1994). Brint's general thesis is confirmed by Wright's comparative class analysis in *Class Counts,* where the author notes, "The bourgeois coalition in the United States extends much deeper into the contradictory [middle] class locations than in Sweden . . . All three managerial class locations as well as expert supervisors are part of the American bourgeois ideological class formation" (425). Among employees in the United States with some kind of college background, only "skilled supervisors" and self-employed "experts" are

part of the "middle class coalition," accompanied in Wright's twelve-class-position model by "small employers" and "petty bourgeoisie" (the self-employed).

17 Radical humanism has much in common with the sophisticated Marxist humanism of another landmark work of the 1970s, Raymond Williams's *Marxism and Literature* (Oxford: Oxford University Press, 1977).

# ACKNOWLEDGMENTS

· · · · · · · · · · · · · · · · · · · · · · · · · ·

Many people helped me learn the things that made this book possible. I was then able to pull its various materials together because of the particular labor and support of some people I'd like to thank individually. Ken Wissoker's patience helped sustain my own interest, while Bruce Robbins and Andrew Ross gave me valuable feedback on two separate versions of the manuscript. Kelly Lynn Mulvey, Gina Valentino, and Sa Zhang offered reliable and illuminating research assistance. In the course of her research for me, Jessica Blaustein provided analysis of some of the earlier texts that helped shape my thinking about them. Members of the University of California staff and administration were quite helpful at several stages, including France Cordova, who commissioned the white paper that served as a foundation for chapter 8, and Sherylle Mills Englander and Carol Mimura, who were crucial sources of my accelerated education in technology policy. I owe thanks to Fred Kameny and his group at Duke University Press for their editing of the manuscript and to Toni Mantych for her excellent work on it in Santa Barbara. I steered perhaps too many long walks with Ann Jensen Adams toward a blow by blow of the book's arguments in all their nonlinear incarnations: I am grateful to her for her stamina and her insight. Ricki Morse read the entire manuscript and helped sustain my belief in its affirmative elements. Avery Gordon supported and inspired me in more ways than I could ever name. Whatever the limitations of this book, which are entirely my own, its writing exposed me to combinations of friendship and intelligence that will for me always be part of the final product.

# INDEX

· · · · · · · · · · · · · · · · · · · · · · · · · · · · ·

Christopher Newfield is a professor of English at
the University of California, Santa Barbara.

Library of Congress Cataloging-in-Publication Data

Newfield, Christopher.

Ivy and industry : business and the making of

the American university, 1880–1980 / Christopher Newfield.

p. cm.

Includes index.

ISBN 0-8223-3201-9 (cloth : alk. paper)

1. Industry and education — United States — History — 19th century.

2. Industry and education — United States — History — 20th century.

3. Education, Higher — Economic aspects — United States. I. Title.

LC1085.2.N39 2003

371.19′5 — dc21

2003010841